Joint Action for Jobs

Joint Action for Jobs

a new internationalism

edited by Ken Coates

With contributions from Michael Barratt Brown, Stephen Bodington, Ken Coates, Mike Cooley, Stuart Holland, John Hughes, Ken Livingstone, Richard Minns, Frances Morrell, Robin Murray, John Palmer, Tony Topham and Terry Ward.

foreword by Stuart Weir

New Socialist / SPOKESMAN

First published in Great Britain in 1986 jointly by New Socialist and Spokesman,
Bertrand Russell House, Gamble Street, Nottingham NG7 4ET
Tel. 0602 708318

British Library Cataloguing in Publication Data

Joint Action for Jobs: a new internationalism

1. Unemployment — Europe
2. Manpower policy — Europe
3. Europe — full employment policies
I. Coates, Ken
331.13'77'094 HD5764.A6

ISBN 0-85124-427-0
ISBN 0-85124-428-9 Pbk

Typeset, printed and bound by the Russell Press Ltd., Nottingham
Tel. 0602 784505

Contents

Foreword

When at *New Socialist* we first began to explore the first shifts in opinion and positions which was to lead to what we described as the "realignment of the left"[1] I was very surprised to discover than one of the cornerstones of the shift was a "new Europeanism". I have to say that I was also very sceptical. Desirable as it was for the leader of Sheffield council to discuss the (west) European-wide phenomeon of unemployment with the mayor of Bologna, and for trade unionists in Ford plants in western Europe to try to coordinate their response to the giant car company's plans, such ideas seemed to me to be subordinate to the urgent need for the Labour Party to develop a coherent national response.

Now it seems to me that a sensible and democratic national response can only emerge within the framework, on the one hand, of local and regional planning for employment — with all kinds of diverse experiments — and on the other hand, a supra-national, probably west European, attempt to plan jointly for economic recovery at the least, and better still, to seek to control the multinationals and bring about reform of the western economic order.

I am not arguing now that Labour does not need to develop a national response. A government must govern. No more am I arguing that a future Labour government can do nothing to restore employment and rebuild our industrial capacity until it has lined up western European allies behind it. But the old corporate, or tripartite, strategies are dead, and you cannot convincingly breathe new life into them by arguing that this time round the government must be actively on the side of the trade unions; and that together they can push the employers in a more radical direction. For the base from which a Labour government and trade unions alike begin is far too narrow to generate the power which would be necessary for such a strategy to win through. The strategy fashioned by Andrew Glyn for the Campaign Group is narrower still: statist at home, isolationalist internationally speaking. Though the idea that a Labour government's bold purpose in launching such a strategy would win over working class support is inherent in the proposals, they are at root profoundly undemocratic.

Certainly, a future Labour government should regard the trade unions as its natural allies in the regeneration of Britain. Certainly it should use state powers to take control of the economy. Certainly it should take into public ownership key industrial and financial institutions. But it can only build a truly popular strategy if it frees working people from fear and gives them opportunities to put their skills and enterprise to work. This implies building on the pioneering work of Labour authorities like the GLC, West Midlands and Sheffield in sponsoring local enterprise. But it also means creating new rights for people at work, as well as in the community, *individual* rights to trade union membership, to information, to power-sharing within their enterprise. These rights should be individual, as they will then be appreciated and defended; but in practice they will require collective (that is, usually trade union) action to make them effective. It means, too, giving local authorities new powers over firms in their areas.

As befits a jounalist, this is a sketchy introduction to a series of important essays and articles. You will find that they do not add up to a coherent strategy or blueprint for action. Rather they are sounding shots which take measure of the problems and tentatively advance answers. Raphael Samuel describes in *New Socialist*[2] how the left coalesced around the idea of *planning* in the early 1930s. That was a watershed which led to the basic strategies of the first postwar Labour government. Hopefully we are at a new point of departure — planning for socialism through people's own endeavours more than through the state and its institutions, and within a new international perspective.

Stuart Weir
November 1985

Footnotes

1. These explorations led finally to Patrick Seyd's article, "Bennism without Benn: realignment on the Labour left," NS May 1985; Ken Coates moved the debate forwards with his article, "A new internationalism", NS September 1985.
2. "The cult of planning," Raphael Samuel, NS January 1986.

Introduction

Ken Coates

Unemployment in Britain has become the central, all-dominating political issue. Even while the British economy registers modest growth, the number of people without work continues to rise.*

Long term unemployment constitutes a growing problem, and the number of those people who have been out of work for three years or more increased by one-third in the twelve months after July 1984. In spite of a range of more or less cosmetic measures, youth unemployment maintains very high levels.

But in this matter, Britain is not at all an island. All over Western Europe, similar complaints may be heard. From Spain through to Greece, economic crisis is the main pre-occupation of both Governments and peoples. In different countries, there are differing possibilities of effective national action for recovery. But the truth is that all such possibilities are steadily diminishing. It is difficult for middle-sized nations to seize the economic initiative. Separate national bids to reflate are successively frustrated, as the reflation attracts foreign imports. These imports all consist of someone else's exports, and contribute to recovery in the other nations from which they are sent. But in the home state, they mean adverse balances of payments, and intimidatory visits from the bankers. A group of socialist economists from several West European countries came together to address this simple but exceedingly difficult problem. After a careful and systematic exchange of views and information, over a period of years, they agreed the text of *Out of Crisis*, which was edited by Stuart Holland, and published by Spokesman in 1983.

Launched at a major conference in Paris, the *Out of Crisis* project agreed the definition of three main strategic aims: reflation,

*Actually, official figures fluctuated, and fell by 4,000 between August and September 1985, but the trend rises constantly, if at a somewhat lower rate during the past months.

restructuring, and redistribution. Varying between one State and another in their implications, these policies nonetheless implied measures of public spending, planning and economic democracy, and public and co-operative enterprise.

Out of Crisis showed in some detail that it would be possible to create several million new jobs within a ten year span, if the European economists were to follow "better my neighbour" reflationary policies instead of the present trend of "beggar my neighbour" deflations. Introducing this argument, Stuart Holland wrote: "The economic arguments are essentially simple. One country's imports are another country's exports. Thus if each country cuts domestic spending to reduce import demand and improve its balance of payments it will deepen the vicious circle of deflation in international production and trade". This vicious circle could, however, be broken by co-ordinated European action to increase public spending and import demand and thus to improve employment, income, and trade performances.

Reflation can take many different forms. The authors of *Out of Crisis* believed that it should be controlled through a programme of restructuring and redistribution, which would reallocate resources between firms and sectors within the overall economy, between advantaged and deprived social groups, and between advanced and more backward countries and regions.

From the beginning, *Out of Crisis* argued that such policies could not be successfully implemented within a narrow European mentality, but would need to be pursued by a number of "northern" countries in co-operation with countries of the "south" and intermediate zones. This thinking has been convincingly developed in the report of the Socialist International Committee on Economic Policy which has met under the chairmanship of Michael Manley. Published in September 1985, under the title *Global Challenge*, this report incorporates the findings of *Out of Crisis* and reflects strong inputs from Stuart Holland and his colleagues. *Global Challenge* goes beyond *Out of Crisis* in its insistence that without a redistribution and restructuring of the power relations between North and South, they will not be able to overcome the opposition to that recovery which all of them need.

Such opposition comes from conservative governments and institutions, from monetarist philosophers and from the powerful transnational companies which are served by these spokespeople. Manley's team are willing to accept "a gradual reform of the international system", but they are rightly insistent that any such reform "must also be fundamental, dealing with the causes of the current crisis rather than . . . only with its symptoms''.

The main international agencies whose policies need to be changed are dominated by the group of 10 states, and more especially by the big five within this group. But, above all, the United States is the dominant influence. Manley shows that this influence has been used quite brutally: ''as instruments of . . . foreign policy — such as the US administration's pressure to block World Bank (or Inter American Development Bank) lending to Nicaragua''. More usually, American pressures are exerted in a subtler manner. They are no less powerful for that. In a document approved by all the Socialist Parties in Europe, as well as those in the Third World, it is a striking thing to read this conclusion:

> ''For much of the post-war period, many countries saw the United States as combining both might and right, with the moral authority of administrations identified with the New Deal, Lend Lease, the fight against Fascism, Marshall Aid, and the establishment of the United Nations. Today, the United States is identified, by many countries, with Vietnam, the invasion of Grenada, support for Pinochet's Chile, political leverage on aid, and nuclear proliferation. Over the last seven years, the United States has not agreed to any outcome of North South negotiations, whether the Common Fund, new or renewed commodity agreements, the Law of the Sea Convention, or a new round of global negotiations. Recently, it has not only withdrawn from UNESCO, but has also refused to recognise International Court of Justice verdicts on Central America, refused to agree a minimally adequate replenishment of International Development Agency funds, and has attempted to relegate the International Fund for Agricultural Development to virtual insignificance.
>
> Lately, the US has also made known that it is going for 'a firmer, more forthright and less patronising attitude in negotiating with developing countries', that it will no longer 'reward the radical and non-serious elements of international organisations by accepting their proposals as bases for negotiation', and that it will sometimes refuse to negotiate . . .
>
> The result has been not only US unwillingness to agree to recovery programmes, reform of institutions or redistribution towards the poorest countries. It has also increasingly meant a rejection by the United States of multilateral institutions, save on its own terms, for its own purposes. The message has not gone unnoticed''.

If the Socialist leaders of Europe have really noticed this message, then they are aware of the need to initiate a European recovery programme without waiting for United States approval, and even, if necessary, against the wishes of the American administration. Of course, as the Manley Report insists, it is possible that a new administration in the United States could prove far more enlightened, in which case the labour of co-ordinated recovery could be greatly eased. Supposing, however, that American policy remains constant. In that case, will the Europeans trail behind it, stumbling deeper into debt and social distress? Or will they seize upon the alternative project, and begin to co-operate to create new initiatives?

It is not necessary here to repeat the detailed arguments of *Out of Crisis* or the Manley Report. Of course, these demand, and will repay, close scrutiny. The bulk of this book is concerned with a different aspect of the problem. It is relatively simple, at the level of political analysis, to see what could and should be done. It is very much harder to mobilise the political force that can enable it to happen. Socialist Prime Ministers may know quite well what would prove to be the best course, in the best of all possible worlds. But when they arrive in office, the worlds in which they find themselves are commonly of the worser sort. Before fraternal solidarity is available from like-minded Governments, the bankers are installed in their ante-rooms, their knives ready for the rending of their pounds of flesh.

If this is true, then the work of realising an autonomous European economic strategy needs the building of grassroots links across frontiers. It needs the development of public opinion. It needs more than propaganda: it needs practical example, to show how our forces might be joined, how such a programme has now become real rather than platonic.

In September 1985, after elaborate consultation with trade unions, church leaders, political spokesmen, and the authors of *Out of Crisis*, the Russell Foundation launched an appeal: Joint Action for Jobs. The intention of this appeal was to provide direct contact between municipalities, community organisations, enterprise level trade unions, and other primary organisations, in order that they should both be able to learn from one another and to help each other in their efforts to generate employment. A large number of British authorities quickly responded, and a preliminary seminar was convened with the help of the Greater London Council, at County Hall, London. This met on 19/20 September 1985, and the papers which were presented to it form the content of this book. The appeal, *Joint Action for Jobs*, which was the agreed platform of the first seminar, and which will serve as the basis for a much larger European conference which is in preparation, reads as follows:

> "Unemployment is laying Europe waste. With twenty million people out of work, the number of direct victims has become intolerable: a

common scandal. But there is every reason to believe that this number is growing steadily, whilst the indirect sufferers already include whole populations.

The direct victims enter poverty for long periods of time, and in some age groups and regions, they stay poor, permanently. Such people are forced outwards to the margins of society. There they live a kind of twilight life, without hope of personal betterment, and without any of those social links that might bring collective improvement. In a world in which men travel to the moon, Europe contains many areas in which a fifth or more of its citizens are in want.

The indirect victims of this wasting disorder are counted in further millions. Low paid workers in declining industries gain no improvement, even while their wages are too small to allow decent existence. Often employees in public services are similarly squeezed. Restriction breeds further restriction: as the economy declines, so public spending is cut over and again, each time aggravating the general decline. Unemployment seeds fear, and this fear breaks up individual personalities and tears apart the fabric of human society. It spawns violence and mental breakdown, riot and repression.

First among the sufferers are young people, women and racial minorities. Four decades of European progress in education are now abruptly reversed in a cataclysm in which vast numbers of school leavers discover that they are completely unnecessary: that their skills and knowledge have no economic value, and that their generation has become a social problem. Hard won advances in the conditions of women workers are brusquely checked as the labour market shunts their employment prospects into casual or part-time occupations, ill protected by trade unions or social conventions. The condition of migrant workers and ethnic minorities is deeply menaced, as they lose the chance to find work and suffer the worsening of xenophobia and heightened community tension.

For individual people unemployment may bring despair or even suicide. For societies, its effects are equally poisonous: within the climate it establishes sprout the seeds of authoritarianism and militarism. Democratic institutions become difficult to maintain when multimillions of the citizens are excluded from constructive economic life. The social base of trade unions and other voluntary associations is often undermined. And fear breeds fear, reinforcing tensions between states, and heightening military power. Previous great slumps have commonly exploded into war: although the world knows that such an outcome today would put an end to human evolution.

There is no reason to believe that unemployment is unavoidable or fore-ordained. A mere fraction of the ingenuity which has transformed our technical capacities could re-arrange our social rules in a way which would guarantee a useful role for all our people.

Of course, action by Governments can improve or worsen this condition. If all, or even some of the European Governments were willing to act together in order to reject mass unemployment, there is no doubt that conditions could be radically improved. But this is not a problem which can be left to Governments. Because it concerns everybody, it needs action by all of us. Just as economic collapse threatens our democratic institutions, so economic recovery calls for an enhancement of our power to respond through democracy. Those who are still employed have a special responsibility to help their fellows who have been squeezed out of work. It is understandable that insecurity breeds fear, but this can only be dispelled by acting together in mutual support. Ideas about economic recovery, and action for employment, are needed at all levels of society, and from all relevant social organisations.

The work which is necessary requires us to find ways of joining needs to resources, of restructuring institutions to regain the democratic initiative in the global economy. As the slump has deepened, want and waste have faced each other out. Europe must discover an answer to this evil process, an agenda for the recovery of output, production, incomes and trade, and for the regeneration of work and hope, not only in our corner of the world but also in the underdeveloped countries and among the victims of a dreadful world-wide crisis of debt which threatens to breed famine, turbulence and war. We must find ways to replace the policies of 'beggar my neighbour' by those which seek instead to 'better my neighbour'.

A part of this agenda involves those social organisations which both shape and voice public opinion. We think that political, religious and cultural associations, trade unions and public authorities need to establish an open European forum from whose platform it will be possible together to generate the self-confidence for renewal. At the same time, there are innumerable democratic bodies which have it in their reach to initiate practical actions to develop prospects of employment, and to overcome the scourge of enforced and unwanted idleness. Trade unions are already concerned to establish co-ordinated moves to establish safer and healthier working conditions, shorter working lifetimes, longer holidays and more educational facilities at work. Local municipalities are often concerned to encourage industrial development, international contact, and improved trade in their own areas, and may find joint action across frontiers a valuable aid in this process.

Proposal: JOINT ACTION FOR JOBS

Joint European action on the remedies for unemployment would give scope for all such interests to work together, reinforcing every positive example by healthy imitation and support. This, therefore, is what we propose, beginning with a series of conferences and working parties which may be a starting point for widespread, common initiatives. These could be linked by a common rubric: Joint Action for Jobs.

Such conferences must be international, because the present trauma of monetarism is itself worldwide, and more, because the growth of private multinational power has itself been very largely responsible for a marked loss of democratic national controls over economic policy. Our response must operate at the same level as the crisis itself. But the wider it ranges across frontiers, the more it must draw upon, and stimulate, the initiatives of local communities, since these are the agencies through which our peoples can begin the work of regeneration.

Therefore, we do not believe that the difficulties in agreement of international policies are an excuse for inaction either nationally or locally. We think it necessary for Europeans to consult with one another, not in order to discover reasons why action must be deferred until all are able to move as one, but rather in order to overcome passivity, to support each initiative that shows itself, and to create a sense of overriding priority, against which the actions of Governments and others in authority may be judged. There is a considerable effort of new thinking, which asks insistent questions about the future of our social lives and personal relationships, in the context of our changing environment. If Europe is to recover wisely, and in unity with the peoples of the rest of the world, we must examine these ideas.

At the same time, the millions of workless people who have been evicted from active influence over many of our democratic processes must be able to find a platform from which to explain their needs, and a movement within which they may recover their hopes.

We circulate this appeal for signature. Those who believe that European meetings on this theme could be a first step towards more co-ordinated progress invite others to join with them in exploring how such contacts may begin. All those groups and individuals who are concerned with this most desperate challenge are invited to help, by bringing their examples and their problems to a common forum. Daunting though this task may be, it will help us to face it together".

It was on the basis of an agreement on this platform that the following papers were prepared. Of course, agreement on a new framework for joint action leaves plenty of room for argument on contingent matters. But this argument increasingly concerns not *whether* to strive for new forms of international co-operation, but *how* to bring it about. As European working people join their forces, they will acquire the means to resolve all such problems, and more which have not yet arisen.

Acknowledgements

These papers were commissioned for a seminar at County Hall, London, on the Scope and Limits of National Action against Unemployment. The question for discussion were formulated by Michael Barratt Brown. It has become widely accepted even among economists who are not convinced by the appeal of monetarism that a simple return to Keynesian policies is not a viable proposition, certainly not for individual state governments, except perhaps for those of the super states. Keynes himself was clear that national policies to create the conditions for full employment would need to be supported by international action. Hence the importance that he attached to the creation of a World Bank, Monetary Fund and Trade Organisation — none of which in the event were established with the resources or the independent international secretariat that he envisaged. Since Keynes died the power of nation states to manage their economic affairs has been eroded by the growing influence of transnational companies. Yet, while the world's statesmen meet regularly at summits to consider what may be done to halt the spread of unemployment, no decision on co-ordinated action ever emerges. Some economists would doubt whether it ever could; others would doubt even if it did whether it would be of lasting benefit to the unemployed. Others still see in meetings of like-minded socialists in and out of government, and perhaps especially in local and regional authorities, the possibility of developing forms of mutual co-operation that might pre-figure a wider international initiative to escape from the current world economic crisis. While some of these see such an initiative necessarily going beyond Keynesian prescriptions, it would seem to be worthwhile seeking whether a concensus might be found on the outlines of a positive internationalist approach to the disaster of European unemployment.

The pressure for a European-wide initiative comes partly because those who have been most pressing live and work in Europe, partly because as compared with the situation in North America, Japan or other industrialised regions, and even as compared with many parts of the Third World, the crisis seems here to be the more serious. Rates of unemployment have shown no sign of declining even in the recovery, small as it is, of world trade and output since 1982. The European Community has a common agricultural policy which is the most protectionist in the world and a free trade policy for industrial products, which barely conceals beggar-my-neighbour actions all round. The results appear to be quite outstandingly disastrous for all concerned and particularly for the poor whose major expenditure is on food, which they must buy at double world prices. Such untoward results of deliberate economic policies offer a severe challenge to economists. Those who believe in the benefits of the free competitive market should presumably set about dismantling the protectionist agricultural policy and breaking up the giant transnational companies' accumulations of capital. They would then, presumably, have to drive industrial wages down to productivity levels and see if the experiment resulted in full employment.

Those, on the other hand, who still believe in state management of the economy have to show how it could be managed by national and international measures so as to re-establish full employment without unacceptable inflation or intolerable loss of freedom. The following questions suggest themselves as ones that need to be answered for a medium-term strategy designed to move towards full employment, greater equality of incomes and wider participation in decision making.

1. Can a sustainable recovery be achieved, i.e. without unacceptable inflation and payments deficits, simply by expanding national state expenditure with borrowed money?
2. Would taxation have to be increased to finance increased state spending, and if so on whom should the extra taxes fall?

Those, on the other hand, who still believe in state management of the economy have to show how it could be managed by national and international measures so as to re-establish full employment without unacceptable inflation or intolerable loss of freedom. The following questions suggest themselves as ones that need to be answered for a medium-term strategy designed to move towards full employment, greater equality of incomes and wider participation in decision making.

1. Can a sustainable recovery be achieved, i.e. without

unacceptable inflation and payments deficits, simply by expanding national state expenditure with borrowed money?

2. Would taxation have to be increased to finance increased state spending, and if so on whom should the extra taxes fall?
3. How can transfer pricing by transnational companies be brought under some control — to ensure tax payments and a limit to exports? How can exchange controls be made effective?
4. Can price controls be made an effective instrument of economic policy without draconian powers and without arbitrarily distorting the indicators of public choice and investment criteria?
5. Is an Incomes Policy, albeit a voluntary one operated by the TUC, a necessary part of any policy of reflation and how can it be prevented from working in favour of capital?
6. Can interest rates be managed nationally?
7. Should import controls of any sort be introduced and if so, should these be against all or only against non-European suppliers?
8. If a common European reflation programme were agreed, how would this relate to the reasonable aspirations of the Third World?
9. Would an agreed Labour Code be helpful in obtaining unity against the transnational companies' power amongst their workers not only in Europe but in the Third World?
10. How could the democratically-arrived-at area and sectoral plans of the kind proposed by the GLC London Industrial Strategy be incorporated into some form of national planning?
11. To avoid a command structure could this be done by some sort of Clearing House for co-ordinating exchanges between areas and sectors, and possibly extending to other regions and nations in Europe and wider still, on the principles established by the Third World Information Network?
12. Would such democratic sectoral plans imply (re)nationalisation of certain sectors or parts of sectors?
13. How can public ownership be decentralised and brought under regional or local accountability?
14. How would national resource allocation within sectors or areas be made accountable to public opinion, i.e. what extension of Parliament's powers and forms are needed to limit the power of the executive (Prime Minister)?
15. How can Trade Unions be more involved in factory, company, area, region and national planning, so as to extend real participation, not just responsibility without power?

By arrangement chapters 1 and 6 have already appeared in the pages of *New Socialist*. Chapter 2 has been published in *Tribune*. Chapter 5 is featured as part of the *Introduction* to the GLC's *London Industrial Strategy,* while chapter 12 consists of two parts of the same Authority's *London Financial Strategy*. The contribution from Mike Cooley has also been published by the International Metalworkers Federation. Chapter 9 is an excerpt from *Trade Unions and Politics* to be published by Basil Blackwell in 1986.

Joint Action for Jobs proposes a series of conferences in which these issues will be further explored. Some of these will, as soon as may be arranged, be international gatherings.

Part I

The Scope and Limits of National Action

Chapter 1

Time for a New Internationalism?

Ken Coates

Britain is being laid waste by unemployment. The precipitate decline of manufacturing industry, temporarily masked by support from oil revenues, has made all thinking people aware of a deep structural crisis. No voices are nowadays heard suggesting that this will all resolve itself, that perhaps tomorrow a new long-wave upturn will carry us all back to yesterday's levels of employment and economic activity. On the contrary, recovery presupposes a rupture with existing policies.

Not surprisingly, Labour Party activists are increasingly unanimous that the return of a Labour Government must be given overriding priority, precisely in order to reverse the drift to what threatens to be irreversible decline. The truth is that such decline is part of an overall crisis, affecting many countries at once. In this, monetarism and militarism are inextricably joined together, and democracy itself becomes an increasingly tenuous commitment for some of those in authority. Here at home this crisis is simply more acute than in most other areas, and its social effects are aggravated by deliberate decisions which actually deepen it. In addition, Mrs Thatcher's serial attacks on local Government autonomy and trade union independence represent an onslaught on political pluralism, which onslaught seeks to limit collective powers of response and self-defence by all the weaker groups in society. The erosion of welfare, a conscious drive to limit low incomes still further, seeding more and worse poverty: all these events form part of a calculated policy, which less than a decade ago would have been deemed unthinkable by the overwhelming majority of politically active people of almost every persuasion. Unfortunately, afflictions like these are also being imposed across a wide territory outside Britain. There, too, they delay recovery, including British recovery.

Previous international collapses of this kind have been resolved by desperate measures, usually involving war. This solution is no longer possible. War might quite possibly result from the intense competition and conflict which seethes beneath this crisis, but it will provoke no regeneration, because it will end in nuclear winter.

Never, certainly not in 1945 when it obtained its most overwhelming popular victory, has the Labour Party in Britain faced such a daunting set of prospects. What can British socialists do to promote recovery, restore employment, and regain the social initiative? The strange thing in 1985 is not that this question is discussed, but that the debate is so subdued.

After the 1979 defeat, Labour was naturally preoccupied with reforming its own structures, in order to avoid the possibility of a recurrence of various apostasies culminating in the winter of discontent, which had revealed a fundamental and wide division between the Labour Government and the people it represented. We were involved at the same time in the debate about an alternative economic strategy. In its consensual form, and at the time it was developed, this offered some realistic choices, assuming that oil revenues could be directed to industrial recovery. But time has been running out, and even if the oil has not, its price has been seriously undermined in the continuing slump. Today, the prospect is dismal. Greater unemployment will be followed by still greater problems, while the wreckage continues unabated. We now have to ask ourselves, what is the scope for a national recovery, and what are the limits set upon it?

The unhappy record of the Callaghan administration no longer stands alone. In France, in spite of some important ameliorative measures, the trajectory of the Mitterrand Government seems from this distance to be very similar to Labour's 1974-79 experience. In Spain, the Gonzalez team presides over staggering levels of unemployment, and begins to encounter strikes and protests on an ascending scale. That the Spanish Socialist Party voted to declare itself 'Marxist' only shortly before its electoral victory has not notably changed its behaviour, which seems uncannily familiar to those of us who were so recently arguing about the identical drift of policy under eminently British Fabians and pragmatists. That Britain has harboured a political tradition of patronage and corporatism is true: but no House of Lords has neutered the reforming zeal of the French. The very least we can say about these European experiments, while hoping that they may yet rescue themselves, is that they reflect a pattern, which shows how very difficult it is for middle-sized nations to escape from the effects of structural crisis.

As we have seen, when any medium-weight states goes for growth it stimulates imports from other nations, and creates jobs for them. Shortly afterwards, it then encounters problems with its balance of payments, and hostile visits from the bankers. Then it retrenches, deepening the slump at home and abroad. To break this jinx, the lesser states will have to act together. In large parts of the world which are crippled by the debt crisis, the same truth applies. But even the best Governments are timid about such co-operation. How can they be encouraged to act? How can the peoples who are the victims of crisis join their forces to re-orient or remove Governments which oppose joint recovery? It is this problem which must figure at the top of the socialist agenda for the next decade.

British and European trade unionists are increasingly aware of the uncontrolled power of multinational corporations. But we do not always link the questions which these place on our agenda. Every recent Labour Party briefing on the economy has stressed the outflow of capital from Britain: nearly £50 billion during the Thatcher years from 1979-83, and over £15 billion a year now.

There are, of course, more modest counterflows, amounting to £4 billion foreign investment in Britain in 1984. But both of these statistics are usually seen as cash-flows, and the larger of them is rightly perceived as a deprivation of the ruined areas of our declining regions. That is a proper and a natural reaction: but it is even more important that they should also be seen as a shifting and concentration of *power,* involving still further transnational encroachments both in Britain, in Europe, and further afield. British capitalism is being abolished, not as Tony Crosland and others thought, by the advance of managerialism, but by the processes of internationalisation. Old capitalism grew when trade followed the flag. Today's trade goes all around the flag, and a large part of it consists of transfers within the giant corporations themselves.

Increasingly, British workers in what is left of the viable (to a frightening degree, transnational) economy in their own country stand in the same bargaining position that the British mineworkers or other trade unionists occupied in the early decades of the 19th century. Area and county associations of labour then linked up, only to find very soon that employers were always a jump ahead, and able to offset their local claims by calling in supplies or resources from other districts.

Already the same logic that forced our British pioneers to take to the trains, and exploit the penny post, to begin to form their links at national level, now positively compels similar, functional association at international level. This becomes urgent, not only in such vital bodies as the European Trade Union Confederation but in the creation of links between enterprise-level trade unions which can enable them to match and outpace their footloose employers.

More: as capital ranges across the world, beyond the reach of national trade union centres, it also escapes the controls of national governments.

The collapse of the old consensus in Britain was the result of the erosion of the 'Keynesian World Order', even if it was reinforced by the decline of Empire and the rotting away of great power status. Post-war full employment was maintained by state intervention in economic management according to Keynesian prescriptions, and this positively assisted the development of giant transnational corporations. Because these gradually acquired the power to override or ignore national economic regulations, they directly seeded the malaise which ultimately destroyed full employment. As more and more trade was carried on 'internally' between different national outposts of the same giant companies, so devices like transfer pricing nullified certain key state economic policies. Companies could duck out of taxes and harvest their profits in the most favourable patch. Governments lost almost all direct power to regulate economic activity by the major enterprises in their territories. A Dutch auction of interest rates (and inflation) between different states resulted from the evolution. Governments which had never opened the door to any constructive involvement by workers in the democratic management of industry, and which only imperfectly understood what was happening in the world of the multinationals, found themselves confronting the trade unions in order to limit this inflation by restricting the one hitherto unchallenged union prerogative, of free collective bargaining. Ultimately incomes policies proved inadequate, as was entirely predictable: whereupon they gave way to attempts at direct physical control of union behaviour. The resultant explosions played their own part in scapegoating trade unions as causes of economic decline, while transnational corporations, the real culprits, remained completely unchallenged. The 1979 Conservative Government actually increased this untrammelled corporate power by the simple device of encouraging the collapse of huge numbers of under-capitalised smaller firms and vulnerable industries, leaving the transnational companies in an even stronger relative position.

This is a rapidly developing problem, and it demands a radical response. If trade unions need to join hands to meet it, how much more do the political organisations of Labour? How long can we be content with purely formal, top-level meetings between Socialist Parties? Do we not need to move towards the creation of an inclusive, comprehensive European Labour forum, bringing together representative activists across the continent, and exploring the possibilities of joint and convergent policy formation? The shape of such a project is outlined below in papers by Terry Ward, Michael Barratt Brown, John Palmer and Frances Morrell.

Already in 1983, the Labour Party fought the European Elections alongside other European Socialist Parties, on an agreed platform. The economic section of this combined Manifesto was strongly influenced by the programme *Out of Crisis,* to which we have already referred in the Introduction. This group was co-ordinated by Stuart Holland. Some of Stuart Holland's phrases were actually highlighted as keynote sections of the new programme: as was the catchword demanding an end to 'Beggar my neighbour' deflation and the adoption of 'Better my neighbour' expansionary policies in a co-ordinated linkage. The European sociailists agreed on this diagnosis, and on a package of proposals which based recovery on a move to joint policies of redistribution and restructuring. Whilst nobody, least of all the original authors of *Out of Crisis*, believed that these proposals represented the last word on how to overcome the slump, such proposals certainly do represent a convincing beginning. As is the case with many major political programmes, *Out of Crisis* contains certain creative ambiguities which leave scope for variations of approach. Whilst committed to participatory involvement in planning, the precise form of such planning would necessarily depend on the initiative and negotiating power of those involved. Stuard Holland returns to some of these issues in the last chapter of this book.

There is room for argument about how such initiative can be exercised within different industrial relations systems: but there is surprisingly general agreement that there will be small chance of recovery unless the initiative and inventiveness of working people can be brought directly into play.

The formal commitment of Socialist Parties to this kind of framework seems to be variable. Neil Kinnock published a strong article along these lines, and took up these themes as a consistent part of his campaign in the European Elections. In Greece, Prime Minister Papandreou has persistently pressed this case, even at the time of his Presidency of the EEC. Other Government leaders have been less consistent. Consistency in advocating international action, however, does not bring it about. Even the Greek Government has at least been compelled to enter the vicious process of enforced austerity and conflict with trade unions. At the same time, governmental pressures are not the only ones which can affect this issue.

The power of multinational companies has called up a variety of responses from trade unionists. The idea of planning agreements, greatly developed in *Out of Crisis*, was originally put forward in Britain in an effort to enlist trade union help in controlling their direction. Throughout the lifetime of the Wilson-Callaghan Governments, however, no real planning agreements were ever concluded. The proposal that such agreements would be mandatory was razored out of the Party's industrial legislation, as a result of business pressures. Only when Chrysler were at the point of collapse was some sort of half-cock planning agreement contrived as part of the process of state-financed resuscitation. Rightly greater attention was attracted by the path-breaking initiative of workers at Lucas Aerospace, who prepared an 'Alternative Corporate Plan' for the conversion of their plants to socially useful production. The Lucas Plan caught the imagination of Labour movement activists as did no other single socialist initiative of that time. Labour Ministers of left and right steadfastly stonewalled when asked to bring pressure for the implementation of the Plan. But a new generation of Labour Councillors drew inspiration from it, and it became the foundation of a whole industrial strategy in Local Enterprise Boards.

Lucas workers may have found their own Labour Government to be deaf: but they attracted prodigious attention from trade unionists overseas. Mike Cooley, a most compelling spokesman of the Stewards' Combine Committee, found himself preaching all over Europe, from Italy up to Sweden. The Shop Stewards' Committee was nominated for a Nobel Prize, but the prize which Mike Cooley actually received was that of victimisation, in which the allegedly left-wing leaders of his trade union played a truly shameful role.

It is not an accident that Cooley soon found himself working with the Greater London Enterprise Board. Mass unemployment and the disciplinary forces of anti-union legislation were a powerful check on trade union rank and file initiative and on the movement for Workers' Control, which burgeoned in the 1960s and 70s. Experiments in industrial democracy, squeezed out of factories, moved into the field of Local Government, where protection could be afforded, not only to co-operatives, but to other sometimes more challenging initiatives.

The development of alternative, and more 'green' technologies became materially possible within this more sympathetic environment. It became thinkable to socialise the entrepreneurial function, and at the same time to vastly increase the scope for action by women, as well as by minority groups against whom discrimination is common.

At this level, we find a potential growth point for ideas of

European recovery. As Local Authorities seek to tackle the malaise of unemployment and enter into a wide variety of job creation schemes, they begin to need links which can facilitate direct meeting and mutual support. Often they find themselves liaising closely with enterprise level trade unions, themselves troubled by the discriminatory effects of multinational company policies. In Britain the Greater London Council has done pioneering work in this field, on which rests a large part of the analyses of Robin Murray, Mike Cooley himself, and Richard Minns in chapters five, seven and twelve.

Neither at the level of Governments and Party General Secretaries, nor at the level of the Town Hall and the trade union combine committee, does European co-operation imply acceptance of the framework of the EEC. But it does imply a resolute rejection of the kind of nationalism so ably voiced by Les Huckfield and some of his colleagues in the European Parliament. As the interpenetration of capital locks the continent into a great transnational vice, such voices sound more and more like the provincial diehards, who, in the last century, saw no point in linking their local trade union to a national movement, or in consulting with fellow workers outside the confines of their own Parish.

Ken Livingstone offers wiser counsel in his contribution to this book. To the extent that each national economy in Europe is still tied to the rules of an external financial regime (however weakened this has been), he argues "independent macro-economic management has been reduced in scope without (developing)* the mechanisms for European macro-management, (so)* that Europe is, as a result, overcast by the shadow of the American economy just as it is overcast militarily by the shadow of the American arsenal". The need to escape from this shade has led him to insist on a "much stronger public interventionary body in the EEC — a European Enterprise Board (EEB)". Such a Board would, he believes, replicate, on a very much larger scale, the experience gathered in London. It could offer a central role to trade unions and user groups in evolving sectoral strategies of genuine benefit to the working community, and it would deploy large investment funds "according to long-term social criteria, not short-term financial returns".

The argument for these kinds of structures is, of course, quite inimical to the original prospectus of the Treaty of Rome, and this gives rise to the need for an either comprehensive review of that Treaty, or for joint action outside its framework, in order to insist

(*insertion by KC).

upon top priority for the restoration of full employment. But whether or not this happens, what is to prevent linkages between municipalities across Europe to build co-operation from the ground up?

Is the Labour Party committed to this kind of strategy, or is it still anchored to the view that Britain must go it alone? It hardly seems plausible that Labour could carve out a truly non-nuclear defence policy, requiring the withdrawal of all American nuclear bases from these islands, and confront friend and opponent alike in Western Europe at the same time. Why not, as one distinguished elder statesman of the unions has whimsically asked, declare war on China as well?

But this is not simply a matter of prudence: a necessary restriction of options for tactical reasons. The fact is that West European nation states, just like Britain, no longer have adequate scope for effective autonomous economic action. Can Europe (all Europe, not simply the EEC) converge upon a common recovery strategy, and create the instruments with which to carry it through? The only practicable approach which offers itself for such a convergence would involve a completely new set of relationships with the Third World, and with developing China. This could be a coalition for peace, as well as development and recovery. It need offer no threat to anyone. There is, of course, another model of European unity, but this is a very ugly one. However, it is not very likely that a European superpower, imitating others which have already arrived on the world scene, could lever itself into existence. Transnational capital is probably too advantageously interlocked readily to sustain the idea of a European super-state. The political space occupied by Mrs Thatcher, hiding behind the ghost of Adam Smith, surely reflects a transnational corporate prejudice in favour of less government, not more. It is trade unions, oppressed and rejected groupings, the poor and the weak who need strong social agencies for their defence, and who could come to see the virtue in establishing these at the transnational level. Indeed, might not the whole struggle against privilege and economic challenge be easier to wage in the process of evolving transnational democratic controls?

It can certainly be argued that whilst any oil money remains, there remains a (continuously diminishing) possibility of an independent British reform strategy. But what is clear is that the British disease is already spreading across Europe, and the scope for joint action against its effects is growing as steadily. Before our time runs out, the sensible thing to do is to use what leverage we have to create the alliances we need for survival.

If this argument is well founded, then it follows that Labour movements throughout Europe should be aiming at a joint representation committee in which rank and file trade unionists and socialists can find a common focus on their problems. Even if it takes time to establish such a forum, it is necessary to try, in order to create the kind of fulcrum from which to lever movement in the political institutions of the states which make up Europe. In Britain, everyone understands that we need a Labour Party which is broadly inclusive of all the relevant strands of thought and organisation present among working people, and that we need such a Party regardless of the shape which may be taken from time to time by Local Government structures, political constituencies, and economic institutions. A European labour forum is also needed, whether there is an EEC or not, or whether that community deploys itself to our advantage or against it. Only by seeking agreement on detailed policy, and arousing general discussion which can bring together all the divergent interests of European working people, can we begin to arrive at the possibility of new choices.

A beginning has been made by the peace movements of Europe, which, in July 1985, held their fourth general assembly in Amsterdam, the END Convention. At Amsterdam representatives of all the major peace movements gathered to take part in a wide series of workshops, some of which have maintained continuous contacts since the first Convention in Brussels back in 1982. If the peace movements can organise this kind of discussion, why not Labour Parties and trade unions as well?

As a step in this direction, the Russell Foundation has been consulting with politicians, trade unionists, religious leaders and town Mayors in order to launch a programme of joint action for jobs, which can work out practical forms of co-operation between towns, enterprises and social institutions. If this kind of initiative catches on, the framework of political response can change. It will begin to be possible to shape resources to meet needs. Perhaps the main reason why recent factional differences in the British Labour Party have been so off-putting has been that to many thinking people, they have been so irrelevant to these present demands. No matter who prevails in a nationalistic Labour Party, many of us have an uneasy feeling that the result may be the same: modest reforms followed by increasing retrenchment, followed by electoral defeat. Worse: nationalism narrows our goals and lowers our sights, just at the time when we need to aim high and free our people's imaginations to tackle the immense tasks which face us.

If we set ourselves the goal of creating a truly European Labour movement before the end of the century, and of elaborating the policies which can unite such a movement, then we can mark out a series of national policies which lead in that direction. We can greatly expand our political activities for shorter working time as well as joint recovery measures, which will give practical solidarity to Danes, Spaniards and Germans who are fighting the same battles, and help to widen the linkages. Our towns can form material as well as political links, exploring all the practical possibilities of job creation and joint production, from Sweden to Greece. To advocate joint action does not mean waiting until all have agreed: it means doing what can be done, and reaching out for support. It means helping others and seeking help. It means a revolutionary change in 'foreign' policy, moving to create a world in which there are no foreigners, only comrades.

The British TUC was launched by local Trades Councils, beginning with a modest initiative from Manchester. Maybe, more than a century on, a 'local' British Labour Movement could help to play a similar role in catalysing a genuine European movement out of crisis, out of division and away from war.

Chapter 2

Why do we Need a European Solution?

Terry Ward

Unemployment in the UK is part of a wider European and global problem. Its origins lie in the economic recession which has persisted with varying degrees of severity in Europe since 1973 and which by the early 1980s had spread to most parts of the world. The causes of this prolonged period of slow growth are the subject of some dispute. But it is difficult to deny that the enormous and destabilising expansion of private capital flows between currencies, the breakdown of global management of international finance and exchange rates in the face of this and the policy response of the major Governments to these phenomena, as well as to the financial problems created by the emergence of large OPEC surpluses in 1974 and again in 1979-80, are key factors.

Governments throughout Europe and in many other parts of the world, whatever their political complexion, have come to attach overriding priority to securing and maintaining the confidence of financial markets which have become truly international in their operations. In order to appease markets, objectives of employment, growth and the achievement of various social goals have been sacrificed in favour of lower State borrowing, the avoidance of balance of payments difficulties and the containment of inflation. Some like the Thatcher Government have adopted this course of action with enthusiastic zeal, many more have done so with reluctance, convinced however that to follow any other course would precipitate speculation against their currencies, the rapid exhaustion of external sources of borrowing and a financial crisis to feed internal opposition to their policies. Examples abound of governments curtailing expansion under pressure from international market forces, monetarist governments in other countries and international organistions like the IMF. The Mitterrand Government in France which was pursuing only very modest expansionary policies is the most familiar recent example in a long list which includes the Labour Government in the UK in

1976, the Carter administration in the US in 1978 and now the present UK Government at the beginning of 1985, demonstrating that even governments committed to monetarist ideals are not immune from market pressure.

In these circumstances, recession spread rapidly from country to country in the 1970s as one government after another, willingly or unwillingly, curtailed growth and became increasingly reluctant to take the lead in initiating expansion for fear of provoking hostile market reaction. This was particularly the case in Europe where the degree of interdependence between nation-states in terms of trade and production had developed much further than anywhere else. In a region where imports typically account for one-third or more of expenditure and exports one-third or more of output and where two-thirds of trade is with other European countries, market contraction in any one place is bound to have significant repercussions elsewhere and can quickly lead to a cumulative process of deflation. The role of financial markets was to reinforce this process, to inhibit the pursuit of mutually beneficial expansionary policies and to turn economic interdependence into a curse rather than the blessing which it had seemed to be in the 1950s and 1960s.

Stagnation of the European market induced by restrictive fiscal and monetary policies is the main cause of present high levels of unemployment in Europe, which few countries have been able to avoid and then only by extensive programmes of subsidising employment. This stagnation is also a major reason for slow growth in the rest of the world and the debt burdens incurred by developing countries. Since Europe is by far the most important market in the world economy, recession here has a powerful depressing effect on the export earnings of other countries and their ability to sustain development programmes without running into borrowing difficulties.

The response of European governments to stagnation of markets and constraints on financial expansion has been to focus increasingly upon competitiveness and the acquisition of larger market shares as the key to faster growth and lower unemployment. This has led to pressure on wages and on social welfare programmes paid for by taxes on businesses. But lower production costs offer no route to general recovery, particularly in Europe where one country's gain tends to be another country's loss and where accordingly attempts at increasing competitiveness can be offset by slower market growth as the losers in the competitive race are forced to adopt ever more restrictive policies.

Alternatively, Europe has looked to the US to initiate global expansion, but recent experience has demonstrated that the leverage exerted by US growth on the European economies is nowhere near strong enough to pull them out of recession without a fundamental change in the policy stance of European governments. This should not be too surprising given the relatively small share of the US market taken by European producers and the relatively small size of that market as compared with the European one.

The only way in which Europe as a whole is likely to regain the rates of real income growth and levels of employment enjoyed before 1973 and thereby facilitate world economic recovery is through the common adoption of more expansionary policies. Then the high degree of interdependence between countries would serve to spread the beneficial effects of growth throughout the region, while expansion of a market as large as the European one would greatly ease the balance of payments problems of developing countries and allow them to achieve more acceptable rates of growth. But for the adoption of expansionary policies to be feasible requires fundamental reform of international finance — or at least of the European monetary system — so that it acts to support recovery and the creation of new jobs instead of enforcing deflation. Equally for expansionary policies to be pushed far enough to make significant inroads into the problem of unemployment in all parts of Europe, let alone into the problem of inadequate growth in the Third World, requires the establishment of a mechanism for correcting the trade imbalances which would inevitably widen as recovery gets under way. International trade flows need to be managed so as to ensure so far as possible that a country's need for growth, in terms of the prevailing level of unemployment, degree of industrialisation and so on, is matched by its ability to grow, in terms of its capacity to generate export earnings in line with its demand for imports.

The conclusion reached in the *Out of Crisis* report published two years ago was that the scope for unilateral action at the national level to secure faster rates of economic growth and thereby to bring down unemployment is extremely limited. What is required is international action to reform the global system of trade and finance to open up the possibility of the adoption of expansionary policies and to allow each country to pursue its own national objectives instead of being constrained to comply with the dictates of world market forces.

It is a conclusion which is no less valid today, even though it is now being contested, at least implicitly, by those who are at present arguing that the recent success of the US in generating employment demonstrates that through a judicious mix of fiscal and monetary policy it is in fact possible for a national government to expand output and create jobs unilaterally. The UK or any other European country could, so the argument goes, emulate the US and bring down unemployment sharply if only the Government were prepared to expand budgetary policy enough to stimulate output growth and at the same time raise interest rates enough to appease the international money market, protect the exchange rate and avoid a financial crisis.

The difficulty with this argument is, first, that it is yet to be seen how long the US can sustain growth in the face of a rapidly mounting trade deficit and foreign debts in the face of a dollar which is becoming increasingly vulnerable to speculative pressure. The lesson of 1978 when the Carter administration was forced to introduce austerity measures only one year before a presidential election is that international financial market forces can be kept at bay only for so long. Secondly, the UK, or any other individual European country, does not possess the same perceived inherent economic strength as the US and a comparable degree of self-sufficiency. The balance of payments, for example, would deteriorate by about twice as much — and foreign debts would accumulate at twice the rate — for any given rise in internal expenditure as that of the US. What level of interest rates would be required to attract money from abroad under these circumstances and could the increasing trade deficit and foreign debts simply be ignored?

A more realistic comparison is between the US and Western Europe as a whole. Co-ordinated European budgetary action to expand output might indeed be capable of reducing unemployment substantially, but that is precisely what the *Out of Crisis* report concludes.

Where does that leave us? Seemingly in the unfortunate, and unacceptable, position of having to wait until there are enough like-minded governments prepared to co-operate in the pursuit of expansion and in the reform of international trade and financial arrangements to take effective action against unemployment. This, however, is much too pessimistic a conclusion. Although limited, there is some scope in a number of countries for the adoption of a more expansionary policy stance without much risk of financial crisis, even without other countries following suit.

Beyond that, policies of redistributing income, wealth and jobs can always in principle reduce unemployment in acceptable levels and ensure that the costs of continued recession are equitably borne. Though growth has proved over the years to be the most effective and reliable way of reducing unemployment, the difficulty, or indeed, the impossibility, of achieving adequate rates of growth should not be used, as so often in the past, as an excuse for abandoning employment objectives and social goals. If public expenditure on job creation or on subsidising employment or various kinds of work-sharing arrangements cannot be financed by additional borrowing then it has to be financed by increasing taxes. While this is a less efficient policy, in the same sense that it does not necessarily produce more income and output in aggregate but merely redistributes the money which is spent from the private sector to the public sector and thereby achieves control over how it is used, it may nevertheless be the only viable means under present circumstances of reducing unemployment. At the same time, changing the composition of domestic expenditure towards social programmes and away from luxury goods which are frequently imported is likely to mean a higher proportion of spending going on domestic production and therefore some loosening of the balance of payments constraint on growth.

A campaign against unemployment can serve a vital function in drawing attention to the possibilities of creating jobs. It can demonstrate that though the obstacles are formidable it *is* possible to provide work to all those who want it. It can put pressure on the Government to adopt more expansionary policies and it can show that through redistribution of both income *and* work — it is essential that the two are considered together otherwise the jobs that are shared will inevitably be those towards the bottom end of the income scale — unemployment can be brought down to tolerable levels. Local authorities have a major potential role to play in this respect, since in the absence of central government interference, they have the capacity to channel income into creating jobs which maximise the effect on the number of people employed while at the same time ensuring that social objectives are not ignored. If these activities are co-ordinated then the likelihood of jobs merely being relocated from one local authority area to another can be minimised.

How far a programme of redistribution can be pushed and how far, therefore, unemployment can be reduced will depend on the prevailing consensus. Although one of the most important aims of the campaign will be to increase the possibilities for redistribution, it has to be recognised that any such programme will have to contend with powerful interest groups which will be able to count on the support of the international financial market in resisting higher taxes and other measures which seem to threaten monetary stability and the cost competitiveness of domestic products.

A campaign against unemployment as well as concrete action to create jobs would, however, have more credibility and more chance of success if carried on at the European rather than the national level. Then common pressure could be exerted against all governments pursuing restrictive policies, increasing the possibility that an expansionary move in one country would lead to similar moves elsewhere. Local authorities and trade unions could co-ordinate their activities across national boundaries, exchanging information and ideas, negotiating agreements on purchasing policies and working practices and mounting a concerted defence against attacks on wages, conditions of employment and social welfare. They could endeavour to ensure that the jobs created, whether in the public or private sector were reasonably secure, useful and tolerably well-paid and that any reduction in unemployment achieved was not at the cost of accepting a deterioration in working conditions and a reversal of the social advances made in the post-war years.

After 12 years of recession and almost continuous increases in unemployment throughout Europe the need for a transnational campaign of this kind which not only draws attention to the common nature of the problem and the unacceptability of it continuing, but also proposes concrete measures for its alleviation and presses for their implementation is long overdue. It will become increasingly urgent as time goes on because without fundamental changes in the operation of the global economic system and without the acceptance of the need for international co-operation to manage trade and finance both within Europe and outside, unemployment will continue to rise and social deprivation will become even more widespread.

Chapter 3
Can European Workers Cope with Transnational Capital?

Michael Barratt Brown

Entry into the European Economic Community in the 1960s was seen by its advocates as a promise of greater opportunities for British industry to compete for a place in a rich and expanding market, for the British people to share in rising standards of living on the Continent. The reality has been that British manufacturing firms have collapsed in face of the competition. Imports have grown in every sector and have only been paid for by the flood of North Sea oil. Giant companies that once exported goods from British plants have moved their production abroad, especially to the Continent. Capital that might once have been invested in British industry has flowed out at a staggering rate, which rose in 1984 to 15 billion pounds. Half of this steady flow over the years has gone to Europe.

Britain's trade has become increasingly concentrated on Europe and as movements of goods inside the transnational companies, at the expense of traditional and more balanced links with partners in the Third World, but the new balance is more and more unfavourable. The UK deficit on trade in goods is no longer even covered by the sale of oil and services. The government cuts back spending to reduce the import bill, but this only weakens the home market for firms manufacturing in Britain. Other countries follow suit in making similar cuts and the volume of world trade, which had been growing steadily at 10 per cent per year up to 1979 failed to grow for four years and has only just begun to recover in 1984-85, with Europe lagging far behind Japan and the USA. The problem is not just a British one. The European boom of the 1960s and 1970s simply ground to a halt after 1979.

To say, as Mrs Thatcher so often does, that we have all been caught in a world-wide slump, appears to transfer to some external force the effects of deliberate actions of governments pursuing policies of 'beggar-my-neighbour' in an increasingly competitive world, through exchange rate and interest rate manipulation and protective tariffs and subsidies. Summit meeting follows summit meeting, at which European and world leaders discuss what measures they are all taking to encourage free movement of goods and capital. But this only means freedom for the largest companies to grow at the expense of small and even medium-sized businesses. Common policies of joint government action to plan for an expansion of purchasing power leading towards increased employment are not merely neglected but firmly rejected as inflationary and likely to distort the workings of the market. It is not made clear that in the case of Coal and Steel and of Agriculture common policies in Europe totally distort the market at the expense of British coal and steel production and of British food consumption, which is priced at double world levels. It would not, however, make for any improvement in Britain's or any other country's position to apply similar methods of protection to manufacturing industry. In this, at least, the government leaders are right. Merely to agree to exclude from the European Community the products of Japanese or United States industry or Third World products would but raise the price of European manufactures, as well as of European agricultural products, to double world levels.

The fact is that it is not simply a crisis of exchange, of circulation as Marx would have called it, which the capitalist world is going through, and the countries building socialism are equally suffering from. It may appear to be a matter of foreign payments and debts, of exchange rates and interest rates, of private and public spending proportions. Behind this there is a crisis of production, which makes impossible a return to things as they were before Thatcher, to a revival of Keynesian measures of national and international deficit budgeting. Thatcher is right about that too. But there is another alternative which we can follow if we will only grasp the nature of this crisis. In one aspect we know what this is only too well. It is the advent of the micro-chip incorporated into information systems in the first stages of a new technology that will reduce the greater part of human mental activity in production. At the same time, the last stages are being reached in the old technology which applied mineral energy to replace much of human physical activity in production. Those enterprises and those countries which have been most effective in combining these two revolutionary changes in the forces of production have been able enormously to reduce the costs of production in terms of human effort. Despite the increased costs of energy inputs they have been able to drive all others out of a wide range of economic activity and to accumulate capital on a scale that has enabled them to dominate industrial development throughout the world.

This development has not been like that of Britain's emergence as the workshop of the world in the 19th century, when what Marx called machino-facture replaced manufacture. Today we have to speak of systemo-facture. The workshop is not in one enterprise or in one country. Production of goods and even of some services is spread right across the world, component parts sourced in a 100 places to be assembled at key points, transported and distributed under the control of one single directing centre, using all the aids of modern information systems. Sources, designs and parts can be switched and costings regularly compared and analysed to provide the most flexible but the most controllable instruments of production on a global scale.

This production system requires not only the most complex and speedy information network and control procedures inside the company, but the involvement of the workforce and appropriate macro-economic policies from local and regional government. The Ford Motor Company in Europe was, for example, making it clear throughout 1984 that (1) only a "joint commitment to change" by workers and management alike would protect jobs in Europe; and (2) only an "improvement in the external environment" created by government agencies, local, national and international (e.g. the EEC) would ensure the survival of Ford itself and the European motor car industry itself against Japanese competition. These two statements from Bill Haydn, vice-president of Ford of Europe, the one to Dagenham's workers, the other to Euro-MPs, clearly indicate the essentially tri-partite nature of the production system, as the big companies see it — company, workforce and government all working together. For this is how it is in Japan.

Outside Japan the way to achieve such integration has been for the companies to seek to divide and conquer, threatening each workforce and government in turn that they will take their business away, unless . . . . As a result each group of workers and each region or national government bids for the company's interest — workers agreeing to reduce wage claims and abandon hard-won controls over the work process, governments agreeing to reduce taxes and other controls. It is obvious that in this Dutch auction no single workforce or government can successfully go it on its own. Attempts at national protection and even nationalisation still have to come to terms with the international law of value. Even the USA with its vast market and resources would be hard put to it to survive in isolation from world markets and world resources. Its sheer size does, however, of course, give it a bargaining position with the giant companies that a smaller state like the UK could not rival. Is the answer, then, to take Bill Haydn's hint and improve the European "external environment", with Europe's workers following suit, to agree together on a "joint commitment to change"?

To answer the question, it is necessary to consider what is involved in each case. The external environment required by Fords included harmonisation of European car tax rates, grants and subsidies, vehicle regulations on emissions, use of lead in petrol, etc., and common measures of protection against Japanese imports, local content specifications etc. They also included a crucial reference to social policies. This means not only a state's legislation on employment protection, health and safety, hours of work, equal opportunities, social security insurance — all the so-called 'social charges' on employers — but also any social legislation that distorts market conditions. Car sales like the sales of many other products of modern industry depend on a distribution of incomes across the population that allows some workers to be paid well enough to afford to run cars, dishwashers, freezers, etc., while others are paid little enough to hold down the costs of producing these goods. The car industry no longer pays wages above the odds and car sales in recent years have grown mainly to meet the demand for a second car from households that already had one. Between 1971 and 1982 the proportion of households in the UK with a car rose only from 56 per cent to 59 per cent. A more equal distribution of income is not an "improvement in the 'external environment'" for the giant companies, whether they are thinking about the market in the UK or in Brazil, about cars or packaged holidays in the sun.

The requirements of the workforce in each country are equally clear. Employee involvement is the key phrase; and this does not mean an increased role for trade unions or increased workers control over their jobs. It means co-operation on the employer's terms with changes in the organisation of work and in the procedures governing it — in pace and effort, in job flexibility, demarcation between jobs, distinction between direct and indirect functions, inspection and supervision. These have all been accepted in Japan, where company unions have for long been the norm in private industry on the guarantee of life-long employment and of continuous consultation offered by the very large companies. The bargain is taken very seriously and the whole system would collapse if the guarantee were not honoured.

The answer to the question about taking up the Ford offer and similar offers at a European level can now be addressed. It is evident that it would depend on the conditions that could be obtained in the bargain. If European governments acted together, instead of bidding against each other, there is no doubt that they could exercise considerable power, and similarly if the workforces of each major company acted together they would enormously enhance their power to make the restructuring of production one that favoured labour rather than capital. They could between them ensure that cars sold in Europe were made in Europe and in conditions that were acceptable to European workers within a generally agreed code of best practice. There are, however, at least four flaws in such a proposal. First, it does nothing to pose a fundamental challenge to the power of the giant companies, but only strengthens the divisions between West European, Japanese and United States capital. Second, and related, it fails to support the demands of workers in the Third World, who can be further exploited without the assistance of their European comrades; and this can only work back to weaken wages and conditions in Europe. Thirdly, it assumes that the production of those goods in which the giant transnational companies specialise should be the main object of production, when we have already seen that the market for such goods by definition meets the needs only of the top half or two-thirds of the population. Fourthly, there is no possibility of manufacturing industry increasing the employment of the available workforce. The new technology means inevitably that jobs will be destroyed throughout industry. It is in the provision of services and particularly in social provision of health, education, the social and recreational services that future employment prospects must lie.

We can now draw some fairly firm conclusions from the arguments examined above for a combined European initiative to attain full employment:

1. It will need to have an opening to the Third World so as to unite their workers also in challenging the power of the giant companies to divide country and country, workforce and workforce;
2. It will need to be organised within an international structure, quite different from the existing EEC institutions — perhaps on the lines of the European Enterprise Board, proposed by Ken Livingstone in Chapter 10 below.
3. it will need to concern itself with expansion of public enterprise and social provision, subject to popular control, to meet social needs which the market fails to provide for and to stop social evils — pollution, land erosion, congestion, ill health that the market permits;
4. It will need to involve the trade unions in such a way that they

can retain their independence and strengthen their influence on behalf of working people, while contributing to the full employment programme.

Such a European initiative can begin from the links already being established between European cities and regions which have developed their own local employment programmes and on trading links already being established between Britain and the Third World. The structure that emerges cannot be imposed as a blueprint from above, but can only be built on the initiatives of local and regional authorities, which have done so much to involve community associations, trade unions, co-operatives, nuclear-free zones etc in their work. It will present a fundamental challenge to the existing institutions of the EEC and will certainly require major revisions in the Rome Treaty and the Common Agricultural Policy. The question is whether the institutions control us or we control the institutions. What are presented to us now as regulations to preserve free choice in a free market are in reality the product of the influence and the decisions of the largely unchallenged power of the giant transnational companies, through which the world's trade now flows and in whose hands capital accumulates.

A Strategy for European Employment Initiatives

The need is now recognised for a European dimension to any policy designed to lower the currently disastrous levels of unemployment and correct the current redistribution of incomes in favour of the rich. The nature of this European dimension is less well established. Yet it must depend on clear understanding of the reasons that have led to this new interest in European co-operation. These can now be summarised.

First, any government that attempts, as the French socialist government did, to reflate its economy on its own will immediately find that goods are pulled in from outside creating severe balance of payments difficulties and financial pressure on that government's currency.

Second, any measures which one government might use to protect plants in its country from competition would contravene EEC and GATT agreements and incur retaliatory measures, and these would in turn reduce the whole level of world trade exchanges.

Third, government measures to redistribute incomes away from the rich by curbing prices or stepping up taxation of large transnational companies and their shareholders, or even by reducing the concessions or other benefits available to them, would find that these companies either by-passed their measures through transfer pricing or switched their investment elsewhere.

Fourth, governments which proceed to take parts of transnational companies into public ownership through nationalisation and similar measures would immediately find not only that foreign markets were closed to them, but that essential parts were not available which were sourced from outside that government's territory.

Fifth, the trade unions and local and regional authorities, which would be needed to develop support for a joint international programme of recovery, are being systematically played off against each other by the trans-national companies, and as they are divided so are they conquered.

This whole situation has led to much pessimism and resignation in face of the seemingly uncontrollable power of the giant trans-national companies in relation to state power, let alone the power of the unions and local authorities. Stuart Holland has argued that nation state power has to be strengthened by international agreement to sustain national sovereignty in face of the increased power of these companies. I agree, but I would want to argue that such international action at state level can only be one arm of a pincer movement that also involves the trade unions and the local authorities where plants are located. The fact is that the transnational manufacturing company is today engaged in what we have called "systemofacture". The system involves not only, as we have seen, the sourcing of the final product from many different plants in several different countries, some plants belonging to the TNC, some to sub-contractors under franchise (and TNCs in the service industries like fast foods, hotels and tourism operate in the same way) but the system involves also joint planning by company, government and trade union; for this is how it is in Japan.

But this does not, however, require that Europe should copy exactly the Japanese model of planning by a central bureaucracy with a wholly incorporated trade union structure and hierarchically organised local authorities. If such a model is rejected, then it is necessary to find a framework for independent contributions to be made by trade unions and by popularly elected local authorities with sufficient power to bargain effectively with the big companies. The framework will have to be constructed by national governments, not on their own but rather as a result of agreement among themselves and not from above but rather from proposals formulated by the unions and local authorities. Such proposals will need to be of the most detailed kind directly related to the specific structures of the different companies and industries, and their elaboration will need to be part of a developing process.

Some firm beginnings have already been made in such a development. There are international trade secretariats of unions for fifteen different industries and these have a programme of regular conferences and special meetings to consider the problems in relation to specific multinational companies. To complement this at a lower level there are already important contacts established on a European scale and even on a wider scale between trade union shop floor representatives in Fords, Kodak, Unilever, Philips and some other transnational companies. These contacts have received considerable support from the city or local and regional authority in which plants are located, but no common action by states, unions and local authorities has so far been attempted with the aim of setting limits to the power of the transnational companies. Yet, the very need of the companies for joint planning offers a weapon that could be employed against them. The shape that this weapon should take has still to be formulated. That this is not an easy task has been demonstrated by the lengthy and detailed deliberations that a GLC Inquiry into the Ford Motor Car company's operations at Dagenham has been engaged in over the last several months.

At the same time there are already links established between different cities and regions in Europe and also outside through twinning initiatives of various sorts, including association through the movement for nuclear free zones. Some cities have reached agreement on the exchange of products, for example Sheffield with Tientsin in China and London with Ho Chi Minh city in Vietnam.

It is now urgently important to consider the nature of the strategy that could be agreed upon for joint union and local authority action to press for a new state framework within which the transnational companies should be required to operate. Some part of this strategy would necessarily have a European wide application but the increasing switch of transnational manufacturing company's operations to sources of production in the Third World suggests that an opening for involvement of Third World governments and trade unions should always be borne in mind. Most of the international contacts of the trade unions and local authorities in Europe have so far been limited to the exchange of information and the general raising of confidence that something can be done.

What is needed is a strategy — a programme of action — to bring trade union and local authority links into a working relationship with nation state planning, so as to operate a pincers movement on the power of the transnational companies. This means moving beyond mere information exchange to practical joint action, but what action? It is no more than an Utopian dream to think of transforming at a stroke the international power of private capital by bringing the giant companies and their financial intermediaries under national state control. Even the long term aim of bringing such institutions into public ownership would imply some prior agreement among several nation state governments that they would act together. But this is not an argument against starting to plan now the stages through which national plans could be linked together. Such a strategy will have to start from the kind of detailed research into the actual European activities of the transnational companies that the GLC has sponsored in relation to Fords and to Kodak.

This strategy could then be conceived in two parts:

1. from below through action by trade unions and local authorities;
2. from above through joint plans by nation states.

1. Action by Trade Unions and Local Authorities

a) the establishment of a continuous flow of information between workers' representatives and local authorities in different countries concerning the activities and forward planning of each of the major transnational companies with which they are involved; this should at the very least help to end the policy of divide and conquer that is now so successfully applied by most transnational companies in their dealings with trade unions and local authorities;

b) A code of employment should be drawn up, based on best practice achieved in any country. This could cover trade union recognition, disclosure of information, consultation on investment policy and future manning, health and safety standards, hours of work and time off for education and training, redundancy payments and procedures, pension rights, anti pollution standards and general protection of the environment. Examples of such model codes can be found in the ILO Resolutions and in the EEC Vredeling directive. Such codes could then be used by workers and governments in Third World countries to support them in their struggles with the transnational companies.

c) Wage levels are bound to vary according to local levels of economic development and of productivity. It is unlikely that agreement could be reached especially in relation to the Third World countries on a common wage level. Nevertheless, a monitoring system could be established to relate workers and productivity in order to protect workers from speed-up and super-exploitation.

d) The preparation of joint international corporate plans for investment and for the development of the several companies' products, so as to challenge the transnational companies' own planning and ensure that identified social needs are being met. It has already been proposed that the GLC should support the preparation of an international corporate plan for Lucas Aerospace. The Lucas shop stewards' original plan was concerned both with averting redundancies and with converting production from armaments. It is not only that many transnational companies' products are anti-social like arms production, but many are designed to meet the needs of a narrow range of consumers. As we saw earlier, even in the UK, for example, over 40 per cent of households have no car and are more interested in a better public transport system than in owning a car.

2. *Action by Nation State Governments*

a) Although wholesale nationalisation of the top several hundred companies is not a viable proposition, a public stake in manufacturing industry and in banking and finance through the deployment of public sector pension funds and in other ways would ensure that investment programmes can be monitored and experience gained and staff trained for managing institutions in a manner that places social need before private profit.

b) Corporate plans prepared by trade unions and local authorities would need to be incorporated into a national plan, prepared in consultation with other European governments and submitted for wide discussion. These plans would imply an important measure of agreement between the several areas and countries involved in the location of plants and production facilities. At the very least, it might be possible to agree that some minimum proportion (e.g. 75 per cent) of a product marketed in any country should be produced in that country.

c) National plans developed on the basis of international negotiation would need to include plans for long-term trade agreements on the level and composition of trade exchanges and on national specialisation, within which transnational companies would be required to conform and smaller companies encouraged to participate.

d) Prices of products would have to be subject to annual review in relation to the movement of world prices and to any special considerations that were agreed should enter into the calculations, especially in relation to the needs of Third World countries.

In conclusion it may bear repeating that the aim of this strategy is to make a serious attempt at curbing the irresponsible power of the giant companies which control so much of the world's output and trade, and to do this in a way that will bring about real improvements in workers' conditions in the short run as well as enabling trade unions and popularly elected local authorities and national governments to establish their authority over the major processes of production and finance in the longer term.

Chapter 4

A Common Programme for Europe's Left?

John Palmer

It has become strikingly evident in recent decades that any socialist strategy based on an isolated national economy — particularly one so far down the path of de-industrialisation and decline as Britain is — is doomed to failure. The growing impotence of the nation state in matters concerned with the international division of labour and the power of multi-national capital is well testified. While it would be wrong to deny the possibility of any serious action by a Left government at a national level, it is important to be realistic about what purely national 'power' can achieve in current circumstances. At best it can 'buy time' and counter the most blatant external subversions of a socialist economy. But a Left government which does not have the perspective of international support will risk isolation, will be vulnerable to de-stabilisation and so failing in its basic objectives as to open the door to radical reaction.

There is a trend in European ruling class politics towards an embryo 'European State'. For two or more decades it has been evident to the majority of large European capital that its interests required the developments of a stronger European economical and political executive. Although the evolution of the European Community 'Common Market' has gone some way to protect the interests of European capital this is now seriously inadequate in the face of the growing international crisis and competition from more advanced capitals based in the United States, Japan and some other countries.

There are also trends towards the 'regionalisation' of the world economy which have accentuated the need for European capital to organise itself on a comparable basis. So it is that European capital has identified the urgent need to bridge the 'technology' gap and to organise production, investment and trade in ways that mitigate intense international competition. The demand of the hardest hit sectors of European capital for defence of their interests at a European level is the strongest single impetus behind the repeated attempts of some West European governments and the EEC institutions to revive progress towards economic and political union. Equally, there are forces pushing for less 'Atlanticist' and more 'European' common foreign and security policies.

The trend towards the consolidation of the power of European capital and its expression in terms of the development of a European State is, of course, subject to the deepest contradiction. At a political level the National States in Western Europe, both within and outside the EEC itself have profound bureaucratic and other interests in resisting supra-nationalisation. Nowhere is this more clearly expressed than in the Thatcher Tory Government whose ideology towards Europe is still a strange admixture of pro-Common Market sentiments on trade and competition combined with a 'neo-Gaullist little Englandism' and a deep pro-Atlanticism in all fundamental matters affecting foreign and security policy.

A more profound obstacle to the creation of a united capitalist Europe is the obvious complicity of a large section of European big business in forms of collaboration with non-European capital. In an effort to counter the commercial and technological backwardness of European business many large European firms have preferred to strike commercial and technology co-operation agreements with American and Japanese companies rather than other European companies. This profound ambiguity will in the end have to be resolved if the political momentum towards European union is to be sustained.

There are a variety of other serious impedimenta in the way of European union. Among them are the imbalance in the development of existing European Community 'common' policies such as agriculture, budgetary disciplines, and the main provisions for an internal market under the treaty of Rome. Because of the unevenness of benefit and contribution already evident within the 10-nation Community it will be extremely difficult to work out an acceptable new treaty which would reconcile these conflicts of interests, particularly with enlargement to 12 or more member states.

The response to these developments of the Labour movement has been singularly deficient. No serious analysis has been made either of the trends towards the Euro-State nor of the mainly reactionary obstacles that still stand in its path. As a result the European Trade Union and Labour movement has not had the ideological means at its disposal to develop a politics capable of exploiting the opportunities in Europe created by the present economic and industrial crisis. Nowhere is the Labour movement suffering under a greater parochial narrowness than in Britain. Yet any serious reading of the situation facing the working-class movement at the present time demands far greater priority to strategies designed to mobilise the European Labour movement.

The striking feature of the present job crisis is that it is almost equally serious in impact throughout Western Europe. Although there are minor differences due, in the main, to variations in national economic policy being pursued by the different West European Governments, these are dwarfed by the common structural crisis affecting Western European industry. On current projections the present period of economic recovery which began some three years ago will peter out at the end of 1985 or in early 1986. Yet there was no interruption of the upward trend of unemployment in Western Europe during the period of so-called recovery. Any new economic recession must risk bringing unemployment throughout Western Europe as a whole to well over 20 million by the end of the decade.

Unemployment also tends to be concentrated in and around the same structurally declining industries — notably steel, coal, vehicle manufacture, construction, and textiles. There is also a common emerging pattern arising from mass unemployment in the fiscal burdens being imposed upon the West European welfare states. Everywhere governments are attempting to fund massive budget deficits induced by the enormous scale of current levels of resources being devoted to unemployment. This same fiscal constraint combined with high international interest rates means that national governments have virtually no maneouvring room to unilaterally reflate their economies. The appalling experience of the Mitterrand Government which reverted from Keynesian expansionism to Thatcherite monetarist austerity after 12 months in office is a striking testimony to these trends. Everywhere social democratic Governments in office are in full flood retreat before the goals of full employment, rising living standards, protected welfare spending and even basic civil and labour rights.

Although it will require sweeping changes made by like-minded governments throughout Western Europe to fundamentally alter the economic situation which has given rise to mass unemployment, a variety of steps can be taken in the immediate by Labour movements in opposition. These include:

1. Support for measures to bring trade unionists working in a common transnational corporations together to form a European combine of shop stewards. The GLC has been able to give direct encouragement to this kind of work with Fords, Kodak and Philips.
2. Such combines can prepare common strategies to force the far

greater disclosure of information about their companies and to lay the basis for a concerted strategy of resistance to plant closures and mass redundancies.

3. These combines, together with the wider European Trade Union Movement, can begin to discuss and raise the issues of alternatives, particularly for those sectors most hard hit by structural decline and mass unemployment. The whole impetus of the approach to workers' plans as first outlined by the Lucas Aerospace Shop Stewards, taken up by such bodies as the Greater London Enterprise Board, have particular relevance at the European level.
4. Such alternative workers' plans for key sectors of the European economy will not only identify areas of unfilled market and social needs, identify, through social audit techniques, unused labour and capital resources, but will also begin to broach at least the rudimentary questions of transnational trade planning. Any strategy, for instance, for the European motor industry, devised by trade unionists in that industry would have to involve some understanding about an appropriate and planned division of labour between the different national plants.
5. Progressive Local Authorities and other bodies in the European Community can also be persuaded to give encouragement to twin trading agreements. This would involve preference being given in the purchasing policies of progressive Local Authorities to enterprises receiving the financial backing of these Local Authorities or their Investment Agencies throughout the European Community.
6. In the same way, a network of mutual support and twin trading can be encouraged between the burgeoning European Worker Co-operative Movement. In this way something of a partial 'sheltered economic environment' can be developed both for worker co-operatives and for enterprises backed by the left Local Authorities which would go some way to enable them to survive in the present economic climate.
7. Conferences of all those engaged in this work should be held to discuss wider issues raised by their work, notably what demands are appropriate to place upon their respective national governments and what demands should be placed upon the institutions of the European Community. As far as the latter is concerned there should be a concerted programme of demands to expand the European Social Fund and to encourage the development of an EEC Enterprise Board to mobilise public sector resources at a European level to be put

behind worker co-operatives and other such enterprises.

8. There should be co-ordinated pressure for national strategies to be adopted by incoming Left governments which maximise European co-operation and minimise the dangers of nationalistic confrontation within Western Europe. One key priority here should be the future of the European Monetary System which could provide the basis for the European planning of exchange rates and currencies in ways that did not subordinate employment and living standards to the hegemony of bankers. Equally, there should be concertation of measures to extend public ownership, to impose controls on foreign trade and on capital movements to maximise reciprocity and mutual interests between like-minded governments.
9. There should be a concerted campaign to introduce European Community 'best practice' in welfare provisions, trade union rights, the contractual conditions for Labour, as well as redundancy and social benefit rights. If we live in a Common Market where the same rules governing the movement of capital or free trade apply we should also live in a community which has West German level unemployment pay, French level social security payments, or Dutch payments to single parent families. At the same time measures should be advanced to campaign for a common programme of equal rights for women and 'guest workers'.
10. Particular and immediate attention should be given to the demand for a shorter working week and the related demand by the trade unions for 'liberated time' that is the diversion of a part of 'excess production' in firms benefiting from new technology to enable them to extend output to socially useful areas outside the market.
11. The whole question of conversion from the arms industries and from nuclear based power must be integrated into any such strategy. Urgent work needs to take place to devise a common European workers' energy programme and a common programme to switch employment from arms to socially useful production.

These are only some of the issues which are possible to raise and to win support for in the perspective of a common European Left political strategy. None of this is to accept either the present Rome Treaty or the present boundaries of the European Community. To the contrary, the above demands are clearly incompatible with the Rome Treaty as it is currently framed and this demands an ultimate programme to replace the Rome Treaty with a new Treaty between West European Socialist Governments enshrining co-operation and co-ordination towards an ultimately common socialist United States of Europe. Such a United States of Europe could not but challenge the iron curtain which divides Europe down the middle. It goes without saying that every effort should be made to establish contact with the oppositional Trade Unions and peace movements in Eastern Europe with whom common cause in the struggle against nuclear alliances and bureaucratic despotism should be established. Finally, at least the beginnings of a dialogue with the Labour and Trade Union movements outside Europe must begin, particularly in the Third World. A European transnational strategy is itself only an interim towards a global internationalism to pose the fundamental question of worldwide socialism. In the meantime Left governments which obtain office must be placed under the maximum pressure to extend public ownership and to make radical changes in the whole character of state power so as to permit the growth of the embryonic institutions for a socialist economy and for democratic working-class power.

Chapter 5

What are the Lessons from London?

Robin Murray

There are today three great issues facing the British economy: de-industrialisation, the economic collapse of Britain's major cities, and the conditions of life and labour of Britain's working people. They are not separate, but three alternative aspects — sectoral, spatial and social — of a common economic problem. In each case London has been at the eye of the storm.

Take de-industrialisation first. As the result of the growth of mass production from the First World War onwards, London became one of the principal manufacturing centres of the UK. In 1951 there were more than one-and-a-half-million people working in London's factories. In 1961 the figure was 1.43 million. By 1983 it has fallen to 594,000 and the prospects are that it will have fallen to 485,000 by the end of the decade.

A similar pattern of industrial loss has occurred in the national economy. Britain lost 25 per cent of its manufacturing jobs in the decade between 1971 and 1981. But the decline has been steeper and more widespread in London. In the same decade London lost 36 per cent of its manufacturing jobs and inner London 41 per cent.

Furthermore, while at the national level the growth of services largely compensated for the decline of manufacturing, the same was not true in London. With the exception of financial, professional and miscellaneous services — which showed a small growth — every major sector of London's economy lost jobs. Table 1 gives a breakdown of the figures. Distribution lost 70,000 jobs, construction 53,000, transport and communications 80,000. Even public sector employment fell and those losses have increased in the last two years. In all, between 1973 and 1982 more than half a million jobs were lost in the London economy.

The result has been unemployment. Substantial even in the 1970s — the figure had reached 132,000 in 1979 — the registered total has trebled since then. In spite of a change in the method of

Table 1

Decline of Employment in Greater London 1973-83

Sector	*Numbers employed 1973*	*1983*	*% change*
Manufacturing			
Food, drink and tobacco	99,766	61,000	−39
Coal, petroleum and chemical products	60,860	44,000	−28
Metal manufacture	19,911	10,000	−50
Engineering and allied industries	404,871	266,000	−34
Textiles, leather and clothing	88,670	40,000	−55
Other manufacturing	250,008	173,000	−31
All manufacturing	924,086	594,000	−36
Infrastructure			
Construction	197,073	144,000	−27
Gas, electricity and water	56,156	41,000	−27
Transport and communications	419,672	340,000	−19
Distribution			
Distributive trades	528,939	459,000	−17
Other Services			
Financial, professional and miscellaneous services	1,397,716	1,468,000	+ 5
Public Administration and defence	344,700	313,000	− 9
All industries	3,872,739	3,366,000	−13

Percentage Unemployment Rate by Parliamentary Constituency, January 1985

calculation, in spite of the women who do not register for employment and in spite of the multiplicity of schemes to keep school leavers, students, and even those over 60 off the register, there were in March 1985 over 400,000 people registered as unemployed in Greater London. We estimate that there are a further 120,000 who are seeking work and would take paid employment if it were available. This is the largest urban concentration of unemployed people in the advanced industrial world. Our own forecasts suggest that registered unemployment in London will rise to at least 545,000 by 1990 if present government policies continue, as cuts in public spending, increased privatisation and the use of new technology bite deep into employment in once buoyant service sectors which alone have offered alternatives as manufacturing declined.

To describe de-industrialisation is to go to the heart of the second main economic issue in Britain, the economic decline of its major cities. In Liverpool, Manchester, the West Midlands, Tyneside, Glasgow, and Belfast the pattern and chronology of decline are similar. Between 1960 and 1981 London and the major conurbations lost 1.7 million manufacturing jobs, that is 79 per cent of the total national loss of 2.1 million jobs. The inner cities have become the newly depressed regions of the 1960s.

The acuteness of the urban crisis has been recognised sooner in the north than in the south. More recently the West Midlands has at last been made eligible for EEC regional aid. But London is still regarded as part of the prosperous south-east, whose pockets of decline can be solved by the trickle down of prosperity from neighbouring areas. The Department of Employment, for example, still insists that most of London should be treated as a single travel to work area and, as such, its unemployment rate of 11.5 per cent is below the national average.

The economies of cities do not work like this. Depression takes hold of particular areas. From the second half of the 1960s until the end of the 1970s, London's de-industrialisation was concentrated in inner London and the east. Docklands was particularly severely hit. In the period 1971-78 east London lost more than 20,000 docks jobs and 53,000 manufacturing jobs. The great names of the past have almost all run down or pulled out: AEI at Woolwich, P&O, Turners, Vestey, Tate and Lyle, Unilever, Spillers, Courage and many wharfside warehouses. Some of these sites still stand empty and broken windowed. Others have been demolished. There are whole roads of corrugated iron and guard dogs. In all there are some 11 million square feet of empty commercial and industrial office space in east London. In Tower Hamlets registered unemployment is now 21 per cent, in Newham 17 per cent. Male unemployment in Poplar is approaching 30 per cent. There are similar rates south of the river, in Greenwich, Deptford, Peckham, Bermondsey, then on into Lambeth and parts of Wandsworth, as well as to the north along the old river and canal industrial belts in Islington, Hackney and up the Lea Valley into Waltham Forest. Depression takes hold of particular sections of the population and particular areas. Inner London has an unemployment rate twice as high as outer London (16.7 per cent compared with 8.3 per cent). Black youths tend to experience as much as twice the level of average unemployment, with levels as high as 50 per cent in some areas.

The 1980s have deepened the economic crises in these areas, but they have also seen the spread of similar destruction to west London. In Hayes and Hounslow, Southall and Park Royal, a once thriving economic landscape has become like an industrial cemetery. The AEC bus factory, for example, which once employed 4,000 workers, has been razed to the ground. The household names of the long consumer boom, Hoover, Pyrene, Macleans, remain as no more than signposts above the old factory doors. The Firestone factory, like Hoover, one of the art deco creations of the 1930s, has gone altogether, demolished at night before the preservation order could be served.

Further west, Heathrow has lost 13,500 jobs in four years between 1979 and 1983, and further losses are forecast following the privatisation of British Airways. The result has been the emergence of rising rates of unemployment in west London: 12 per cent in Southall, 15 per cent in Brent, 15 per cent in Hammersmith and Fulham.

The jobs in the new warehouses and hotels in west London are not sufficient to provide employment in their immediate neighbourhoods, let alone for those in Docklands and London's inner ring of decline. From studies in these areas, it is clear that many workers are restricted to their neighbourhoods — by their dependence on council housing on the one hand and their lack of time and money to travel longer distances to work on the other. London is not a single labour market, but a set of overlapping ones: wider in range for the better paid, for men and those without domestic responsibilities (there are still more than one million commuters into central London every day), narrow for manual workers, particularly women, and many of London's 314,000 black workers. There is no clearer example of the distance between them than in Tower Hamlets. There, the council tower blocks stand facing the commercial skyscrapers of the City: the one representing

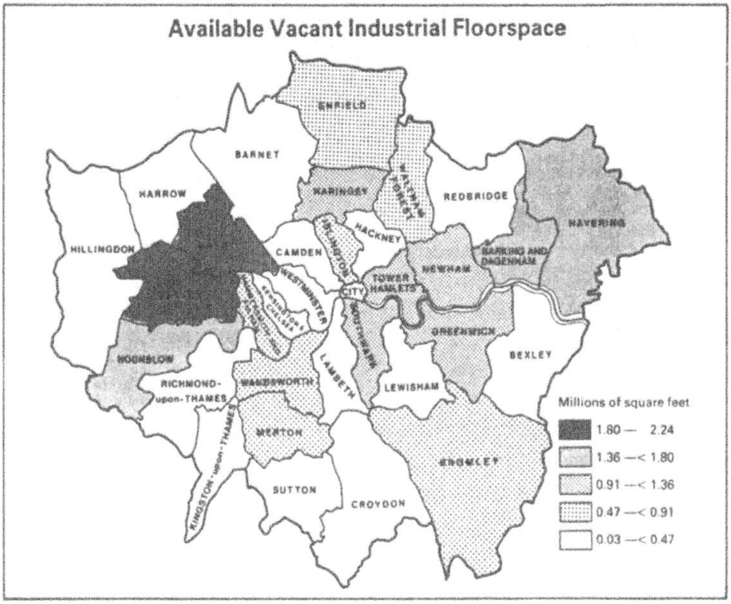

one of the most depressed areas in Britain, the other sited in one of the richest square miles in the world. It is a contrast that has been seen before in London's past. It is well known in the Third World. But lacking a modern Mayhew or a Charles Booth, it still today awaits some wider recognition.

Charles Booth undertook his great study of London Life and Labour nearly a century ago to answer a challenge put to him by Henry Hyndman to explain why were the poor. He hoped, with the full confidence of Victorian empiricism, that the facts would produce the answer and he ended his 17 volumes disillusioned that they had not. But what he left was a description of Londoners at home and at work at the end of the 19th century which was far richer and more suggestive of alternatives than those same lives and experiences expressed through statistics alone. To work with statistics can give us the impression that we have grasped a problem and pinned it down. Certainly the fact that, for example, one-third of London's parliamentary constituencies have unemployment rates above the national average has a force and a meaning but it is only the beginning of the work. It does not show what skills exist, what hopes, how life has changed for those in work, as well as for those without, how fast the production line is moving, how shift work grows, how part-time labour and casual work replace the steady jobs on which a lifetime can be built. When we come to these questions we soon find the statistics are inadequate, or not available for London, or out-of-date. Or that some more qualitative forms of enquiry are required — beyond the sample survey and the counting from above.

All this is relevant to the third great issue — the changes that have taken place in the conditions of London's life and labour. We know from innumerable sources — from word of mouth, or writing in community and trade union papers, or adult education classes — that conditions at work have for many people worsened over the last five years, that budgets are tighter, that local services have been cut and queues lengthened. But that statistics about these changes are still imperfect. We know that shift work has risen: 24 per cent of manual men and 17 per cent of manual women in London earned shift premiums in 1982 as against figures of 17 per cent and 9 per cent respectively in 1974. Casual work has increased in many sectors; in local authorities, the health services and in the many ancillary services that have been privatised in the past three years. Part-time work has spread in the retailing sector (Sainsbury employ some 60 per cent of their staff on a part-time basis) and in the catering trade. Industry studies also suggest an increase in sweating, with an estimated 30,000 homeworkers in the clothing trade and worsening pay and conditions in hotels, cleaning, food processing and branches of the retail trade. We also know that there has been a marked increase in inequality in London, both in income and in the availability and scope of jobs. The GLC has just sponsored a study to chronicle these changes in more detail. Already we know enough to say that London's economic crisis is a crisis for its labour force as well as its industry, for those in work as well as the half million who are seeking it.

These three issues are recognised and debated. There are conferences on the inner city and on Britain's industrial decline. Large sums of public money are spent in countering the problems, in regional aid, in urban aid, in support for small businesses and in unemployment and social security pay. London's depressed districts received £296 million (in 1982 prices) from the urban programme between 1979-80 and 1983-84. London's unemployed receive an estimated £600 million a year. The MSC spends £70 million a year in London. The great proportion of this spending is elastoplast aid. It does not address the causes of London's decline, nor offer any general way forward out of that decline. It largely funds current spending not investment — and with the exception of some infrastructural aid — is explicitly separated from the 'productive economy'. Such patching is already utterly inadequate and will become more so as London's unemployment increases.

Traditional Strategies

There have been two traditional strategies relevant to the London economy; the monetarist and the Keynesian. The first is based on a cheap labour policy, enforced through market competition. It has been vigorously pursued over the past five years, has been disastrous for the London economy, and in our view offers little hope for full employment or adequate jobs over the next decade.

The second argues for deficit finance by the government, a managed labour market (through incomes policy), and controlled markets for foreign trade and payments. Its re-introduction could at most be expected to reduce London's unemployment by a third. In what follows we summarise our views on the limitations of the two traditional approaches, and in the following at the GLC and which if adopted nationally would, we believe, offer some more substantial hope for London's sweated workers and the unemployed.

Monetarism

For the monetarists, the main means of solving unemployment is for Londoners to price themselves back into work. If British industry is losing out to overseas competition, there will be some wage rate (and work rate) which will restore competitiveness. If the sunset industries are past recall, then new industries will emerge to take their place. Tourism — founded on cheap labour — is significantly growing in London, while furniture and food processing are not. If Ford has cut its London workforce by a third over the last five years (from 25,129 to 16,839) this is because London's workers have failed to match the levels of productivity achieved on the Continent, or the wages set in Brazil. The price of labour and its effective use become the main levers of economic policy.

The government has argued that the state should stand back from the private economy. In fact, it has been highly interventionist with respect to its goal of weakening labour. There have been the following main strands to this policy:

a. *Private sector monetarism.* On the surface the aim of the government's restrictive monetary policies was to control inflation. But as its theorists made clear before the 1979 election, it had a deeper goal of contributing to the cheap labour policy. The mechanism was as follows. To cut the money supply, the government raised interest rates. This attracted money from abroad and drove up the exchange rate (from $2.07 to $2.40 in 18 months). Exporting became harder, importing easier. Domestic profits were squeezed, forcing some firms out of business and the remainder to shed labour and resist wage demands in order to survive. It was an explicit policy and it was put into effect with remarkable success in the private sector. It did not cause the recession of the early 1980s — let alone the decline of London — but it doubled its severity, according to the OECD. In London more than 500 major redundancies and factory closures were announced between 1979 and 1982. Unemployment trebled. By the time the exchange rate fell in 1983, manufacturing jobs had declined by nearly a quarter (23 per cent) and industry appeared so traumatised that an upswing was slow to emerge. From the quarterly reports of the London Chamber of Commerce and Industry, the prime benefit of the recession for the employers had been the discipline that large-scale unemployment had exerted on those at work.

b. *Public sector cuts and privatisation.* In the public sector the strategy faced greater difficulties. The government attempted to cut back jobs in public corporations and in central and local government by a variety of controls: changing capital structures, cuts in government grants and budgets. But these tactics met with more unified resistance than had been possible in the private sector; both from users and national unions. In the case of local government, the rapidly changing systems of penalties became ever more complex and contradictory. It was matched by some councils raising rates to maintain services and cutting capital investment and bought-in materials rather than direct service labour. In London, local government employment fell by only 6 per cent between 1979 and 1982. After the 1983 election, the strategy changes to a much greater emphasis on privatisation and on the direct control of local authority rates (through rate capping) together with the proposed abolition of the metropolitan counties and the GLC. Privatisation in particular has led to cuts in jobs, a worsening of conditions at work and a switch from service-oriented to profit-oriented public provision. British Telecom alone is expected to lose 15,000 of its 82,000 jobs in London as the result of privatisation.

c. *Anti-trade union legislation.* The Employment Acts of 1980-84 are best known for the outlawing of secondary picketing and the insistence on formalised balloting as a condition for legal industrial action. In London these have had some effect (the latter in relation to action in the Post Office for example) but they have had less impact than in some other parts of the country, in part because the scale of job loss has itself profoundly weakened London's traditional manufacturing unions. The National Union of Tailor and Garment Workers has declined from a London membership of 20,000 in the 1940s to approximately 3,000 today. The furniture union FTAT has suffered a similar decline, as has the docks section of the TGWU and the AUEW more generally. The unions in retailing, in finance, in hotels and catering have always faced difficulties and have been further squeezed by the recession. More significant for many sections of London labour have been the clauses in the acts which have increased the possibilities of unfair dismissal, weakened trade unions in smaller firms, and removed the requirements for paying union rates in non-union firms.

d. *The internationalisation of the economy.* By removing exchange controls the government allowed large quantities of capital to move abroad, part of which might otherwise have been invested and provided employment at home. It has also allowed increased domination by multinational companies of the UK economy. The importance of the latter point is less about ownership than about the tying of UK production into an international division of labour. This has taken place at Kodak in Harrow from 1976 and at Ford, where the integrated plant at Dagenham has been run down, process by process and replaced by investments elsewhere serving the whole of the European market. The multinationalisation of production is the step which allows workforces in London to be played off against those abroad as Ford has done in the body plant and on the Escort assembly line. More generally, of London's largest 75 factories in 1982, 73 were owned by multinationals and many were open to this form of multinational production that had been made easier by an open exchange policy.

e. *The assault on skill.* The main strand here of the government's policy has been to cut apprentice training. In 1981 it abolished 17 of the Industry Training Boards (leaving seven in operation) and withdrew grants for apprentice training in 1983-84. Apprenticeships in London fell sharply. The intake of engineering apprentices in 1984-85 was the lowest on record (500 apprentices in an industry which still employs 170,000 workers in London). The number of apprentices in road transport has fallen by a half between 1978-79 and 1982-83, mainly in the vehicle retail and repair. In construction the number of apprentices has fallen by 20 per cent between 1980 and 1983 and already skill shortages are re-emerging in spite of the depressed state of the market. What is behind these policies is first a downgrading of skills — the YTS schemes for example specify 13 weeks off the job training, as against the 24-40 weeks received by apprentices on ITB schemes. Secondly, the government wanted to shift control of the training that was necessary unequivocally to the employers. It was this which lay behind the abolition of the ITB's which had trade unions represented upon them.

The results of this assault on labour have been economically disastrous. The policies have contributed as much as 150,000 to the unemployment totals in London. They have deepened the desolation and eliminated a whole swathe of London industry which is unlikely ever to appear again. The growing inequality in London can be seen to be a result of conscious policy — providing incentives to the industrial 'head' and discipline to the unskilled 'hand'.

Even in its own terms, of market profitability and private capitalist growth, the cheap labour strategy is demonstrably not working. The reasons emerge from sector studies. Take furniture for example. In 1951 there were 62,000 people employed in London's furniture trade, some 40 per cent of the UK total. Today there are 12,000. Imports which were 7 per cent of the national market in 1973 are now 27 per cent. The main cause of this drastic decline is not the cost of labour. It is that the new growth sectors in furniture are based on design, flexible production and an integration with retailing. London's main mass producers have lost out because they have failed to respond to this trend. They compete at the cheap end of the market in which there is over-capacity. The great names, with the longest runs and greatest efficiency, Harry Lebus, Schreiber, Beautility and Cabinet Industry, were too inflexible to cope with the recession. The workings of the market therefore hit the most efficient. They did not lead to a new system of production as developed by the Italians and the Germans. Design remained largely unapplied, in spite of the strength of the London furniture design capacity, since design investment is so easily copied by competitors. The entry of the Scandinavian retail giant IKEA into the London market, drawing on continental supplies, threatens to weaken further what remains of the London-based industry.

There is a similar picture in the motor industry. Ford has argued that its rundown at Dagenham has been the result of lower productivity levels than in Europe. Apart from the problematical nature of the comparisons (Dagenham tended to be run at a lower capacity than the European plants) and apart from the fact that Dagenham's wages were amongst the lowest in Europe, an internal

Ford document which compared Ford Europe to Toyo Kogo (Mazda) in Japan, showed that differences in work intensity accounted for only one tenth of the difference in manufacturing cost. "More than two-thirds of the excess cost compared to TK are the product (not the sum) of design, build complexity, schedule instability and consequential low level of mechanisation and automation." Ford, in short, had been under pressure from the Japanese not because of labour cost or labour effort, but because its management had been less efficient in production engineering and less responsive to market variations.

Furniture and motor vehicles are both sectors where a cheap labour policy can run directly against the requirements of modern flexible production, with its need for skill and stability. Clothing is another, where there is recent evidence that the London clothing industry has been losing orders because of the quality control problems of sweatshop work. Instead of innovating, London clothing manufacturers have been forcing down wages, and worsening conditions in order to remain competitive.

In other sectors where British industry is competitive in production, it is the limited size of the internal market which has laid it open to destructive competition from abroad.

Software is one example, television another. In each the large fixed costs of production are more easily covered in their home market by US rather than British firms. In each, the sector studies suggest London production is unlikely to be able to compete against US imports priced in relation to marginal rather than average costs.

For the monetarists, such destruction of London industry is not of immediate concern. For them, international economic welfare will be increased if US firms dominate the software market or the supply of programming to cable TV. The displaced workers in London will be attracted to other trades in which they are relatively more efficient; tourism once more. The problem with this argument is that it presumes that there is enough work to go round and that the question is one of how to distribute it appropriately. But what we now witness is ever-growing unemployment on a world scale. Those thrown out of work in one place may never get another job. This is the clear experience of London over the last decade. The doctrine of free trade, as the Cambridge economist Joan Robinson once put it, is the 'mercantilism of the strong'. It is an argument put forward by the strong to justify the lowering of trade barriers by the weak. The difference in contemporary Britain is that free trade is being promoted by a government of the weak, as part of its cheap labour strategy.

In summary the cheap labour strategy is unsatisfactory even on its own terms:

— it emphasises labour costs when the key issue is the size of markets and/or the switch towards flexible specialisation;
— it provides no mechanism for the restructuring of fragmented industries;
— by cutting labour costs it is also cutting demand and therefore the size of the home market;
— it runs down skill at the moment when an extension of skill is needed;
— it fails to protect industry in the process of restructuring and has thus caused the disappearance of large slices of manufacturing from Britain;
— it fails to acknowledge that there is now and is likely to be for the foreseeable future, a massive labour surplus internationally even at a subsistence wage. The labour market cannot 'clear' itself. The trend in London has been for new industry not to emerge in sufficient strength to compensate for the destruction of the old.

It has been a tradition of private capital when in crisis to turn first against its own labour force. The present government's policy represents this response at a national level. Industrialists, though squeezed themselves by this policy, have remained loyal to the government because of its effect on labour and the labour market. What they cannot see, any more it seems than the government itself, is that this policy is destroying the domestic economy to a point from which important parts of it may never revive.

The Keynesian Alternative

The second major strategy is centred around Keynesian policy. It is the strategy which was followed in the post-war period until 1979. Whereas monetarism uses macro-economic policy to influence production — mainly by disciplining labour, Keynesian policy separates macro-economic management from production and deals almost exclusively with the former. For Keynesianism, if the general macro-economic conditions can be got right — the level of consumption and investment, of interest and exchange rates — then production will look after itself. Like monetarists the Keynesians concentrate on the world of markets but they see the role of the state not as using the market as a discipline but rather as providing the conditions within which enterprise can grow. Montetarism sees the state's prime task as removing the obstacles (including itself) from the free operations of the market. Keynesianism sees the task as intervening in markets to ensure they work well.

For Keynesianism the main answer to de-industrialisation and recession is to reflate the economy and to protect the new growth of industry from foreign competition. Within this broad framework there are different tendencies in policy. Some would reflate by tax cuts, others by expanding public spending. Some would devalue, others would use import controls. If investment does not respond to the improved conditions, then more radical measures are needed: measures to repatriate British capital from abroad; to ensure pension funds are invested in long-term growth rather than distributed as dividends. There are variations along all these lines between the left, right and centre of the post-war consensus. But the key point is that all shades of the consensus work within the common categories of the Keynesian world.

For London the Keynesian solution is wholly inadequate. De-industrialisation set in from the mid-1960s principally because of corporate restructuring and competition from abroad. Unemployment rose during the 1970s period of Keynesian strategy and would have continued to rise in the 1980s at perhaps half the rate it achieved under monetarism. There would still be some quarter of a million people out of work in London if Keynes and not Friedman had won the general election in 1979.

The limit of Keynesianism is that it does not address the main issues in production. For the Keynesian, production is like a black box with investment going in and goods coming out in search of a market. The organisation of production, what is produced, under what working conditions, with what technology, in alliance with whom — all this is left to the capitalist. In a period of expansion this limitation is not so apparent. London's consumer goods factories were producing things which had a wide and unsatisfied market. Their expansion fed back into demand for machines and materials. This allowed an increase in wages, as labour's share of growth. It led to requirements for new infrastructure, financed out of public funds. But when the upward curve of demand for the new goods approached saturation, when international competition sharpened for the demand that remained and when outlets for new profitable investment failed to appear, then profitability, investment and the rate of growth all fell. To maintain profitability, manufacturers tried to speed up and increase the intensity of labour. They sought cheaper sources of labour in smaller towns and the peripheral regions of Europe and the Third World. The banks, both directly and through funding state spending and consumer credit, provided the finance for potential growth. But such credit could not reverse the decline of profit whose prime causes were located in production. With insufficient profit, the debt payments on credit could only be met through inflation, which had the effect of preserving the money value of assets, while undermining their real value. Keynesianism sees credit expansion as a source of demand, and demand as the key condition for expanding production. It is certainly true that credit is a necessary condition for expanding production. But the approach fails to deal adequately with the more important question of profitability, and whether conditions are favourable for profitable production. This is not primarily a matter of effective demand. Economic crises occur even when demand has been inflated — as it was in the UK in 1973.

Traditionally capitalism has responded to crises of profitability in ways which are both sharp and brutal. Bank crashes and widespread bankruptcies mark down the value of capital and thus reduce the base against which profit is measured. Secondly, these slumps increase unemployment and the pressure on labour. Thirdly, they speed up the switch to new branches and methods of production. Monetarism has attempted just such a strategy through a consciously engineered crisis — but it has found that mechanisms of earlier capitalism no longer work for an economy which is already weak and backward.

Keynesianism on the other hand suspends these mechanisms without offering an alternative. It bails out the banks and the major corporations. It provides padding for demand but no necessity to encourage restructuring. It also finds that its traditional instruments of international control are weakened in an age of multi-nationals and that both industrial and financial capital are seeping away to areas where production is stronger and profitability higher.

Most seriously, the failures to deal with production and the continued slump in profitability, led Keynesianism to turn on the foundation of its consent. Cuts in public spending and increased control of wages, appeared as inevitable to those caught in the categories of Keynes and the institutions which had been formed around Keynesian policy. But they neither limited inflation nor stimulated profitability and instead paved the way for the introduction of monetarism.

The post-war consensus believed that the production of income and its distribution could be separated. Income distribution either socially or geographically, could be tackled independently. There had long been a tacit pact. Private enterprise should be allowed to run production and the state could look after redistribution, the one efficient, the other fair. By the mid-1970s this pact had collapsed. Private enterprise in Britain was clearly not efficient, while wage controls and state cuts meant that the state was seen as very far from fair.

The separation of production and distribution had a parallel in regional policy. The 'Inner City Problem' as it became known was tackled largely financially. The Urban Programme applied tasteful financial first aid to the worst sores on the urban body politic: grants were given to 'social' projects, defined as quite separate from the market economy. Later the programme was extended by adopting instruments used in regional policy in support of the market grants to firms, industrial promotion, incentives for small firms, and property development. Urban problems were acknowledged by a redistribution of funds. But none of the expenditure touched even the first base of the central problems of urban industrial production.

The point about the Keynesian strategy is not so much that it is wrong but that it is inadequate. Any strategy will have to have a policy on interest rates, on the exchange rate, on investment and the level of demand. These are real parts of the economy which like markets, cannot be ignored. But they are bound by what happens in that other sphere of the economy — in production. It is production that in the present system determines the limits of distribution, that is reflected in the level of the exchange rate, and in the level and form of demand. So while a measure of reflation, of public works and protection may all be necessary, they can only make long-term sense if they are part of a wider strategy centred on the material, and not merely the financial, aspects of the economy.

In summary a Keynesian reflationary strategy is inadequate because:

— it is concerned primarily with the general level of spending in the economy (the demand side) rather than the detailed economics of supply;

— having no strategy for production, it has no long-term answer to overseas competition nor the low level of profitability;

— its instruments for insulating the national from the international economy are increasingly limited in a period of multinational corporate control of production and finance.

— in recent years it has subordinated the public economy, full employment and the direct provision for social needs to the requirements of profitability in the private sector: hence the tendency to limit wages and cut state spending in order to encourage the private sector.

Reclaiming Production

Monetarism and Keynesianism have been the two poles of

mainstream economic debate. Yet in many ways their similarities are more striking than their differences. Both are preoccupied with markets, and with removing or counteracting its imperfections. Theirs is the world of the stockmarket, the foreign exchange dealer and the retail price index in whose terms we see traced out daily the economic fever chart. Both strategies rely on interventions in these markets to restore our economic health, yet both have virtually nothing to say about the other part of the economy on which that health is based — namely production.

Ignored by economists, production has been left as the province of the engineer, the production manager and the industrial relations consultant. They have a dual concern; first with the physical process of production, with the layout of the plant, the smooth running of the machinery and the quality of work; secondly with the economics of production, with how fast the work is being done, how hard people are working, how quickly a machine can be reset to meet changes in demand. New technology is introduced to meet both concerns, to improve the speed and synchronisation of physical production on the one hand, and to increase managerial control over labour on the other. Wages and recruitment systems are designed to similar ends.

These issues, which vary from industry to industry, are at the core of any economy. It is in the process of production that competitivity and profitability are determined. It is the conditions in production which explain the long-term movements in the indices of the fever chart, the value of the pound or the city's closing prices. It is decisions about production — what is produced, in what quantities, and by whom — which determine the extent to which an economy meets the needs of its people. Mainstream economics believes all these can be adequately influenced from outside by adjusting the market. The growth of unemployment, and unmet need, the decline of private industries and public services — all indicate a deep failure of such policies. What is required is a change of direction in economic strategy, towards direct intervention in production.

We need to go further than this. For once we step from the City's world of abstract numbers to the concrete detail of the factory floor, it is clear that there are alternative policies towards production: that of the manager is very different from that of the machine worker. The former is concerned with speed and control in order to increase profits, the latter with maintaining some control over how the job is done, with the use of skill to produce useful products, with a working life that enhances rather than degrades. There is also an interest of users in the quality of products, in the overall balance between sectors, and between what is produced for sale on the market, and what requires an alternative public provision. At the moment overriding priority is given to private market production and to the military sector, to increased intensity of work within the factory, and the technological replacement of awkward labour. We can call this *militarised market production.* It represents the economics of capital. There is an alternative which we shall call *socially useful production,* which takes as its starting point not the priorities of the balance sheet, but the provision of work for all who wish it in jobs that are geared to meeting social need. William Morris referred to it as useful work rather than useless toil. It represents the economics of labour.

The importance of this alternative perspective is not that it promises an easy technical solution to the current economic depression. Rather it raises a whole set of issues which have been kept on the sidelines of political and economic debate. Few major politicians and fewer economists have given the quality of work any significance in their analyses or programmes. Yet it remains a grim truth that the majority of Londoners spend their working lives in jobs which have been designed to dispense with human skill, and under a domination which stands in profound contradiction to the principles of all political democracies. The social control of what technology is developed and how it is used; the control of products which threaten health (in the food industry, through leaded petrol, or pharmaceuticals); these, like the quality of work are all issues which arise from the material character of production and its outputs, and which are quite lost to an economics that is limited to the play of the market. They are more difficult for a government to manage than the traditional instruments of the Chancellor's budget and the Bank of England. They involve a contest of two opposing economic forces at many levels. Unless they are addressed the deep rooted problems of the British economy and the quality of ordinary people's working lives cannot be expected to improve.

Not for a hundred years have want and waste stood so clearly facing each other in London as they do today. There are half a million people in London wanting work while there are families in need of food, elderly people in need of heat and care and the London's infrastructure requires £12,000 million worth of investment to restore it to even a modicum of repair. This is the central irrationality of our present economic condition. It arises from taking the needs of the financial mechanisms of the economy as a priority. The market, money and profit which were intended as servants to bring want and work together, have become the masters and are now keeping them apart.

There is an alternative — that starts directly from production and from need — which has a different priority and offers a different vision. It is this alternative which the GLC has been attempting to put into practice over the last four years.

In what follows we outline our experience of that strategy as it applies to the three main spheres of the London economy, the household, the public sector and the private market economy. In each of them production takes place and the fruits of that production are financed and distributed in quite different ways. Between them and within them we find a conflict of priorities, of understanding and of power. New social forces — in the trade unions, in local communities, among women and black people — have forced their alternatives on to the political agenda. What has yet to happen is the consolidation of these alternatives into a new national economic strategy.

Productive Intervention in Practice: Popular Planning

A central task for the *London Industrial Strategy* is to increase social control over the process of restructuring. By and large, the immediate power to restructure has been in the hands of private companies and public sector managers. Trade unions have had to concentrate on defensive campaigns. In the nationalised industries industrial restructuring has been extensive but it has largely been dominated by commercial criteria. In the large public corporations, managers are usually recruited from the private sector and are neither encouraged nor inclined to involve workers and consumers in reorganising public enterprise. The battle that the GLC had in bringing London Transport under control exhibits the difficulties faced by any strategy of 'restructuring for labour'.

One of these is that commitment by politicians and planners to alternative strategies is not enough. They lack the range of knowledge that is necessary to survive, let alone transform, the complex commercial world of marketing, technology and finance. It becomes necessary to depend on managers and experts who, in general, are unsympathetic to alternative forms of restructuring and economic control. How can this be changed?

The development of an alternative investment institution is a necessary first step, staffed with people who understand the practices of management, and the principles of the alternative. This is the purpose of GLEB. But our experience has shown that new public investment institutions like GLEB are not enough. They and the political authorities to which they are accountable need the power and the knowledge of both trade union and community organisations if they are to carry out restructuring for labour. Without them, the GLC with its limited resources, and a handful of GLEB managers, will be quite isolated and forced back into a dependence on traditional managers. They will end up against all their good intentions, restructuring for capital.

The manifesto embodied that understanding, and in doing so reflected the new directions in trade union action that had grown in the 1970s. As industrial restructuring gathered pace from the late 1960s, trade unions developed fresh forms of action. Between 1969 and 1972 there were over 100 occupations against redundancies in the north-east alone. In the traditional but declining industrial conurbations, for instance Merseyside, Tyneside and the West Midlands, shop stewards, trades councils and various trade union resource centres tried to develop a more strategic, less reactive trade unionism in defence of their communities. In London, the Lucas Aerospace stewards in west London played a central part in developing an alternative corporate plan with which to resist management's redundancy plans. In east London the fight to save the upper docks took a more offensive form as the 1970s progressed. In the public sector there were many hospital occupations in the late 1970s, and both NUPE and the NCU (previously POEU) have taken up and adapted themes developed in an industrial context — early warning through investigating employers, alternative plans and public enquiries — as a focus of campaigning. They have emphasized the involvement of users and the community.

These new kinds of trade union and community initiatives have come up against limitations through lack of political support. For groups in London the GLC's industrial strategy has provided the opportunity to achieve this support and the resources and platform it entails. On the other hand for GLEB and the GLC the new developments in trade unionism have provided a vital, albeit precarious, base within production.

It is a new development in economic strategy for a local authority, or indeed any state body within the UK, to base its industrial policies on support for the initiatives and organisations of labour. The only other move in this direction was the drastically foreshortened attempts of Tony Benn and others at the Department of Industry in 1974-75. Normally the resources and the powers to plan have remained at the centre within the state or shared with management. Worker or community involvement has taken on a secondary consultative form commenting on plans drawn up within the public authority. Popular planning by contrast involves sharing power, empowering those without official power. The end result on many occasions, for instance the People's Plans in docklands and Coin Street, the campaigns against hospital closures, and the alternative plan at Ramparts engineering, is an alliance around policies worked out together. Such alliances allow more power than either the GLC or the trade union and community groups would have on their own.

These alliances have taken a variety of forms. The Industry and Employment Branch has financed a network of trade union resource centres based in 20 different areas and different sectors of London. The Industrial Development Unit has been set up to work with trade unionists to anticipate management's redundancy plans and prepare strategies for resistance and alternatives. The Popular Planning Unit has provided support for trade unionists especially in the public sector. The unit has worked closely with shop stewards in multinationals seeking to establish international links. Trade unions have been involved in the conferences, public inquiries, hearings and working groups which are reflected in many of the chapters in this volume. There has been a close working relationship with the South East Region of the TUC. GLEB, whose chair is a noted London trade unionist, has developed enterprise planning through a support team drawn largely from the trade unions. There has been a programme of work around the use of GLC purchasing power (contracts compliance) and also trade union discussions fighting discrimination against black people within the workplace and within trade unions — discrimination which has often served to weaken the trade union movement.

This work has taken place against the background of recession. Industrial decline has seriously reduced the numbers and political weight of shopfloor organisation in manufacturing. Large sections of workers in London are in unorganised workplaces or, if formally recognised, are not actively organised. In many areas the destruction of industry has gone so far that, in Docklands for instance, people's livelihoods depend not on the future of the factories — there are none left — but on the future of the land itself.

For these reasons the original tools we inherited — enterprise planning, early warning, popular planning — have had to be modified. Enterprise planning has often been concerned not with extending the scope of collective bargaining but with establishing a framework for collective bargaining in the first place. Work on early warning has rarely been about anticipating crises. More usually it has been about bringing together the power of the GLC and GLEB with that of the trade unions to save something out of a crisis. The idea of alternative plans has been taken forward most in the public sector where sections of the trade union movement have been able to maintain a strength to mount positive campaigns and bargaining positions, rather than in the manufacturing sector where it first began.

In spite of these difficulties, the steps that have been taken both by the trade unions and the GLC have been of importance in developing the ideas and perspectives that are reflected here.

A second perspective of the manifesto was the importance of linking users and local communities with trade unions in the making and practice of strategy. The significance of this has been brought home in the public sector campaigns against the cuts. Unions in Direct Labour Organisations and tenants organisations, for example, have often been in conflict with each other. The same divisions existed on London Transport, or among caretakers and tenants on council estates. There have been notable achievements in overcoming these divisions in the past few years. The campaign against STOLport was one instance. The Hayes hospital occupation another. There has been slow but significant progress on some estates with tenants groups working out compromises with local DLO organisations. There has been some coming together of transport workers and users in the campaign against the government takeover of London Transport. Where these links have taken place it has greatly strengthened the campaign for maintaining and improving jobs and services.

A number of the public sector ventures raise and reflect these problems. But it is important for a number of private sectors as well. The movement for the conversion of the arms industry to peaceful purposes is one example, the food industry another. In terms of employment GLEB has concentrated on meat products, wholefood and ethnic minority food. On the user side, the GLC has funded a Food Commission to work for the improvement of food products, while the ILEA has adopted a new food policy for the school meals service.

Another way in which the interests of people as workers and users has been linked is through industrial area initiatives — in the King's Cross area, in the Hackney Road, in the Royals, in south Docklands, and west London. Here sites have been developed which provide local housing and local work opportunities together (this is the aim behind the Coin Street and the Courage developments on the south side of the river, and in the Battlebridge Basin area in King's Cross). In other places, the area offices support community enterprises, and provide premises and services for local industries which use local skills.

There are two basic points underlying this part of the GLC

strategy. First, no alternative plan for an industry can be developed adequately without the central involvement of workers and users in that industry. Second, any strategy must not only address the question of alternatives. It must also take account of how such alternatives can be brought about. It must deal with the question of power as well as direction.

The struggle between the economics of capital and the economics of labour has taken place within each of the three main sectors of the London economy. It has also taken place over the boundaries between them and their relations one with the other. At the present time, the government is attempting to reduce the public economy, pushing labour back into the home and colonising areas of public production by private capital.

A strategy for socially useful production would aim to reverse this movement. Its first task is to re-assert social control over the public economy itself, and having done that to use this base to strengthen those forces that are arguing for an economics of labour in the private economy. There are a number of ways this can be done:

— by extending direct labour to produce goods and services required by public bodies and their employees;
— removing restrictions on public producers which prevent them from selling in the private market. In the public market, direct labour organisations should be assessed against private competitors employing workers on parallel wages and conditions to those of public sector workers;
— the planned consolidation of the public economy to extend the public sector for direct labour production and increasing the bargaining power of public sector bodies with the external market. In 1979 public corporations alone spent £12,500 million on goods and services from the private sector. At the moment there is severe fragmentation in the public sector. Different public authorities run their own laundries, canteens, maintenance departments, purchasing organisations, with no reference to others. Why should not the GLC Supplies Department purchase as full a range of products for the NHS as the LCC did when it organised most of London's hospitals through the 1930s and 1940s;
— purchases from the private sector should be restricted to firms on an approved list who adhere to a code designed to maintain fair wages and equal opportunities on a par with requirements prevailing in the public sector;
— taking back into social control those public enterprises and services which have been sold off to the private sector,

particularly the transport and telecommunications networks;
— insisting on public ownership of technological innovations funded by the state;
— ensuring that any public funds advanced to the private sector carry with them a share in the equity of the receiving firms. This is particularly important in the case of interventionary rescues;
— selected interventions in key parts of industrial sectors to ensure a programme of effective restructuring.

Much of the discussion of British industrial policy has centred on institutions: public ownership, a national investment bank, a national enterprise board, and so on. From the perspective of alternative production all these are necessary but they mean little if not geared to a strategy. How would Unilever be different if it were taken under public control? What would restructuring for labour mean in that instance? What is the key point of control in the food industry — research and development, the supply of materials, food processing plants, marketing or retailing? Which is the relevant public instrument will depend on the strategy to be pursued. There is no point in extending public power for its own sake, particularly if that power is not organised to support trade unions and users in developing alternative strategies in the industry.

There is one more general point about the public sector which relates to employment. There is currently little prospect of a return to full employment through the expansion of private sector jobs. The attack on the public economy has reduced employment and the provision of necessary services. Its expansion could improve both. The basic principle of the public economy is to employ labour to meet specific needs. The barrier to providing work for all who want it in the public sector has faced one overriding barrier: that it would have to be financed from taxation and thus in part from withdrawal of funds from the private economy. According to Keynesianism, the return to full employment would expand national output so that the funds would effectively generate themselves. We have seen that there are limits to this. Nevertheless, if new jobs were provided both to expand services and to contribute to the productive restructuring of both private and public economics, the inflationary effect would be reduced. We should remember that two-thirds of the increase in service sector jobs in western Europe in the post-war years have been in the public sector.

In summary, an interventionist strategy based on production has the following main features:
— an emphasis on long-term strategic production planning of industries;
— a concern that restructuring in all sectors of the economy should

be carried out in the interests of those who work in the industry and use its products;
— a commitment to the development and application of human-centred technology;
— a strategic concern with improving the conditions and hours of work in the domestic economy, and with improved means of integrating domestic work with other parts of the economy in order to improve the living and working conditions of women;
— a priority to extending social control over the public economy through increasing political, trade union and user control;
— a commitment to popular involvement in all aspects of strategic policy making (popular planning) and in the operation of enterprises (enterprise planning).

In both the monetarist and Keynesian strategies there is little room for local government in the development and implementation of economic strategy. For monetarists, the main task of local councils is to reduce their interference with the market and, where they do intervene, ensure that this intervention removes barriers to the market. In the property market, they argue that councils should put surplus sites on the market and that planning restrictions should be eased. Enterprise Zones are an example of the monetarist strategy of restoring employment through reducing controls.

The most important monetarist employment policy for local government is the cutting of rates. The CBI has for long said that it is the rates which are cutting employment in London and have used this as their principal argument for supporting proposals for the abolition of the GLC.

Recent research undertaken for the Department of the Environment has now effectively undercut this argument by showing that there is no evident relationship between the levels of rates and employment. This is confirmed by the GLC's own research, which suggests that the main effect of a rate rise is to reduce property prices. In the short-run small firms may have to bear the cost of this increase until their next rent review, but even if they do go out of business, new firms will start or old firms expand to take up the gap in the market. For these sectors are predominantly local. In the case of larger firms with national and international markets, rates are a trivial portion of total cost and are not cited as significant in the large firm surveys that have been conducted.

The argument can be extended to support the proposition that financing employment through rates is likely to expand overall employment in London. If rates are lowered, property prices rise and with them the rents received by property owners. Some of this increased rental income might be spent locally — on the consumption of services or on local investment. But there is likely to be a high leakage out of the local economy, both through consumption on imported goods and on investment outflows. The same sum if held by the local authority through a rate increase would be largely spent locally. A local council's propensity to import or transfer funds out of London is almost certainly less than that of the owners of property and the recipients of rent.

Part of the evidence for the inverse relationship of rents and rates has come from the Enterprise Zones. The rate exemptions in the Zones have meant that property prices and thus rents have risen within the Zones, so that much of the incentive for new development has been lost. Certainly the Isle of Dogs Enterprise Zone has created few new jobs in its initial years of operation, apart from the impact arising from the large public investment in its infrastructure.

The urban property market is inherently imperfect. Reductions in rates or the offer of other incentives attached to land (such as are found in the Enterprise Zones and Freeports) merely serve to increase land prices and provide windfall gains for property owners.

This is the basis of the case against monetarist policy on the land market. But there is a more general point. The reliance on the market by local authorities cannot be expected to expand employment, since London's present unemployment is the result not of the market working imperfectly, but of it working too well.

Keynesians too have given little place to local councils in broader economic strategy. For them the problems of London require national reflation rather than local intervention. Local councils have only marginal significance. They should step in where local markets fail — in the training of labour for example, or the provisions of small industrial premises, business advice or economic information. Again, as with the monetarists, the emphasis is placed on getting the market to work, and as with the monetarists, the weakness of the strategy at a local level is that it has been the market that has been the bearer of London's recession.

With an interventionist approach to production, however, local authorities have an important place in national strategy. They are in a position to support changes in the domestic economy and to consolidate their own public economies. They can extend the influence of their public economies, through municipalisation and the use of purchasing power and pension funds, and intervene in the private economy through direct investment. Furthermore, if strategies and institutions are to be built from below then local councils form one of the principal building blocks.

It has been in part the economic initiatives taken by local authorities over the last four years that has focused interest on the production-led approach. The emphasis has varied. Sheffield has sought to extend direct labour production to provide goods previously bought from the open market. They have also emphasised the improvement of the working conditions of women, at home and in wage work, and on extending democratic control within the public sector. Lancashire has developed through their Enterprise Board an industrial complex centred on the fishing industry in Fleetwood. The West Midlands have concentrated on measures to provide long-term funds to medium and large firms, linked into a restructuring plan for key segments of the engineering industry. Leeds have developed a substantial programme of co-operative development and training. In London, the GLC and, now, Hackney and Haringey have set up Enterprise Boards, and have been pursuing similar policies. In each case these councils have refused to remain on the sidelines, offering a grant here, running an advertising campaign there. They have entered directly into production and, in doing so, have shown the potential and the difficulties of this approach in practice.

What emerges from these experiences is that the local and the national are not alternatives, with local councils extending municipal production while the national government takes care of reflation. Rather, in case after case, it has been clear how local initiatives need the power and scope of national government to be fully effective. With multinationals, for example, alternative strategies can be developed by the unions working in conjunction with relevant local authorities. But it needs the power of a central government to bargain with Ford over its location of investment and its access to both national and public sector markets. With cable, energy, software, food, airports and the docks, national policies are immediately called for as the result of the studies of these sectors in London. In some cases it is a questions of finance, in others one of tariff policy or national regulations. But beyond this in almost every private sector we have studied, the extension of social control for the purposes of restructuring requires intervention at the national level.

These studies indicate that a national public investment body is needed with the powers, the staff and the funds to control the commanding heights of the main sectors of the economy. In one sector it will be a strong social presence in distribution. In another it might be in research and development. In a third, the best approach will be the takeover of a leading firm that integrates different parts of the sector. In each case a strategy of public intervention will need an understanding of the structure and direction of the industry, in order to identify the key points for social control.

We would see a national production board standing in a federal relation to local enterprise boards, providing a forum for the co-ordination of local municipal initiatives and a framework for linking national and local interventions in the same sector. The same would be true of the development of sector strategy, for if a national production board is to avoid a discredited planning from above, it must build on the work that emerges from below. Learning from the experiences of GLEB it would be important to devise appropriate forms of democratic control based on parliamentary accountability, a strong trade union input and a federal relation to local and regional enterprise boards. It would provide a framework for linking national and local interventions in the same sector. It would develop sector strategy in a way that built on plans put forward by trade union organisations and local authorities. It would be part of a newly constituted Ministry of Industry. It would co-ordinate sectoral policy and implementation, linking with unions, local councils and a co-ordinated public sector.

Traditionally local government has been seen as performing tasks delegated to it by national government. But the approach of popular planning suggests a different model, one that starts from the local and ends with a role for the national by virtue of its power over law, tax, money and the foreign exchanges.

Work towards this has already begun. Local authorities who have been concerned with the clothing industry are meeting to develop their local strategies into a national one. There have been similar meetings on food, and on a number of multinational firms who dominate particular sectors. These discussions need to be extended, so that over the next three years a set of national sector strategies emerge from municipal, trade union and user initiatives.

Chapter 6

Atlanticism, Isolation or a European Alternative?

Frances Morrell

The credibility gap that Labour needs to close exists not only between the party and the electorate, but also between the leadership and many of its supporters. The party urgently needs to consolidate its claim to be able to win the next election — and then to deliver for working people when in office.

Despite the wistful dreams of Harold Wilson, Labour has never been the natural party of government in this country. We have, as the party of change, always had to work harder than the Conservatives at explaining the practicality of our proposals to the voters. The legacy of the 1974-79 government is that today doubts about their practicality disturb many party members and trade unionists.

Such doubts are not disloyal. They are an honest acknowledgement that the party needs to be able to explain to itself and everybody else just what is Labour's strategy for the economic and social survival of the United Kingdom.

More significantly, the unease derives from a sense that the party's strategic perspective is incomplete. For the foreseeable future, Labour must reason from a simple first principle. The true political divide in the west is between the democratic socialist forces within Europe and elsewhere, and the Atlanticist hegemony. Labour needs an alternative European strategy in response.

Acceptance of that perspective would lead to three things. First, a decisive break with the ruling principles that have governed Labour's policy-making, both in its first "isolationist" phase after 1918 and its second "revisionist" phase from 1947 to the present day. Second, it would involve a profound reconsideration of the interlocking economic, industrial and military relationships between Britain and the United States on the one hand, and Britain and Europe on the other. The strategy would effectively involve a realignment of Britain's position within the west.

At the next general election, Labour will probably declare to the electors its intention to protect and expand the welfare state; to increase employment; to modernise our collapsing manufacturing capability; to move to a non-nuclear defence system, and to expel the American nuclear bases; and to bring back into public ownership and control privatised resources like oil and gas, and key privatised assets like British Telecom.

Labour manifestos are frequently discussed in party circles as if they were unique expressions of socialism on our planet. Actually, such a programme is a conventional European democratic socialist response to the current crisis. More importantly, in international terms it is anti-Atlanticist. If it is to be carried through, then conflict with the current presidency of the United States is inevitable. Equally inevitable is some conflict with major American and Japanese multinationals trading in Europe, with international financial institutions like the IMF, and with the EEC over some of the clauses of the Treaty of Rome.

However, it is a mistake to believe that these institutions collude to control world economic affairs. Matters are worse than that. The reality is that international financial and economic relationships are out of control. National economies and international companies can be likened to ships, all separately adrift, in a huge and stormy ocean, desperately trying to steer a course which avoids disaster.

Even a big economy like the United States is not fully in control of its own affairs. The speculation against the dollar in 1978 showed that. Equally, even policies as ferociously monetarist as Mrs Thatcher's have not guaranteed a safe passage through the storm. The speculative crisis against the pound is likely to recur, particularly if Mrs Thatcher tries to introduce policies to reduce unemployment. We are presented with the notion that Mrs Thatcher's personality is the reason for the non-introduction of these policies. If only it were true. The financial managers of major currency holdings, anxious to protect their investments, are taking these decisions for her. Her role is to legitimise them.

Two previous Labour governments — in 1964-70 and 1974-79 — were elected to carry through programmes similar to those being developed by Labour now. Both were driven by currency speculation and the IMF to adopt weak versions of the present government's strategy. Other European democratic socialist parties have developed similar programmes in response to domestic economic circumstances like our own, since recession, industrial decline and rising unemployment is a phenomenon which specifically affects countries in western Europe. In government, they face the same conflicts; Mitterrand's inability to carry through the French Socialist Party's original programme is an outstanding case in point.

Plainly, we have to consider how we can break out of this cycle of election, capitulation, and then rejection by the electorate. It is too easy to argue that strength of will alone is enough. The Labour Party believes in heroes. However, the election of a Superman as party leader is not the complete answer.

Labour is in many ways a prisoner of its own traditions. We are locked into a permanent internal debate between two polar positions — one is essentially isolationist, the other Atlanticist. The party's first strategy was essentially insular. The plan was to build democratic socialism in one country. In 1918, when the party constitution was adopted, Britain was the metropolitan centre of a world empire. It was perhaps legitimate to assume that a Labour victory in a national parliamentary contest would be decisive and unconstrained. The need for alliances with democratic socialist forces in Europe was scarcely relevant in a country which ruled so many others by right of conquest and which had just — in alliance with the United States — defeated Germany in an imperialist war. Britain's economic and naval power would protect a domestic socialist transformation from external intervention.

The isolationism of the Labour Party socialism dates from that time — and has two aspects. One is the unquestioning faith in unilateral action; the other the assumption of conflict of interest with other European countries.

By 1945, Labour finally took power with a huge majority. It seemed the vindication of the first phase strategy. Socialism in one country would be brought about by electoral victory, followed by a programme of public ownership which would systematically bring Britain's capitalist economy into democratic control. This was the strategy of an imperialist Labour Party; it rested on the unspoken assumption that Britain remained powerful enough to act free from external interference. However, as Labour's leaders entered their inheritance, the world changed.

During the lifetime of the 1945-51 government the United States exerted its power. Britain's old imperial trading alliances were swept away to be replaced by a global market in which companies would trade freely across frontiers without let or hindrance. The need for a new strategy became apparent.

Labour leaders feared that Britain, no longer strong enough to act unilaterally, was going to become a third-rank European power in the American sphere of influence. A second "revisionist" political strategy was adopted. Economic co-operation in western Europe was rejected by Labour-led Britain. Atlanticism replaced isolationism. Labour hoped to preserve Britain's influence through the special relationship with the United States, Britain's defence capacity through the NATO alliance, her economic independence and growth through the Commonwealth. At home, equality and full employment were to be secured through Keynesian economics and support for the mixed economy. The revisionist strategy hung on the special relationship. This came to mean acceptance of the American analysis of world affairs and a defence budget out of all proportion to Britain's economic means.

From the day in 1951 when Bevan resigned over cuts in the health service to pay for a defence programme the US required through the 1974-79 Labour government decision to cut spending on public services, but to maintain the nuclear programme, to the present day commitment to Trident, a simple truth has held. Our welfare state and public investment programmes have been consistently sacrificed, not because the country's economy could not afford them, but because it could not afford them *and* an extravagant defence policy. The postwar reconstruction boom masked this trend at first. It is now very clear.

Particularly Atlanticist was the stress by Labour's revisionist theoreticians on the free market element in the mixed economy, and its relationship to democratic freedom. In practice, this essentially American political equation of managerial and democratic freedom caused Labour leaders to tolerate the sustained disinvestment in British manufacturing industry that has taken place since 1945, and the loss of control by government over large sections of the economy. The acceptance of that free market ethic around the world has led directly to the current crisis.

Bevan and his colleagues challenged the Atlanticism of the postwar Labour government, but they challenged it from the vantage point of a historic isolationism that has become increasingly inappropriate.

After the vote in 1975 to remain in the EEC, Britain's world changed again. For a second time, our trading alliances were drastically altered. The Commonwealth was abandoned and the west European market was embraced. Both the isolationist perspective, and the governing revisionist strategy were rendered obsolete. The succeeding Labour governments then proved undeniably the inability of Keynesian economics to deliver equality and full employment. By 1979, all that remained of Labour's postwar package was the huge nuclear defence bill — the legacy of the special relationship and the price of our leading position in NATO.

Mrs Thatcher is, of course, the ultimate Atlanticist. Our

domestic industry continues to collapse as capital flows freely out of the country, oil revenues go to waste, the welfare state is being dismantled, and privatisation reduces still more the government's capacity to control the economy in the interest of the people. Yet the defence budget is the biggest in Europe.

No wonder Mrs Thatcher was feted by President Reagan at a recent dinner in Washington. No leader of a vassall state could have been more compliant to his wishes or make sedulous in support of the free market ethic. In that sense, she is the agent of the crisis.

Membership of the EEC was supposed to afford protection against United States and multinational management pressures. That was a major reason given by some leading figures in the labour movement — for example, Harold Wilson — who wished to join. It does not. The philosophy of the commission, the EEC bureaucracy, reflects faithfully the free market ethos of the Treaty of Rome. This is why dyed-in-the-wool Atlanticists like David Owen happily support it. A Labour government cannot be bound by the Treaty's provisions which prevent a national re-industrialisation programme. We should simply ignore them, as other member states have successfully done.

The Treaty of Rome is not our main problem. This country's biggest single vulnerability is the instability of our currency. Unless we can control our currency, we cannot hope to implement our programme. The European Monetary System — of which all EEC countries, except ourselves, are members — is designed to protect currencies against speculation. We are not members because the conditions of its operation reinforce deflation. Unfortunately, non-membership has precisely the same effect — though the deflation is enforced by speculation.

Labour's strategy objective must be to work with our European socialist allies to bring about a reform of the EMS so that it both protects economies against speculation and operates in support of policies to reduce unemployment. Since this is both technically possible, and in the interests of other democratic socialist governments, it should be possible to achieve. Britain could then enter the EMS, stabilise the pound, and reflate — hopefully in partnering other west European economies.

Party critics of the performance of the last two Labour governments have tended to emphasise the irresolution of cabinet members and their conservative ideological framework. Confident leadership exercised in the national interest does make a difference. Some important policies could quite easily be carried through unilaterally — for example, the re-nationalisation of our oil resources or the cancellation of the Sizewell B Pressure Water Reactor in favour of coal.

Ford Europe, however, provides an example of a characteristic *industrial* problem which cannot be solved either by amendment of the Treaty or by confident and ideologically correct domestic leadership alone. Earlier this year, Ford Europe announced its intention to close one of its European plants. The unions from the different plants have come together to seek to devise a common negotiating strategy. Their efforts are vitiated by the absence of a political framework.

If they acted collectively, the five west European countries would have a very strong bargaining position with Ford. Essentially they could negotiate access to European markets against investment in research and manufacturing facilities to create jobs in their areas. Since they do not act collectively, it is childishly simple for Ford to play one country off against another and to secure anxious offers of subsidy as their price for not closing a plant.

The expulsion of the American nuclear bases will cause a crisis in our relationship with the United States. The public support of democratic socialist leaders in Europe would strengthen our position in that crisis, yet there is no evidence that we have seriously tried to achieve it. There is a groundswell of support within Europe for a new relationship with the United States and with eastern Europe. We will not help to secure these objectives by our current posture of aloofness.

Britain is a second-rank European country in the American sphere of influence. Labour has to offer a strategy for economic survival that relates to this reality. There is much that a Labour government, acting alone, can do, but some major strategic objectives will need the support of other west European governments and the labour movement in Europe generally. The bureaucratic paraphernalia of the Common Market cannot help. A common strategy, supported by the west European socialist and labour movements, can.

Part II

Technology, Resources and Needs

Introductory

Ken Coates

The relationship between jobs and technology seems, to many people, all too simple. New inventions eat up jobs. There is a sense in which this has always been true, even when the problem has been ameliorated by fast economic expansion. Long ago, Karl Marx pointed out that new inventions were not deployed in order to save the time of working people. There is a brilliant chapter in the first volume of *Capital* on the length of the working day. "A horse . . . can only work from day to day, eight hours."[1] But men and women are more resilient. Under the rule of capital, eight hours is nothing: "time for education, for intellectual development, for the fulfilling of social functions and for social intercourse, for the free play . . . of bodily and mental activity"[2]: all are eaten away by the demands of production, including institutional overtime.

The justice of this judgement of Marx is still apparent after more than a hundred years. Indeed, workers living under the shadow of great nuclear power plants are probably working more intensively, and perhaps even physically longer than their forebears in medieval times, where the most advanced technology was built into windmills. Every reduction in working time has had to be fought for, and often vigorously fought for. That is why Marx himself celebrated the achievement of the ten hours act in Britain as "the first victory of the political economy of labour over the political economy of capital". Tom Mann, as a boy learning the trade of engineer, later greeted the establishment of the nine-hour day as the dawn of a true liberation. He was then able to take himself to nightschool, and learn those skills which made him so passionate an advocate for the eight hours movement.

Shortening of working time has become more urgent than ever, in the dawning age of robotics. In his groundwork for the writing of *Capital,* Marx prepared a huge text, which was not published in England until more than a century after the appearance of *Capital* itself. The *Grundrisse* contains important thoughts on these matters. "The true economy is economy of labour time" is one of these. "Free time is the most productive time of all" is another. Joining these two slogans together, it has been easy for socialists to arrive at the view that free time is a process of personal development, outside the zone of compulsory labour. Too easily this can be identified simply with leisure, personal recreation. Undoubtedly leisure is crucial to the development of culture, and to moral growth. But widespread robotics offer a positive flood of leisure, quite unlike that anticipated in the age of Marx. While every reduction in working time is bitterly contested, and institutional overtime is endemic, we are threatened with the formation of a whole class of unemployed persons, maintained on public relief, and yet permanently locked out of social creativity. Such victims can hardly be described as "free". Nor are they simply "a reserve army of labour" since the prospect of their ever obtaining employment, even during times of boom, is shrinking all the time. Bread and circuses by day, and riots by night, are the future of this new underclass, unless alternatives can be defined.

Telephone workers in Australia, facing the threat of new technology which promised to confiscate one-fifth of their jobs, have opened up entirely new possibilities in coping with these issues. Not only did they negotiate shorter working hours but they also hit on a formula of genius. They exacted from their employers an agreement to provide free *social* time, in which the telephone network would be placed at the service of the community, and in which all employees would devote approximately one-fifth of their working hours to the new "welfare" sector, serving Citizens' Advice networks, Samaritan calls and similar needs. The idea of free *social* time is one of the key thoughts which has been developed in the work of Mike Cooley.

The technological threat to humanity is real. In order to stay in front in the field of informatics, micro-electronics, bio-technology, and lasers, the United States has launched its "Star Wars" programme. The motive for this otherwise bizarre adventure is the need to maintain American leadership in the world economy, and to stay on top of the Japanese and European oppositions. Western Europe has been discussing a similar response, under the code name Eureka. Advocating this, the French Government has argued that by the early 1990s European capacity in the technology of informatics will be less than half that of either the United States or Japan. To remain competitive, Europe would need to expand its electronics production to 30 per cent of the world market within 10 years, which would involve a 100 per cent increase on present capacity. Without vast expenditure and effort, the French argued,

West Europeans' share of the electronic market would in fact decline from its present 15 per cent level to only 10 per cent of world capacity during the same decade.

It is not at all an accident that the development of these profoundly important components of what is now usually called the Third Industrial Revolution requires, in the United States, a military motor. The civilian expenditure of billions of dollars by the Government would be seen as Communistic by all President Reagan's most ardent supporters. Military expenditures on quite similar items are paradoxically perceived as an antidote to Communism. Unfortunately, in the Soviet Union, these considerations cannot be preponderant. There, all those trillions of dollars are seen to constitute an overwhelming threat.

In the pioneering work of the Lucas Aerospace Combine, which focused the energies of a workforce engaged in military production on the problems of conversion to meet civilian, social needs, we can find a parable about this dreadful condition. Michael Parry Evans, a worker who had been engaged in the fine arts of rocketry, perfecting systems capable of pinpointing an explosion on the other side of the moon, found himself working on prototypes for the assistance of handicapped people.

> "Before we even started the corporate plan our members at the Wolverhampton plant visited a centre for children with Spina Bifida and were horrified to see that the only way they could propel themselves about was literally by crawling on the floor. So they designed a vehicle which subsequently became known as Hobcart — it was highly successful and the Spina Bifida Association of Australia wanted to order 2,000 of these. Lucas would not agree to manufacture these because they said it was incompatible with their product range and at that time the corporate plan was not developed and we were not able to press for this. But the design and development of this product were significant in another sense: Mike Parry Evans, its designer, said that it was one of the most enriching experiences of his life when he actually took the Hobcart down and saw the pleasure on the child's face — it meant more to him, he said, than all the design activity he had been involved in up to then."[3]

In what follows, Mike Cooley opens questions of the greatest importance. The new technology will not go away, and it is in the interests of no-one that it should. The question is different, and much more fundamental than that raised by ancient and modern Luddites. Luddism has had a distinctly bad press, and has been a perfectly respectable, if inadequate response to mechanical servitude. But the really humane answer requires the subordination of machines to truly human purposes: and nowhere is this more plain than in the place we now occupy. Our world contains mass unemployment, and its major public investments, greater than all previous investments in anything, are committed to its ultimate destruction. All that money, and all that genius could unlock the door to a new and incomparably richer civilization, in which people become the true measure of all things, and their powers of creativity and love opened the doors to a new moral world.

Footnotes

1. Karl Marx, *Capital,* Torr Edition, Allen and Unwin, p.215.
2. *Ibid.* pp.249-50.
3. Michael Cooley: 'Design, Technology and Production for Social Needs' in Ken Coates (ed.) *The Right to Useful Work,* Spokesman, pp.201-202.

Chapter 7

Who will Harness the New Technology?

Mike Cooley

There persists a widespread belief that computerisation, automation and the use of robotic equipment will free human beings from soul destroying, routine, back-breaking tasks and leave them free to engage in more creative, fulfilling activities. It is further suggested that it will automatically lead to a shorter working week, longer holidays and more leisure time. Viewed thus these new technologies are perceived to be liberatory and positive and seen as the transmission lines along which will flow an ever increasing 'quality of life'. There is however, another side to this somewhat simplistic scenario. Those who work in industry often find that such a view of technology is a cynical attempt by industrialists and politicians to placate the well-founded fears of the community at large about the wider social-multiplier effects of these new technologies in general and their impact on their employment in particular.

This dual nature of new technology was pointed out by Herman Rebhan in his introduction to *Microelectronics and Employment:* "It has been hailed as unlocking the door to a new world in which hard, manual, dirty labour becomes a thing of the past and the way is opened to new vistas of leisure. It has also been condemned as a number one job killer ushering in a new world division of labour in which unemployment grows, jobs lose their skill and interest while a handful of multinational corporations make super profits which are beyond re-distributive reach". Having pointed out that new technology is neither inherently good nor inherently evil he concluded, "the new technology was introduced by man, it has been applied by man, and under man's control, the problem is that such control is currently kept in too few hands whose chief interest is profit maximisation. Our task is to place the new technology at the disposal of human need, we must master it or it will master us". If we are to master new technology it is necessary to understand its nature and the wider effects it is having on the structure of society and our work.

One of the most remarkable features of modern industrial societies is the gap between what technology could provide (its potential) and that which it actually does provide (its reality). We have on the one hand a level of technological sophistication such that we can guide missiles to another continent with the accuracy of a few metres yet the blind and the disabled stagger around our cities in very much the same way as they did in medieval times. We are of course assured that there will be a whole host of 'spin-offs' from these technologies which will then in the long term enhance the quality of our lives. Frequently such spin-offs result in something as elegant and complex as Concorde — designed and produced jointly by both Britain and France — but such technology takes place in a society which is not meeting even the most basic human needs.

In Britain at the moment literally thousands of old age pensioners die each year because they cannot get a simple effective heating system, whilst Concorde zooms on its supersonic way to reduce international travel time for businessmen by a few hours. There are senior electronics engineers working out international communication network systems so that messages can be sent round the world in fractions of a second, but it does frequently take longer to send an ordinary letter from Washington to New York than it did in the days of the stage coach. The aerodynamic techniques developed by these industries are sometimes used to optimise car bodies so that they are aerodynamically stable at about 120 miles per hour (mph) when the average speed of a car through some parts of New York at peak travel time is 6.2mph. It is said it was 8mph at the turn of the century when they were horse-drawn.

There are therefore grounds for believing that technology and manufacturing is developing along narrow esoteric lines to meet the wishes and the needs of the vast multinational corporations when on the other hand the requirements of ordinary people are increasingly ignored. All around we see unmet needs. There is no shortage of work: there is only a shortage of the political will and mechanism which will allow human beings to use their great ingenuity and talent to meet those needs.

Appalling though the gap is between unmet needs and the level of technology in the metropolitan countries it pales into insignificance if we look at the requirements of Third World countries. Frequently, very simple forms of agricultural equipment, pumping systems, irrigation schemes and simple medical equipment would enormously enhance the quality of lives there. Of the 122 million babies born in the developing countries in 1982, 11 million died before their first birthday and a further five million before they were five. Five million children die every year from dehydration resulting from diarrhoea; such dehydration can in fact be simply treated. Another five million children are killed in developing countries every year by six diseases — measles, diphtheria, tenanus, whooping cough, polio and tuberculosis.

Cheap mass production methods for vaccine and immunising agents have been developed and it is now feasible to immunise all these children against them. The medical knowledge is there but not the money. Yet closing the gap would cost only £33bn per year or £8.50 per head with money left over for improving water sanitation facilities which are vital foundations for disease prevention.

Malnutrition is widespread in these countries and it undermines the resistance of the Third World to disease and is responsible for the death of 40,000 young children a day while £30,000m a year is spent on weapons by the governments of the world. The growing numbers of the unemployed in the industrially advanced nations could be used to begin to meet these basic human requirements. Displaced workers from automotive plants could be working on simple tractor systems for Third World countries. Indeed the workers at Chryslers in the United Kingdom proposed a range of universal agricultural implements and machinery for Third World countries. Those working in instrument industries could help to make a range of basic medical equipment, whilst others could be engaged in developing and building food processing plants. There is an urgent need for simple refrigeration plants which will provide an adequate environment for the storage of medicines and vaccines.

There is a glaring need for robust repairable buses which are designed in an energy conscious fashion to provide an infrastructure of transport systems for many of these countries. Similarly, lightweight guided transport systems could also be gradually made available. Those International Metalworkers' Federation (IMF) members working in the pump manufacturing and compressor industries could be providing equipment for urgently required irrigation schemes, and those in shipbuilding and heavy construction could be building large-scale solar activated, desalination plants in many of the Third World countries. Many of the Third World Countries have significant hydro power potential. In others considerable use could be made of bio-mass fired systems, solar generators and wind generating equipment. Frequently there is a requirement for good quality recycled machine tools or even complete plants.

Workers in the metropolitan countries could be providing all of these if international mechanisms existed to allow the skills and talents to be used to support the sisters and brothers in Third World countries in this way. The whole arrangement could be based on a form of mutually supported but non-exploitative trading. In the developed countries the requirement for services and equipment is likewise glaring and will be explored in greater detail below. The IMF might well consider setting up an international commission to look at the requirements for equipment which the metalworkers could produce on the one hand, for the Third World countries and, on the other hand, in those countries where its membership is concentrated.

There is much talk in the technologically advanced nations, and correctly so, about the wastage of energy and materials but precious little is said about the wastage of society's most precious asset which is the skill, the ingenuity, the creativity and the sheer enthusiasm of its ordinary people. Yet in spite of this terrible wastage in dole queues in all the technologically advanced nations no serious attempt has been made to provide an infrastructure through which skill and knowledge could be used to meet unmet human needs. So we have thousands of skilled manual workers out of work at a time when we urgently need safe, effective, ecologically desirable transport systems. Thousands of auto workers are being displaced as a result of automated systems when it would be possible to restructure part of those industries to produce, for example, natural gas-fired heat pumps which would reduce energy consumption in the long term.

In all the technologically advanced nations there is an acute shortage of housing, hospitals, schools and public amenity buildings. Building workers could be providing this but in doing so would also be creating a demand for a range of products from steel joists right the way through to heating and ventilating equipment which would be produced by metalworkers. Yet far from developing mechanisms which allow unemployed metalworkers to engage in these socially desirable activities the tendency is for the dole queues to grow in all the technolgically advanced nations.

A major feature of technological change is that it changes the organic composition of capital; it makes processes capital intensive rather than labour intensive. This pattern has been evident since the 1800s. At the beginning of the 1800s in the United States some 86 per cent used to work in agriculture; gradually that was mechanised and increased use was made of chemicals and there are now many systems which might be said to be automatic. Today 4 per cent of the workforce is producing an agricultural produce many times greater than the 86 per cent did at the beginning of the 1800s. (It should be pointed out that the calorific value of the food so produced is actually less than the equivalent energy input if one takes into account the tractors, harvesters and chemicals. This is a problem society may have to address in the long term.)

Change in Composition of US Workforce by Percentage 1860-1980

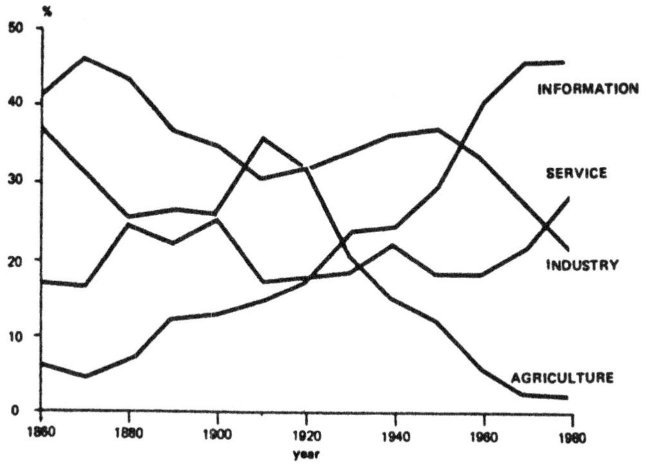

In the meantime the manufacturing industries were growing up to the 1970s but the increases in productivity could no longer be met with the increases in production thus, although the total level of production was going up slowly, those employed in the industries were reducing. In the meantime the white collar administrative staff area was growing but that in turn is being subjected to a growing use of computers so that we are now getting a large scale displacement of workers in banking, insurance, local and central government departments. Thus unemployment is tending to develop in an all round sense.

If we look at given sectors of industries, for example, the manufacture of telecommunication exchanges we will see that whereas it required 26 workers to produce one equivalent unit of switching power in the electro-mechanical field, with a first generation electronic it is 10, and with fully electronic systems in the year 1990 it will require only one worker.

Such productivity increases of 26/1 cannot be met by increases in production. Our inability to do so results from the constraints of energy and materials. Thus there is growing acceptance that we are going to face structural unemployment as distinct from cyclical unemployment.

It used to be suggested that as jobs were lost in the manufacturing industries as a result of technological change new jobs would become available in the white collar and service sectors but computerisation is taking its toll there as well. A recent report in France (the NORA report) suggested that modern computing technology in banks over the next 10 years will reduce the staff in that area by 30 per cent. Similar figures apply to the insurance industry. A survey in West Germany suggests that by 1990, 40 per cent of the present office work will be carried out by computerised systems. The West German unions have translated this into figures and calculated that it would mean a staggering loss of two million jobs out of West Germany's five million clerical and office activities. Thus not only will there be labour displacement in the manufacturing industries but those displaced and their children will be in competition with growing numbers of other white collar workers who have themselves been displaced by these systems.

Unemployment Rates in the EEC

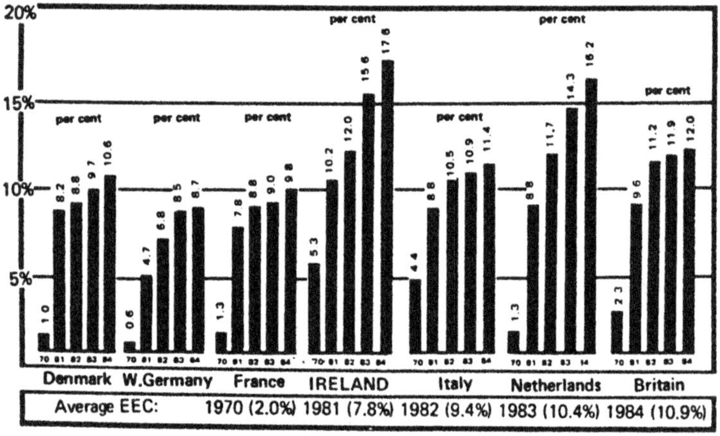

It is being suggested that even if the EEC countries could maintain their present growth rates there would still be 20 million people out of work by 1988. Two issues arise here. First, we are underestimating how important work is to human beings. We are not suggesting that the future lies in more and more people working on productive production lines but rather work in its historical context which links hand and brain in a meaningful production process. Work is central to our lives, if you ask anybody what they are, they will not say a Beethoven lover, a Bob Dylan fan, or a James Joyce reader (I sometimes think it's a pity that they don't), they will say, a teacher, a nurse, a metalworker. We relate to society and to other people by the work we do. It is an important learning, socialising and developing process and society must provide mechanisms for people to engage in socially useful activity as an alternative to structural unemployment.

Secondly, we should recognise that these jobs are not ours to give away. We are the guardians of those jobs for future generations, and in guarding them we can also ensure that there are jobs which are more fulfilling and creative than the ones which we have now got. Once society begins to accept that the unemployment problem it is facing is structural rather than cyclical there should then be the basis for mobilising public opinion and political and other movements to begin to redress the situation. It is felt that the IMF has a profound role to play in this process and there follows examples of job creation attempts in a number of countries.

II The Trade Union Response

The changing structure of industry is now having enormous societal multiplier effects. At one end it is soaking up massive resources of capital equipment and human knowledge in the military industrial complex, and growing peace movements worldwide express basic concern for the future of humanity. In many countries, in particular West Germany, the trade unions are playing an increasing role in discussing these issues. In the non-military sector there is concern at the ever-increasing rate of production and consumption and the exhaustion of energy and material resources. Further, there is the growing concern about the impact this is having on the environment with environmental groups and others drawing attention to the long-term dangers and pointing out, as do the *Environmentalists for Full Employment* in Australia, that jobs could be created by producing pollution control systems and socially useful and environmentally desirable product ranges. Those who work in the industries themselves are likewise confronted with growing problems. At one level there are the effects of automation on skills and then there are the problems of plant relocation and rationalisation worldwide. It may be said that the trade union movement is only now beginning to respond to the scale and nature of these problems, and a reappraisal of the relationship of trade unions to these developments is just beginning to take place.

Likewise within the metalworking manufacturing industries,

technological change is in itself proletarianising a large number of metalworkers, including designers, metallurgists and engineers, and these will be important allies in the battles for socially useful and desirable products during the coming years.

Furthermore, there is growing recognition that it is legitimate for those who work in industries to question what is to be made, why it is to be made, how it is to be made and in whose interest it is being made. This applies particularly in connection with arms production.

Industrial workers are realising that through the trade unions they should begin to question the nature of the products they are making and their impact on society at large, but this they must do not only in a critical fashion: they should go on to say what type of products they believe should be produced as an alternative to the degredation and suffering of growing unemployment. Probably the best known and best documented example of this is the plan for socially useful production by the trade unions at Lucas Aerospace in the United Kingdom.

However, similar questioning has been going on in Nordic countries, in Italy, France, West Germany and elsewhere.

It has to be stated that parts of the trade union movement have not always been willing to respond positively to these initiatives which have come primarily from the base.

But given that the problems are not going to go away many trade union leaderships are now recognising that, if they are adequately to look after the long term interests of their members, they have a profound responsibility to look at alternative forms of production as a basis for providing useful employment for their members and, by doing that, to continue to bring about a more equitable distribution of wealth and services. As the trade union leaderships begin to do this they will have a rich tradition of rank and file activity to draw on. Individual factories will work out detailed plans for alternative forms of work.

In addition, sectors of industry, in particular shipbuilding and the armaments industry, will begin to produce at a factory level creative plans for more long term sustainable employment.

Specific Initiatives

(a) Great Britain

At the end of the 1960s Lucas Aerospace employed some 18,000 workers in 17 plants throughout the United Kingdom. At the beginning of the 1970s the company embarked on a dramatic rationalisation programme. By 1972 it was suggested that some 4,000 jobs would go. Initially the workforce responded in the traditional fashion by occupying plants and preventing the company moving equipment from one location to another, but they were simply campaigning for the right to work on the same old products in the same old way. There was no real long-term vision around which the workforce could begin to organise. Having experienced defeats in the first closures, the workforce felt there was a need for more radical solutions.

They formed a combined committee which organised all the unions (13 of them) working in the Lucas Aerospace plants in to a combined Shop Stewards Committee. They developed an elaborate inter-factory communication network and produced their own newspaper. When further redundancies were threatened the workforce decided to draw up a plan for alternative production. The steps they took could probably be carried out in any sector of industry, in any district or perhaps even in any nation state. The first thing they did was to make an assessment of their own skills and abilities. They analysed the types of products they had made in the past, the means of production to produce them and human skills required to make that possible. Having created an inventory of these, they then did what society often conditions industrial workers to do. They asked 180 authorities and experts what they could be doing with this skill and equipment as an alternative to the degradation of unemployment; they contacted university professors who had given profound lectures in the monastic quiet of their institutions; they wrote to people who had written voluminous books as to how science and technology would be made more relevant; they wrote to 'expert' bodies such as the Institute of Engineering. Out of the 180 world authorities only three were able to say anything that was remotely useful; from the rest they got the vague kind of generalisations that one has come to expect from people of that kind. Then they did what they should have done in the first instance. They asked their own workforce what they thought they could be making; if people have spent a lifetime making products and developing them they are easily capable of saying how they can be adapted and modified.

Almost tragically no-one had thought of asking the metalworker for his or her ideas. By holding a series of meetings and by the use of a unique questionnaire, there was an incredible out-pouring of creativity from the Lucas workers. The questionnaire was so designed as to cause the workforce to think of its members in their dual role in society both as producers and as consumers and to think of a product with a use value rather than of its exchange value, to consider long-term environmental impacts and to look at the means by which Third World countries might be assisted in their development. In asking the workers to present their ideas, they did not insist that they wrote a great thesis about each product. (There is a tendency in our society to confuse linguistic ability with intelligence — we are far more impressed by what people say and write rather than what they can actually do. Industrial workers express their intelligence by what they do and how they do it). If therefore workers wanted to make models of the products they had in mind or make sketches of them all that was accepted as valid design proposals. All these were fed into the Trade Union Corporate Planning Committee which sifted through the ideas and drew them up into plan in six volumes. The plan included proposals for 150 products which could be made in Lucas Aerospace and indeed other manufacturing companies as an alternative to unemployment. They included on the one hand simple medical equipment, for example, dialysis machines. The workforce had learnt to their alarm that every year 3,000 people were dying in Britain because they could not get one of these simple devices. They proposed that the existing kidney machines could be redesigned and made much smaller so that they could be worn like a rucksack on the patient's back. This would then give the patient the dignity of being mobile and active rather than lying there like a block of wood acted upon by the technology which is frequently what Western medical technology does.

They took the view that the unionists had a responsibility to look at the long term questions of the use of energy and materials, they felt that it was desirable to design equipment that would conserve energy rather than waste it. They therefore designed together with research institutions a number of heat pumps using natural gas in internal combustion engines. These pumps, which work somewhat like refrigerators in reverse, would mean that when you get zero degrees outside the building you get 2.8 times as much useful energy as you would if you were to burn the gas directly.

Although there was a report which suggested that the market for these in the EEC countries by 1988 would be £1,000m the company refused to produce them. As the journal the *New Statesman* so perceptively put it, the company was probably determined to demonstrate that it and it alone decided what was made, where it was made, how it was made and in whose interest it was made. We are in fact dealing not merely with an economic system but also with the political one which is determined to retain its so-called 'managerial prerogative' and decision making powers. A number of local governments in the United Kingdom are now looking at the possibility of manufacturing these heat pumps. A number of multinationals have also begun to manufacture them on short batch production scale.

The Lucas workers also proposed and developed power units for cars, coaches or trains which were of hybrid variety. That is to say they made best use of an internal combustion engine and an electric motor: in that way it was possible to reduce fuel consumption in an urban cycle by 50 per cent and toxic emissions by 80 per cent. In addition to this the unit was designed in such a fashion that it really could be repaired and would have a life of some 20 years. It was originally argued by some other trade unionists that this would therefore give rise to structural unemployment. The Lucas workers believed on the other hand that, if throughout the country there was set up infrastructures in repair workshops where units of this kind could be rebuilt and repaired, that would create as much work as would be lost if they were no longer simply mass-produced as throw-away products.

There has since been an important report from the Battelle Institute in Geneva called *On the Potential of Substituting Manpower for Energy* which supports this contention. It broadly indicates that if one designs products to last for 20 years, not only could one conserve energy and materials, one could create in some instances up to 65 per cent more work and the jobs that would be created would be the interesting fiddling diagnostic type of jobs which human beings like doing. This report has gone to the EEC and is receiving serious consideration.

The Lucas workforce also produced a unique road/rail vehicle capable of running through cities as a coach and using the branch lines which were now being closed down in many parts of the industrial world. The vehicle uses rubber tyres of both modes and is therefore capable of going up an incline of 1 in 6; this would also have enormous applications in Third World countries.

On a larger scale they proposed designing and building airships which use helium rather than hydrogen which is normally associated with airships. The idea was to have a constant ballast system in which the airship would be charged only once so the cost of recharging would therefore be avoided. Calculations showed that it would be possible to transport 400 tons of cargo at a velocity of 100 miles per hour using two 200hp diesel engines. There is still considerable interest in this proposal worldwide. The Lucas workers therefore demonstrated in a very practical way that alternative socially useful production is not merely about 2Kw wind generators but can involve large-scale products and systems which would be a challenge to the ingenuity and skill of those working in many sectors of the metalworking industries at the moment. They were however not just talking about alternative products but alternative ways of producing them, and they therefore proposed a range of telechiric devices which would not de-skill the workers involved.

Following the Lucas example trade unions at Vickers and Chryslers in the United Kingdom put forward a series of proposals for alternative products to cope with the growing structure of unemployment. Similar developments were taking place in different forms and at different levels of sophistication worldwide. In Sweden at Götaverken the workforce in the shipbuilding industry there looked at alternatives to the structural problems that their industries were facing.

(b) Federal Republic of Germany

In West Berlin a group involving trade unionists made an examination of the possibility of socially useful products to counter unemployment at the AEG plant in West Berlin.

First stage calculations were carried out with the help of the Berlin trade union transport experts and economists, calculations intended to substantiate the realistic appraisal of the project. It was suggested that there should be constructed 440 new S-Bahn (subway) carriages with 112 rail cars which could be produced over a five to seven year period. Berlin's carriage construction industry would likewise have profited from the project through carriage body construction; in addition another 250 to 300 jobs would have been created at the Brunnenstrasse plant to carry out the orders and in addition to all of this there would have been many training places. Apart from the effects of jobs on the AEG factories, the S-Bahn redevelopment would have meant work for colleagues at Siemens in manufacturing signals, for carriage construction and building industries in Berlin as a whole. A further 2,000-3,000 jobs would have been created for the S-Bahn project in terms of drivers, guards, maintenance and railway staff etc.

(c) North America

With plant closures in the steel industry in North America and Canada, workers in those industries are likewise looking at alternative products and services which they could provide. In some instances they are uniting with other unions to see how they could provide and improve services to the community while at the same time creating jobs for themselves.

Proposals of a similar kind are also emerging in the United States around the *Rebuilding America* programme. This programme is very actively supported by the International Association of Machinists. Just as the initiatives in the metalworking industries will have multiplier effects on jobs outside that industry (e.g. the AEG example above) so also initiatives from those outside the metal industries will ultimately create jobs for those who now produce a range of components and equipment which other industries require.

(d) Australia

An interesting example is the initiative by the Building Workers Union in Australia which has proposed a massive re-housing programme. The president of the Australian Congress of Trade Unions, Cliff Dolan has pointed out, "the housing industry can play a significant role in stimulating the economy and providing many jobs give correct policies. Fifty-one industries depend on housing to some extent for their business. There is no better job creator than the housing industry. It supports industries which are labour intensive and mainly based in Australia, across the whole range of manufacturing industry. Housing creates much needed jobs and a vital social need for people".

In another Australian example, the Amalgamated Metals, Foundry and Shipwrights Union has got together with those working in the railways to propose a modernisation programme for the whole of the railway systems in Australia with new rolling stock and better quality signalling systems. In addition they have proposed to completely refit the railway workshops with new and better quality equipment which would ultimately result in better jobs for their members and a better service to the community as a whole.

Thus we can see that throughout the world trade unionists are beginning to look creatively at alternatives to unemployment. This they are doing using the collective strength of the unions and the organisational forms which they have developed over the years. This will mean that they have a strong and powerful base from which to project their ideas and to bargain with local and national governments.

Reduced Working time

These developments should not be seen as alternatives to the tremendous campaign for a shorter working week, longer holidays and more leisure time. These proposals should in fact run in parallell, and therefore metal unions fighting for a 35-hour week and thereby seeking to reduce unemployment are also supporting aspirations of those who would like to see full employment linked to socially useful production. The metalworkers in Italy have been looking creatively at the possibility of 150 hours sabbatical for workers in the metalworking industries as a form of creative job sharing. Thus we should see the introduction of alternative forms of production and new product ranges as linking in with an overall job creation programme which will also result in a shorter working week, and better more satisfying conditions. These initiatives are vitally important in their own right, but are also important exemplary projects which will animate masses of people to think about the possibilities of fulfilling unmet needs by using the skill of workers who would otherwise lose their jobs in plants which would stand idle.

It is very important to work all such initiatives through the political system. A good example of this has been the initiative by the Labour-controlled Greater London Council in England. This is a local government which represents directly some eight million people and indirectly about 11 million people. In its Election Manifesto the present Labour administration in London pledged to create socially useful long-term sustainable jobs as an alternative to growing structural unemploymnent. (There are 400,000 unemployed in the London area). It set up an Economy Policy Group which together with the people of London and the trade unions in given sectors of industry, are producing reports on each of the major sectors. Thus there are reports on Engineering, Transport, Energy, etc. In order that these proposals could be put into effect it has established a Greater London Enterprise Board — GLEB. This body has got £32m in its first year of operation to establish new forms of industry throughout London. In its first year of operation up to March 1984 it has established 146 projects or companies and created directly over 2,000 new jobs at a cost of about £9,000 per job and very many more jobs created indirectly. Not only can it invest in companies or start up new companies or take over bankrupt companies, it can also invest in existing companies; in all cases it seeks to establish an enterprise plan which gives those who work in the industries a real voice about what is made, how it is made and why it is made. In this way it is hoped that the tremendous creativity which was demonstrated at Lucas can be released since as the Greater London Enterprise Board puts it, "the greatest asset we have is skill, ingenuity and imagination of the people of London themselves".

A vitally important part of GLEB's work has been to establish Technology Networks throughout London. This is a way of opening up London's educational facilities, seven polytechnics and three universities, to the community at large. Buildings are established close to the universities and polytechnics and could produce a range of equipment so that those facing unemployment can work in a very practical environment to develop new product ranges and services. There are four Networks throughout London and they have established a product bank. The product bank is the outcome of the creativity and knowledge of ordinary people. The disabled for example have identified 457 products and services they require. Groups of trade unionists in sectors of industry going into decline have proposed alternative products which they can make. Once a product idea has emerged and looks practical, those involved can come into one of the Technology Network buildings, and together with the help of sympathetic technologists develop the first prototype which can then be tested and even developed into a short batch production stage. This is already happening with power and assisted bicycles, with unique transport vehicles, with a range of energy systems and a whole host of equipment for the medical profession. The idea is then to set up co-operatives, or as part of a bargaining situation around new technology, introduce these products as an alternative to structural unemployment. In some instances the local government will itself purchase the products as an improvement in the services it intends to provide for those in its area. The Greater London Enterprise Board has as its chairperson the Regional Secretary of the Transport and General Workers Union and at every level and in every industry it is receiving widespread support from active trade unionists. Up to now however, it has, like most bodies attempting to deal with unemployment, including the trade unions, been largely reactive. In order to overcome this it has now established an early warning unit which together with trade unionists in sectors of industry will analyse the main trends of those industries and begin to develop mechanisms and policies to cope with job losses before it is too late.

Some other local governments in England including those in Sheffield, the West Midlands and Liverpool are developing similar employment initiatives with the trade unions in their area. Certain municipalities in France, Italy, West Germany and the Netherlands are developing similar projects. These projects although modest in scale compared with the nature of the problems, are powerful exemplary projects which hopefully will prompt trade unions at a national level and political parties to begin to develop programmes of alternative work at the nation state level. In this way, with the full backing of the state, skills and talents of people could be used more fully, rather than declining in the dole queue.

As the true cost in society of unemployment becomes more evident it is hoped that by practical example and political pressure governments will be compelled to look seriously at the possibility of providing better services and equipment to the community at large, whilst at the same time beginning to deal creatively with the problems of unemployment. Trade unions have a profound role in bringing about such changes; through their history trade unionists have demonstrated the courage and energy to act as agents of change and as powerful countervailing forces to those who control industry. Above all they can begin to help their members to get back some control over their own destiny, and to be involved in a process in which they will realise that they are the subjects rather than the objects of history. Given real creative alternatives, workforces will respond with courage and dignity to see that their skills can be used to improve the quality of life for the community as a whole.

Chapter 8

Action at How Many Levels?

Stephen Bodington

Academic and political discussion of employment and unemployment has in the past assumed, almost always, that there is just one level of economic activity — the level of the national, or sometimes the world market. Remedies for unemployment have usually been assumed to be national policies such as cause employers to offer more jobs. However, in recent years the social and economic situation in Britain has so radically changed that policies focused on the national market — important as they still are — would on their own be quite inadequate.

A new approach is forced upon us by the transnationalisation of capital, management's use of the new technology, British capital's strength and know-how in financial institutions internationally and diminished concern for the older industries, and other factors due to changes in the structure of the market and capitalism itself. But a new approach is also needed because people's attitudes to jobs are changing; this opens up positive possibilities that may in the past have been regarded as unrealistic and utopian. Employment policies formerly related too narrowly to 'public employment'; 'the economy' has in effect been equated with economic activity in which work is undertaken for wages and salaries. The logic behind this approach was quite simply, and realistically, that 'the economy' is that system which is unified and organised by the market. (It is for this reason that there always tends to be an ambiguity as to whether the economy we are considering is a national or international system).

Of course the 'public economy' in which people work for wages was never more than a fraction of the social total of activity through which economic needs are catered for. Traditionally what happens outside the money economy is not the concern of policy-makers; so it was something altogether unusual to find the GLC's industrial strategy for London looking at economic activity in London as a whole as opposed to just 'public employment for money' — which they found to be somewhat less than half the total. There are of course a host of interactions of importance between unpaid activities in households and in the community and the money- or market-regulated economy; such interactions enter into childcare, part-time working, DIY and very much else. Alternative employment policies need to take account of social needs overall, how people want to work, where they want to work, when they want to work. Employment policy can no longer be just about generating job offers for people to take or leave; it has to include enlargement of social choice.

We are compelled to explore alternatives and so address these wider issues because the lazier approach of simply cranking up the old apparatus to get it working again as it did in the 1950s, say, simply is not on. It is quite inconceivable that market economics on its own, however sophisticatedly serviced and reconditioned, can provide an adequate economic basis for the kind of social life that we, the British people as we now are, have come to expect and require. Failure to provide conditions in which people have reasonable scope for meeting their demands on life is bound to lead to appalling political and social consequences. But this necessity to think through alternatives is also an opportunity — an opportunity to take a wider view of what economic resources are and to adapt their use to a wider spectrum of social needs. So the problem boils down to making the best we can of market mechanisms (which inescapably will be part of all scenarios of change for the foreseeable future) and *at the same time* catering for employment-creating need-satisfying activities that will coexist with market economics *without being subservient to the dynamic of the market.* Indeed so far from being dragged back by market recessions, economic activity that directly responds to needs actively fills the waste lands left by market failures. Alternatives to be effective in themselves and to exert leverage against decision-makers in market-regulated enterprises must have a dynamic that is independent of the market.

To many this approach seems 'unrealistic', 'extreme', 'utopian'; but such reactions, I would argue, are not so much factual as responses to an ideological climate. Political and academic economics has focused so narrowly on the public economy and financial management at a national level, that the very existence of other forms of economic activity is disregarded and so also, of course, policies directed towards them. Economics is conceived as having just one level — that of the national (or international) market and the financial system geared to it.

Control over market mechanisms and the financial system so as to make it more socially useful and, in particular, following Keynesian or central planning theory, to make it generate more jobs, is *one* aspect of policies for coping with the crisis of unemployment, but it is only one aspect and, if necessary, far from sufficient for Britain in the context of the capitalist world as it is today. The other approach, that today is essential for us, starts from democratic devolution of decision-making, enabling people to control some resources for themselves and inspiring them to become conscious of their own potential resources and to relate them to their own needs. This approach takes many different forms at many different levels. It is the philosophy behind workers' corporate plans (such as that worked out at Lucas Aerospace) and also that behind 'local employment plans', 'popular planning' and so forth, stimulated by Local Authorities trying to put life into their local economies (as in Sheffield, London, West Midlands and elsewhere). But once resources and needs are looked at concretely, 'qualitatively', the question of 'levels' assumes paramount importance. The potential of specific resources — people with skills, particular teams with particular facilities — exists in specific places and sites; similarly needs are the needs of specific people in specific communities. By contrast exchange value, which motivates and measures market activity, overrides specific needs, for work or goods; it generalises, universalises and translates into money that is acceptable here, there or elsewhere.

The question of levels of activity and organisation is obscured by quantitative measures that apply universally. So when the market and money economics fail, one has to look beyond its generalisations to specifics; but it is important to do so in such a way as not to fragment and parochialise specific activity 'at the base'. On the contrary the point is to nurture the social benefits of belonging to the wider system.

Like it or not the economic bond that holds together the wider systems is money. Extraordinarily little thought has been given to financial mechanisms from the standpoint of democratic control over resources, and, what obviously goes with this, the stimulation of local projects to meet local needs. One of the most remarkable achievements of capital — that is, from its owns point of view — is the skill with which the dictatorial power of money has escaped political and moral accountability and obloquy. Nuremburg arraigned politicians and generals but the money-power that had backed them remained to grace the new political scene as if it were simply part of the natural environment. Paradoxically, however, the financial system, which through the youth and maturity of capitalism was regulated by the market forces that turned gold and silver into money commodities embodying exchange value, now can no longer be left to automatisms of the market but has to be 'planned' and regulated by conscious policy decisions which determine the availability of credit and, in effect, the value of *de facto* units of money. 'Financial politicians of integrity' find themselves planning to simulate the behaviour that a gold-based system might have followed had it been possible to leave things to market forces! But financial politicians of not so great integrity are less scrupulous about the use of money-power.

Is it possible to challenge the power that financial management gives and the philosophy by which it is customarily guided? If this is not possible, we might as well give up, because it is hardly conceivable — within any foreseeable future — that money should cease to serve as the instrument of co-ordination between social units engaged each in their specific forms of economic activity. So the question becomes — can money as basis of social power be divorced from money as instrument of co-ordination? Clearly this must be possible now that the financial system has to be regulated by conscious policy and no longer can be left to the automatisms of market regulation. But socialists have given far too little thought to possibilities of using financial policies and financial mechanisms to devolve control over resources and to facilitate democratic initiatives. Democratic financial policies provide a means of building countervailing economic power against the money power of private capital. But the implementation of such policies needs the backing of an alternative economic philosophy and popular support for new ideas about how the financial system should be managed. In particular, new criteria should govern decisions about making credits available. Reactionary finance is cocooned in mystery and it is not easy to build confidence in the feasibility of using quite different criteria for credit policy. The practical difficulties in other respects are not, in my view, half so difficult as they at first may seem. Pethwick Lawrence said in 1943: "The financial prosecution of this war has taught us one striking fact, which is that nothing which is economically possible ought to be financially impossible" (*Hansard,* 17, vi, 1943). This means that it is possible to make socially desirable resource use an overriding criterion for giving credit.

Grassroot groups in industry and in the community, co-operatives and other organisations with 'legitimate interest' (see below) when they have worked out feasible projects should automatically receive credits, once the project has received approval from an appropriate sanctioning authority. Sanctioning powers would need to exist at many levels, starting, in my view, well below the bottom tier of British local government as it now is, adding 'Parish' or 'Neighbourhood Councils' to cover communities of a few thousand and extending up to international bodies capable, for example, of dealing with proposals for transnational companies worked out by shop stewards from different countries. Power due to private wealth or institutional control by an elite which hides behind such dogmas as "management's right to manage" needs to be smoked out and "legitimate interests" in each enterprise (e.g. workers, Local Authorities and local communities, consumers) need to be defined and given rights to determine how resources are used. The application of a new economic philosphy and new criteria to the management of international projects and finance could only be the end result of prolonged and sophisticated political struggle and negotiation; but it would be possible very quickly, given a political will, to apply new credit criteria to the financing of local projects. Campaigning against "the inevitability of unemployment" has to start here and now and go on at many levels simultaneously. Resource-use projects and policies (and financial policies to match them) make the struggle concrete, specific and convincing; and such policies will take different forms at different levels of activity and organisation. They should, however, be guided by the principle that lower levels be empowered and given facilities to develop their own policies for problems that admit at least partial solutions independently of decisions taken at higher levels. At present finance, which is the main instrument of economic co-ordination, is dictatorially centralised; inconspicuous power dictates that money is or is not available. Serious solutions to problems of employment and unemployment are not feasible unless and until financial principles and criteria are established which allow decision-making to be decentralised and related to the place-by-place availability of resources. Workers in specific enterprises and people living in specific communities can see for themselves 'what is economically possible' at the base, at the level where life is lived and work is done. Analogous perceptions of 'economic possibility' will define goals and policies for co-ordination at local, regional, national and international levels. The job is so to control the mechanisms of finance as to guarantee 'financial possibility' to match 'the economic possibility' as perceived by the people by whom and for whom possibilities are to be realised, that is, to give substance to a cliché-worn word, 'democratically'.

Chapter 9

What Prospects for Shorter Working Time?

Ken Coates and Tony Topham

There is a classic example of a campaign by trade unionists for political solutions to industrial problems. It was born in the heyday of the new unions, towards the end of the last century, and, we should never forget, it was linked with a major development of labour internationalism. The first modern day May Day demonstrations were summoned around the international demand for a legal eight-hour day. Responding to a call of the American Federation of Labour, the Paris Congress which consituted the Second Inernational in 1889, proposed that the 1st of May 1890 be the occasion for worldwide demonstrations for shorter working time. The London May Day demonstration was an extraordinary success, and as a result there emerged a pressure group for the "legal eight hours."[1] There was an unremitting campaign to persuade the TUC to support legislation bringing in an eight hour day. Tom Mann became known all over the country as the most persistent advocate of this cause. His first pamplet was called *What a Compulsory Eight Hour Day Means,*[2] but he was soon diversifying to explore the possibilities of local political action to enforce reductions in the working day. Sidney Webb followed Tom Mann into print, with a major study entitled *The Eight Hour Day.*[3] William Morris was involved in a joint appeal by the different socialist groupings to centre attention on an eight hour Bill. During this campaign, throughout the early part of the 1890s, liberal voters among that relatively small part of the working class which was enfranchised were forced to think and think again. The eight hour agitation drew support from working people, but it divided politicians along a distinctly radical axis. Trade unionists learned about the fickleness of their traditional alliances, and became steadily more ready to rely on their own resources. There can be no doubt that this agitation played a major part in turning over the ground in which the new Labour Party was later to grow. Of course, in the last years of the century, the unions were strongly on the defensive as a result of an outbreak of provocations which was orchestrated by the employers' organizations. But the Second International was still emphasizing that the eight hour day was the most crucial demand of the parts of its immediate programme, when it conferred in London in 1896. The engineers who were locked out the following year, while responding to the attacks of the employers, still felt able to make this call their main priority, thus joining an offensive of their own to the defensive manoeuvres they were forced to undertake. Once people had decided to try to found a committee for the representation of labour, they discovered that employers' onslaughts such as that of Taff Vale could actually assist them in their work. But the eight hours movement had established the need for separate representation in a constructive way, and without this example, the opening years of Labour history might have been altogether different. No doubt it is time to reinvent this movement. Perhaps our middle-term strategy, to be reached partly be legislation of longer holidays, and partly by collective bargaining, is for a working year of 1000 hours.

Shorter Working Time by Law

In 1981, the TUC adopted a motion moved by Clive Jenkins of the ASTMS, instructing the General Council to campaign for a limit on the number of hours worked annually, reducing the working week "by statute to a maximum of 35 hours", providing a "minimum holiday entitlement of six weeks per annum, plus sabbatical leave after a stipulated number of years for all employees" and reducing "the qualifying age for retirement pensions to 60 years". In an eloquent support for this case, Clive Jenkins showed that engineering workers in Sweden were, at the time, working 1,500 hours annually, while in Belgium and Germany they were working 1,600 and 1,700 hours respectively. But "the British engineering worker is working 1,902 hours a year."[4]

We must face it that there are a number of difficulties about implementing the call for a statute to fix a 35-hour week.

Even though unemployment waxes, institutional overtime in British industry never wanes. In December 1982, while three million people were already out of work, British manufacturing industry worked 9.66 million hours overtime. In December 1983, this figure had risen to 11.36 million hours, whilst the incidence of short-time had fallen from 1.61 million hours at the end of 1982 to 0.46 million at the end of 1983. If it became magically possible to outlaw overtime, overnight a quarter of a million new jobs could be created. The number would increase as working hours were reduced. Negotiations have been tending to secure reductions in agreed working hours, even though these are often not reflected in reductions in actual hours worked. The TUC has been carefully monitoring progress, and publishing a regular progress report. By 1983, it had monitored 57 separate agreements reducing hours by varying amounts from 40 down to 39 or 36½. Only one agreement was reported implementing a 35-hour week, in the exhibition industry, but this does not take effect until 1987.

The killer in this process is, of course, overtime. Overtime is concentrated and does not fall equally across the labour force. Workers who are doing overtime are thus, normally, doing far more than the average hours of overtime. From April 1981 to April 1982, the average weekly hours of overtime per male manual worker actually rose from 4.5 to 4.9, having fallen the previous year. But average overtime hours per male manual overtime worker rose from 9.4 to 9.7 during the same period. The following year both these statistics fell, back to 4.7 and 9.3 respectively. The TUC is well aware of this problem which continues to be intractable. Indeed, in February 1984 it pointed out the fact that the percentage of workers who do overtime has actually been rising since 1981 from 46.8 to 49.8. The small decline in the number of overtime hours is more likely to reflect the depression than the results of trade union limitations. And in their scrutiny of these figures, the TUC tell us that "the tendency . . . for the percentage of people working overtime to rise from April 1981 must be a matter of concern".

The agreed basic weekly hours have been slowly declining, and manual male workers now average a 39.2 hour week, compared to 39.9 hours which they would have expected to work in 1979. The following conclusions have been drawn by TUC researchers from the movement of working hours during recent years: men who are manual workers work a lot longer than other people. They average a 44 hour week, of which five hours are overtime. But the average is misleading, because half the manual male workers do not work overtime, which means that the other half who do average 9½ hours of it a week. Women manual workers average 39.7 hours, of which only one hour is overtime. Only one-fifth of these women workers get any overtime at all, and so they average six hours of it a week. Non-manual working men work some 38½ hours, of which 1½ are overtime; but only one-fifth of these people actually do work overtime which means that those who get it average six hours a week. Non-manual women workers are on a 36½ hour week, of which only half-an-hour is overtime, and in fact only 12 per cent of these women get to work overtime at all, and they average three hours a week.

Between 1979 and 1983 the total hours worked by men who were manual workers declined by 2⅓, of which 1.6 were accounted for by a decline in the availability of overtime. Decline among other groups was very much less significant.

The TUC's campaign, and the efforts of affiliated unions, have effectively broken through the barrier of the 40-hour basic week, and it is clear that the legislation could make a major contribution if only the unions could agree on how it should be framed. The problem is extremely simple to state, and very difficult to solve. Trade unionists will not say thank you for a law which cuts their earnings, and if overtime is forbidden then approximately half the male manual workers will be much worse off unless they are compensated for its loss. There is a very strong need for parliamentary draftsmen to consult with the TUC, if the Congress resolution of 1981 is to be implemented.

In West Germany, the trade union campaign for the 35-hour week was to become the most severe and important struggle in which that hitherto quiescent labour movement has engaged since 1945. British trade unions promised solidarity with it. The German unions case has been developed with characteristic comprehensiveness. They argue the job creation potential of a shorter work week, calling for commensurate new jobs to replace the hours 'lost' by the reduction in working time. They also point to its beneficial effects on health and safety, and on the equalisation of domestic duties within the family life as male workers in particular obtain more free time. They look forward to the liberating effect upon social awareness of a decisive breach in the customary trade union goal of "eight hours work, eight hours sleep and eight hours play". The German metalworkers' strike makes a pointed contrast with the British miners' strike, not only because it won an important breakthrough, but also because it was orientated outwards at winning public opinion as a major strategic objective.[5]

The Campaign for Shorter Working-Time in Western Europe[6]

In Western Europe, there is a widespread debate, amounting to a ferment, over the reduction of working-time. Much of this movement has received Governmental and EEC support. In September 1984, the European Parliament passed a resolution, moved by the Socialist Group, calling on the EEC Commission to "support forthwith all trade union and management initiatives likely to provide industries, individual undertakings and regions with suitable approaches to the re-organisation and reduction of working-time". It also called for the "opening of a European Commission Enquiry into the structure of the working week in Europe and possibly the creation of an observation centre whose role would be to provide information".

Many agreements, however, have been made bilaterally through union-employer negotiation. The objective is always clearly related to the creation of new employment. Not all the agreements are unambiguous in trade union terms; some reductions in working-time have been paid for by loss of wages, or by wage freezes. Not all have led directly to increased employment. But there is in this trend the basis on which to build a concerted multinational trade union and labour campaign as a major contribution to full employment through work-sharing.

In Germany, the trade union federation DGB adopted the 35-hour week policy in 1978. This was followed by a strike and lock-outs in the steel industry, which lasted six weeks. The settlement, which was adopted also by most of the private sector, introduced a standard six-weeks annual leave entitlement which is now applicable throughout a large part of German industry. But the working week of 40 hours was retained at that stage. The engineering industry took up the campaign in 1984 with the largest post-war German strike, lasting seven weeks. The settlement provided for a cut in the working-week to 38.5 hours from April 1985, without loss of pay. IG Metall, the union which led the strike, regards the objective of the 35-hour week as an absolute priority, surpassing any advances in pay. The employers' opposition was fierce and was endorsed by the Government, both parties arguing that reduced working time would increase labour costs. They countered with offers of flexible working time, early retirement, part-time work, and job-sharing.

The arbitration award which ended the conflict provided that each company could negotiate its own interpretation of the terms; hours could vary between 37 and 40, but must average 38.5. Overtime up to 10 hours per week, with a limit of 20 hours per month, is permitted; it will normally be compensated with overtime rates of pay, but time-off in lieu may be negotiated. An early-retirement scheme was included in the deal, under which workers with 20 years' service might retire at 58 on 70 per cent of gross earnings, about 75 per cent of former net pay. The printing industry has subsequently adopted the same terms.

The progress in West Germany over holiday entitlement in the early 1980s was spectacular.

	Percentage of Employees.		
No. of weeks holiday	*1980*	*1981*	*1982*
3 but less than 4	5	4	4
4 but less than 5	22	19	13
5 but less than 6	69	52	45
6 weeks	4	25	38

About 94 per cent of all employees covered by collective agreements in 1982 were entitled to additional holiday pay on top of their basic pay entitlement during annual holidays. It took the following forms; 42 per cent received a percentage of their basic holiday pay, averaging an additional 46 per cent; 33 per cent received a lump sum, averaging £148.50; 19 per cent received a "13th month's salary" equivalent to 65 per cent of a month's salary, and 54 per cent of employees received full salary beyond the statutory six-weeks' period in sickness. In 1983, the German government introduced legislation granting employees the right to opt for early retirement at age 59, through agreements negotiated by the trade unions. The following year, early retirement at 58 was supported by government subsidy. The employers' costs in pension payments are subsidised providing they take on unemployed people as replacements. Minimum early pension levels are at least 65 per cent of former gross earnings, or about 70 per cent of net earnings. The subsidy covers 35 per cent of the pension costs up to 65 per cent of former earnings. Retirement at this age remains voluntary.

The Belgian government had to set the pace for reduced working time linked to job creation in 1983, when it had set a dead-line for company or industry-level agreements to cut working time by five per cent, with accompanying increases of 3 per cent in employment levels. Where no agreement was reached,companies must pay a penalty into a newly created Employment Fund. In the first few months, a total of between 50,000 and 60,000 jobs had been preserved or created, and agreements were made covering more than 1 million workers, embracing more than 90 per cent of the private sector. Volkswagen in Belgium provided 18 days additional holidays, equivalent to a reduction of average hours to 37 per week, accompanied by a three per cent employment increase. The Caterpiller company provided four more days holiday, and provided for retirement at 55; 100 jobs were created. In the insurance sector, the working week was reduced by stages to 36 hours in 1984, and in textiles, the week was cut to 37 hours and 20 minutes. In 1984, the Belgian cabinet approved a Bill granting 240 hours paid leave per year for training, and an additional 160 hours for more general education. By April 1985, average hours in Belgium were down to 38.5, and still falling. In addition, paid leave has been granted for workers temporarily replaced by an unemployed person; the employer receives £144 per month in state aid under this scheme. The worker's leave in such cases must be for periods of six months to one year.

The Dutch trade union movement has now taken over the lead from the Belgians in the shorter hours movement. Their key demand for 1985-86 is the 36 hour week.. The printing industry has already achieved this target while 32 per cent of the overall work-force is now below a 40 hour week. Government support for the moves is strong. In February 1984, the Dutch Cabinet announced that it might propose legal measures to bring down working time in 1985-6, although hoping that this could be achieved earlier by negotiation.

It argued that a planned reduction of 10 per cent in hours by 1986 was essential to cut unemployment. The engineering industry had made a tentative start during 1984 by agreeing 26 extra half-days "free time" from 1985, although the agreement provides for workers to forgo part of their price-indexed wage increases to pay for the deal. The Philips company introduced 26 additional half-days leave from 1st January 1985.

The French government has initiated a number of measures. In 1982, it decreed that men should have the right to retire on full state pension at age 60; a full pension is 50 per cent of pay based on the ten best years of earnings. It decreed a 39 hour week affecting 15 million workers in the private sector, a move seen as a first step towards the 35 hour week. Those on shift work should achieve the 35 hour week by 1985. Compensation for the loss of hourly earnings are subject to industry-level negotiations, though many of the agreements signed do in fact provided full compensation, and the statutory minimum wage was fully protected by law. At the same time, a fifth week's holiday was introduced — again by law — for all employees. In 1983, the French Cabinet took further steps to cut working time in order to increase employment. It extended financial incentives to employers to recruit staff for 30 hour week jobs, and extended parental leave to fathers as well as to mothers. It is encouraging phased early retirement in particularly arduous jobs, a measure to be accompanied by the recruitment of the young unemployed.

The Swedish LO has demanded the 38 hour week in 1985 for double-day shift workers, and an additional three days leave for all workers. The Danish movement — including revulsion against pay levels as well as the claim for 35 hours — generated a general strike wave in March and April of 1985, which produced the largest industrial action since the war, mass demonstrations on an unprecedented scale, and the nearest thing to civil disorder which the peaceable post-war Danish society has ever witnessed. 300,000 workers were on strike or locked-out, and were met with uncharacteristically visible hostility from government, employers, and police. Private manufacturing was chiefly affected, but food, petrol and oil distribution were also halted, as well as public transport. The dispute reached the proportions of a General Strike at the end of March with its extension into the public sector. There it was led unofficially by left-wing shop stewards who expressed the widespread social opposition to the Government's monetarist policies. Thousands stayed on strike for several days after its statutory termination by Government decree in early April.

The Danish system of centralised collective bargaining is normally a ritual bi-annual affair, practised continuously since 1899. After agreement between unions and employers, the settlement becomes legally enforceable. When major conflicts arise in this process, the Government steps in with a compulsory solution. The last previous occassion for such intervention was in 1973. The unusual feature of the 1985 dispute was that the average worker would have been better off with the employers' final offer than with the unions' demands, at least in terms of take-home pay. For the unions demanded a cut in the working week without seeking full hourly wage compensation. Their demand was for a 35-hour week, (a reduction of five hours), though they were eventually prepared to settle for an immediate fall of 2 hours. This was to be coupled with a substantial pay increase for the low-paid, but no increases for the higher paid. The unions' whole case was grounded on the need to generate employment through reduction of working time. The employers' final offer was for a cut of only half-an-hour per week, and the government ended the crisis with a statutory award of a one-hour reduction by the end of 1986, combined with a two per cent wage increase. The law was used to force the strikers back to work.

The European Trade Union Institute (ETUI) has attempted to distil general lessons from all these experiences[7]. It finds that throughout Western Europe, the unions' goal is the 35-hour week, although some have demanded restrictions on over-time, longer holidays, or other forms of reduction in annual hours. Progress is piece-meal, but the ETUI claims that the over-all effect upon employment is favourable. New jobs have been created, existing jobs under threat have been preserved, and more part-time jobs and training places have been brought into being.

European governments have shown varying degrees of appreciation of the connection between hours-reduction and employment creation. Most have been markedly interventionist in the process, in sharp contrast to the British government's determined laissez-faire attitude. Of course, whilst the Danish government's hostile response shows the closest affinity with Mrs. Thatcher's approach, all the administrations share, by conviction or compulsion, a common ambivalence deriving from the dominant monetarist emphasis on "supply-side" solutions to the labour-market "problem". There is a discernable general trend towards the "de-regulation" of the labour market, which matches the British government's relaxation of laws and state practice in the fields of health and safety, employee protections, welfare provision, and other statutory provisions, as well as the tendency towards forcing workers to pay for hours-reduction with reduced hourly earnings, or with pay freezes, statutory incomes policies, and the like. As in Britain, trade union membership figures are falling generally, and substained industrial action leading to unambiguous victories are commonly difficult in these circumstances.

The conclusion must be a re-inforcement of the general theme which we have emphasised through this book; without international co-ordination of national policies and campaigns elevated to a *political* level, the drive for full employment in Europe and the reduction in working-time will founder on the rocks of national isolation, governmental resistance, and the superior power of employers, deriving from the integration of multinational capital.

During the Referendum on British membership of the EEC, and then again in the first elections for the European Assembly, according to those who favoured Britain's adherence to the Common Market, a cornucopia of benefits was expected to open. Perhaps the most prominent among these was the benefit of increased holiday time. It was pointed out that the Europeans enjoyed far better holiday entitlements than British workers: that they had longer annual vacations and more of them; that their statutory holidays outnumbered ours, sometimes by two or three times. The same TUC resolution of 1981 which sought a statutory 35-hour week also addressed the problem of holiday starvation which afflicts workers in British industry. But when we look at the problem with care, it seems very clear that legislation on weekly hours to be worked. Basic annual holiday entitlement in France and the Netherlands run at five weeks, and in many enterprises in Italy this is also true. Ninety per cent of workers in West Germany have obtained six weeks' or more annual holiday.

The TUC's official objective of six weeks holiday is in fact a modest one, although it would represent a substantial improvement in the conditions of most workers. It would be relatively simple to legislate a statutory holiday entitlement of six weeks. It would even be feasible to legislate to enlarge the size of the labour force in every firm by an amount commensurate with the increase in holiday entitlement. To invent an example which embodies the principle simply: if we were to legislate to give every person an additional month's holiday, it might well be possible simultaneously to require every employer to expand his or her labour force by 10 per cent. This would at once create some two million jobs, even allowing for the fact that some smaller employers would slip between the mesh of a net which would have to be loosely strung. Any such large redeployment of formerly unemployed people would liberate vast sums of dole money which could be used to ease the burdens of those employers who fell into resultant difficulties. Of course, some people will argue that a month's additional holiday is a dramatically over-generous improvement in conditions. In that case, we could opt for a fortnight's additional improvement, and a five per cent increase in the size of labour forces. Indeed, we could create a sliding scale, upwards or downwards, aimed at directly facilitating work-sharing without loss of pay.

Footnotes

1. Cf Allen Hutt: 'The Hours of Labour', in *Marxist Quarterly,* II, 1, January 1955, pp2-13.
2. Reprinted in *Archives in Trade Union History,* published by the Institute for Workers' Control, 1968.
3. Sidney Webb and Harold Cox: *The Eight Hours' Day,* Walter Scott.
4. TUC *Report,* 1981.
5. International Metalworkers' Federation: *The 1984 Collective Bargaining Dispute.* (Mines, 1985).
6. Data in this survey are derived from Incomes Data Services *International Reports,* 1982-5.
7. The ETUI has issued two relevant reports: *Practical Experiences with the Reduction of Working-time in Western Europe,* and *Collective Bargaining in Western Europe, 1983, and Prospects for 1984.*

Part III
Planning for Recovery

Introductory

Ken Coates

National economic planning has been afflicted by many ills. We have been arguing that most of these have been caused by the growth of private multinational power. Certainly, the kinds of indicative plans which grew up during the later periods of the Keynesian world settlement are no longer seriously canvassed. The word "plan" itself has become, for many, a four-letter word. "Hope" is also a four-letter word, but so, we would remind those in authority, is "dole".

The fact that so daunting a proportion of world exchanges are now internal transfers within the major transnational corporations, has meant that big industry can ignore national economic policies when they bid to become a nuisance. Years of transfer pricing have piled up profits in the most accommodating centres, with favourable tax policies and weak trade unions. They have also pushed governments into insane competition with one another, raising interest rates and inflation to economically suffocating levels. What scope remains for national economic controls? Of course, this is bound to be, partly, a matter of suck it and see. The contributors to this section of our debate are well aware of this. John Hughes has unrivalled experience in the field of price controls, and he is the first to admit to a degree of uncertainty about how this process will be affected by the increasing concentration of transnational forces.

Evidently recovery and co-operation between states are becoming virtually inseparable concepts. But what are the mechanisms of recovery? Ken Livingstone opens one perspective on this question. The programme, Joint Action for Jobs, offers a varient approach. Stuart Holland, in conclusion, seeks to generalize in a way which can enable us to think through policies for convergent co-operation, and to determine their relationships to national sovereignty.

Chapter 10

Planning on a European Scale?

Ken Livingstone

The fortunes of the London economy have always been closely bound up with its position in the international division of labour. In the late 19th century London's position as the centre of the world's dominant economic empire determined the nature and growth of much of its industry. In the 1930s, by contrast, London's industrial development depended on import substitution and the national market. In the 1980s, the London economy has again switched direction. Since trade liberalisation in the late 1950s, and particularly after British entry into the EEC in 1973, London has been drawn increasingly into the European division of labour. We can speak of the 'Europeanisation' of the London economy.

The change is clearest in the service and communications industries. In finance, London became the centre of the Eurodollar market from the mid-1960s, and the site for 485 foreign banks and security houses employing 38,000 people in 1983. In business services, there has been a steady growth of multinational accounting and consultancy firms, top advertising agencies, and major engineering and design companies. In all these cases, the new multinational service activities are not confined to Europe. But from Euro-banking to advertising, Europe and the areas of traditional European influence (Africa, the Middle East and parts of Asia) have been the principal focus of the London offices.

One reflection of this is in the growth of air transport. While the North American routes have been declining in volume (London's passenger traffic with New York declined by 39 per cent between 1979-80 and 1982-83) European routes have been growing (passengers between London and Amsterdam grew by 8 per cent over the same three years, between London and Paris by 11 per cent; while Brussels, Frankfurt, Zurich and Geneva have all moved into London's top 10 table in terms of passengers handled through London's airports). Heathrow is Europe's largest airport, and Gatwick the fourth largest. From a total of 6,500,000 passengers passing through London area airports in 1960, the total had risen to 40,000,000 by 1980. London has become a European junction for passengers with a rapid growth in hotels to accommodate them. In 1982 people on business spent approximately 22,000,000 nights in London and £550,000,000, a significant proportion of them linked to London's European connections.

Similarly with goods, London and the surrounding area has been developing as a marshalling yard for European distribution systems entering and leaving Britain. The new automatic warehouses which have grown so rapidly in London over the last decade commonly service the whole region or even the country as part of a European network. The IBM warehouse in West London is one example. Lucas CAV's warehousing in London and Gillingham is another.

IBM is an example of another clear trend since the mid-1970s, which is the Europeanisation of production within multinational companies. IBM was one of the first to develop a productive specialisation on a European scale, with each national factory specialising in one part of the computer for the European market. Other firms have now followed suit: Ford, General Motors, Kodak, ICI, Honeywell, ITT. Many of London's multinational manufacturing plants have been reorganised, and some closed down, as part of the development of centrally planned, integrated European factory systems. In each of these firms, the European headquarters is now the central focus of direct co-ordination, just as the national headquarters once was.

There are three key results of this 'Europeanising' of London's economy. First, London now finds itself competing not just with other parts of Britain but with other parts of Europe as a site for these functions. In telecommunications for example there has been an acute competitive battle over international traffic. For the time being British Telecom (and this means London) has been winning, by virtue of cutting international charges and funding deficits from domestic charges. Britain has the lowest international charges and the highest domestic charges of any European country. This has evoked protests from other European countries, most recently from Italy who have protested to the European Court about British telex charges. In finance there is similar competition. A good telecommunications network together with the right time bands, and an established financial tradition, have been crucial for London holding its own as part of an international financial system in which Britain is no longer the dominant force.

As far as offices go, Britain has one of the lowest clerical labour costs of major European centres, and this has served to increase land prices and rents that international firms are willing to pay to be in London. Yet London has its disadvantages. It is separated from the Continent by sea. It is not at the centre of European political and administrative affairs. It has only 14 per cent of multinational regional head offices in Europe (other than British), and these are largely North American. Also London has so far been allocated no EEC institutions. The crucial point is, however, that over the last 15-20 years London has been drawn into a European property market, with prime office land prices being set in relation to European levels rather than British ones. This has been one factor in the blight of manufacturing, for property prices have been a principal reason for manufacturing leaving London.

Secondly, Europeanisation has led to a switch in the geographical balance of the London economy. When London was the centre of the Empire, the main focus in London was the docks, the City, Westminster and the railway terminals. Now, though the City and Westminster remain, it is to Heathrow that the balance has shifted. As the largest airport in Europe, Heathrow has given London and the South-East an important advantage in the new European knowledge economy. The development of the M4 corridor has been based on the interlink between road and air, and has extended not only westwards from Heathrow, but back into London as well. It is Heathrow which has forced up land prices in West London for offices and hotels.

Meanwhile the core of East London's traditional economy — the docks — has collapsed. With London's deep-sea trade being moved down to Tilbury, and the Port of London Authority (PLA) forfeiting the new short haul European trade to the expanding non-scheme ports of the South-East — Felixstowe, Harwich, Dover, Shoreham — not only did 20,000 East London dock jobs go between 1967 and 1981, but a further 80,000 jobs in dock-related industries, and in services geared to the locality. The result has been rates of unemployment matching other depressed areas, and acre upon acre of waste land and empty property.

Thirdly, multinational firms have been increasingly able to play off London's workers and its local and national government against their counterparts on the Continent and beyond. Many manufacturing companies now operate systems of dual sourcing, with two plants in different countries producing the same product for the European market. No only is this a safeguard against industrial action but it allows companies like Ford to expand and contract production as part of playing off one workforce against another. As far as playing off one government against another is concerned, the most serious area is taxation and grants for new investment. But it also applies to whole systems of public regulation. Take finance for example. In the words of the *Banker:* "The internationalisation of key financial markets is a major constraint on the Bank of England's role in supervising the regulation of the London Stock Exchange. If restrictions are too tight, large sections of the market will simply disappear elsewhere — something that has already happened to the business in South African gold shares" (November 1983).

The overall picture has become increasingly clear. On the one hand London has been drawn into the European market economy. The main core of the Treaty of Rome and the bulk of the work of the Commission over 25 years has been to ensure the conditions for the perfecting of that market: cutting tariffs, encouraging standardisation, harmonising laws and forms of taxation, improving European communications, and the circulation of information (on public contracts for example), eroding restrictions on competition within industries, and between countries, in finance as in industry. In some areas London has benefited. But in others, this new European market economy has been disastrous, particularly in manufacturing. The rise in property prices has blighted factory after factory. British multinationals have tended to move investment to the continent at the expense of London and the UK. Between 1977 and 1981 British firms invested £2.3bn in the EEC, which was more than twice the £1bn invested by other EEC countries in the UK. Furthermore, European competition has reduced many of London's traditional industries, of which furniture is perhaps the most striking example. An industry which once employed 60,000 Londoners now employs 6,000. Over the last ten years imports (mainly from the Continent) have risen from 7 per cent to 27 per cent of the UK market. EEC entry is not the main cause of London's de-industrialisation. But British entry has substantially helped to deepen London's industrial crisis, a crisis that has seen London lose more than 500,000 jobs since 1973.

Some have suggested that London's manufacturing industries should be written off, and that the EEC will provide the opportunities for new growth. But there is no mechanism in the market economy to ensure that new jobs are created in their place and for those workers where the old jobs have been destroyed. A recent European Commission document on south-east England (March 1984) could provide only a thin catalogue of advantages for London enterprises who had benefited from the EEC. They quoted a London Chamber of Commerce and Industry (LCCI) survey which showed that a third of larger companies and less than a quarter of the smaller ones had increased their exports to the EEC. They cited the expansion of banking, and US direct investment (mostly outside London), tourism and business travel. That the EEC has stimulated the growth of some sectors is not in doubt. It accords with my argument about the Europeanisation of the London economy. The main question is of the overall balance. In this context the evidence is unambiguous. The new service industries within a European context are failing to provide alternative jobs for those from manufacturing industries whose relocation has been hastened by the European market economy.

Nor has the Community budget served to balance London's industrial disadvantage. It was also forseen that Britain would pay more into the Community budget than it received back. This was the price to be paid for British industry's access to the EEC market. Thus in 1980 the UK was to contribute 20 per cent of the community budget, and receive only 10 per cent back. In the event much of Britain's national industrial capital has lost out in competition with other EEC countries, while Britain's multinationals have on balance tended to move to the continent. The EEC may have strengthened them (as it has strengthened British banking capital) but left the British private economy weak. The outcome is that the UK has had the worse of both worlds: losing out in the market economy, and on the Community budget. For London the imbalance is even worse. Not only were its industrial losses among the worst in the country (with manufacturing jobs being cut by a third in the decade after EEC entry) but London has contributed far more to the community budget than it has had in return. London pays a greater proportion of VAT and hence of tax contributions to the EEC than its share in the UK economy (nearly £400,000,000). Conversely, London receives almost nothing from the Common Agricultural Policy (CAP) budget (62 per cent of the total EEC budget), and little from the rest. Excluding any community funding of the transport programme, we can find evidence of only some £6,000,000 in EEC grants to London projects.

Clearly it would help for EEC regional policy to take account of the fact that the depressed regions of the 1980s are the cores of metropolitan areas and not just the traditional depressed regions. Since entry, the UK has received grants and loans totalling £5.4bn from the European Regional Development Fund, the European Social Fund, and the European Investment Bank (EIB). The great bulk of this has gone to assisted areas. A proportion — I would suggest £400,000,000 a year from the Community budget, and a matching sum from the EIB — should certainly be directed to London, and would go some way to offset the current Government's cuts of public funds to London (£4.2bn since 1979).

But the danger of confining ourselves to discussions of the budget is that it sets Hackney against Toxteth, and London against Calabria. Increased funds for London should not be at the expense of areas with similar problems, but at the expense of large agricapital (including British agribusiness) who have been the main beneficiaries of the CAP.

Part of these funds are needed to reconstruct London's declining infrastructure. But even more important is London's industrial economy. This should be our starting point and the budget discussions should be related to that. What London needs is public intervention to counter the inequalities of the market, to restructure its industries and expand useful jobs. Yet it is here that the EEC has notably failed. Apart from the continent's old industries — agriculture, coal, steel and textiles — the European project has failed to establish institutions of effective industrial intervention. Both the regional and social funds, and the European Investment Bank are primarily transfers of cash rather than financial support for a planned programme of productive restructuring. D'Avignon's initiatives in the field of advanced electronics and informatics is an exception, but runs consistently into the barriers of national non-planning. The national vetoes are a built-in mechanism against concerted interventionary policies, while letting the market rule. Worse, the development of integrated multinational capital in Europe has blunted the effectiveness of national state policies (particularly in the field of macro-economic management) and led to the dismantling of regulations and to the cutting of taxes. The EEC has reduced the capacity of nation states to plan and intervene in their own economies, without providing an alternative capacity at the European level. A strengthening of the market, and an economic weakening of the state: that is the balance sheet of 25 years of the EEC which has had such serious consequences for London.

There has been a similar pattern in the field of labour. The freeing of trade and the Europeanisation of capital was always seen by the right in Europe as a way of weakening labour — organised as it still is on a predominantly national and local basis. The EEC has intervened to liberalise the Community's labour markets, and free them from what it regards as outdated prejudices — and some of these interventions have been progressive. This was particularly the case with the 1975 and 1976 directives on equal pay and equal opportunities for women, and the directive of 1978 on equal treatment for women in social security. There have also been important directives on health and safety provisions. Beyond this, attempts to cut the working week and to protect and improve labour conditions (and not just liberalise the labour market) for temporary and part-time workers have run into the national veto, used in particular by Britain. With labour as with capital, the Treaty of Rome has strengthened and widened the market, but limited the capacity for equivalent public intervention.

There is growing evidence that this position cannot last. The main cause is the world slump, which has led to a sustained restructuring of industry on a world basis. The lead is being taken by the USA and Japan, both national economies using strong state intervention and international mercantilism to support their strategies. In Europe (with one or two notable exceptions such as the Airbus) the Treaty of Rome does not provide a structure for such co-ordinated initiatives. The Commission in a number of sectoral reports is clearly aware of the problems. In information technology for example, of every 10 personal computers sold in Europe, eight were made in the US. Of every 10 video recorders, nine were made in Japan. European producers of integrated circuits supply only 30 per cent of the Community market and 13 per cent of the world market. In mainframe computers, as in motor components, and many other sectors the picture for the European economy is similarly dismal. But the whole structure of the EEC is such that it is extremely difficult to do anything substantial about it.

It is equally clear that each national economy in Europe is still tied to the US fashioned Bretton Woods international financial regime, that independent macro economic management has been reduced in scope without the mechanisms for European macro management, and that Europe is as a result overcast by the shadow of the American economy just as it is overcast militarily by the shadow of the American arsenal.

In the face of this, a distinct split is emerging within the EEC. On the one hand there are those who are pressing for a further liberalisation in world trade as a response to the world slump. On the other, there are supporters of a Fortress Europe strategy, supported principally by the second rank, less worldwide companies, in sectors such as steel, motor vehicles, chemicals and synthetic textiles. They argue for greater European protection, an uncoupling of the European monetary system from Bretton Woods, and a crash programme of technological development and restructuring, of which the Esprit fund is a first step. They see a 10-year breathing space, within which Europe's economic future will be decided.

The economic differences are paralleled by political ones. The Paris Club — which was set up to resist the Fortress Europe movement — not only favours further world economic liberalisation, but the continuation of the Atlantic alliance politically and militarily. Against this there is emerging a distinct view on Europe's global role, with respect to Eastern Europe, the Third World, in favour of detente in the Middle East, and a military strategy independent of that of the United States.

The UK stands in the middle of the argument: Atlanticist and monetarist on the one hand, but decimated economically and increasingly integrated with the European economy on the other. It is against this background that the Greater London Council (GLC) needs to assess its policy towards the EEC in order to counter the effects that the Community has had on the London economy.

New Policies for Europe

Firstly, there is a need for a much stronger public interventionary body in the EEC — a European Enterprise Board (EEB). It should have seven major characteristics:

i. A large *strategic staff* responsible for drawing up sectoral strategies;
ii. A central role for the *trade unions and user groups* to ensure that these strategies are developed in the interests of working people and not at their expense;
iii. An *enterprise staff* made up of experienced people, drawn from industry, finance, the trade unions, and consultancies, sympathetic with the aims of the Board, and with a capacity to restructure industries directly;
iv. A large *investment fund* to be used according to long-term social criteria not short-term financial returns;
v. A capacity to invest directly and run *European public companies* as and when necessary;
vi. A *technological section* linked into European research institutions; and
vii. A close *direct working relation* with national and local enterprise boards and planning bodies. The EEB should be seen as building on and supporting local and national economic intervention (through expanded public enterprise and public control of finance) not replacing it. The control of the EEB should reflect these links and those with the trade unions and the wider community.

The European Investment Bank, the Esprit funds and the existing programme of industrial restructuring should be reorganised into the new board.

Secondly, there is an urgent need for new ways of controlling multinational companies. In Brussels, the Vredeling directive —

itself a very modest set of proposals relating to worker access to information about multinational companies' strategic decisions — was strongly opposed by the multinational lobby and vetoed by the UK. A much more stringent regime than Vredeling is required; preventing the tax/grant competitions between member states and localities, opening the multinationals' books, using public purchasing, tariffs, taxation and investment controls to bargain with the multinational companies on their investment and production plans.

Thirdly, there should be a much closer integration of European public economies, so that each public economy could increase its links with other public economies, rather than relate fragmentally to internationally integrated private suppliers.

Fourthly, there is need to radically alter the CAP. Its original conception was in part progressive. It involved planned public intervention into the agricultural sector, and addressed real social needs. But its system of support payments has led to massive over-production, a bonanza for large agribusiness, and worst of all, subsidised exports which have undercut Third World agricultural production. There should be an immediate move to a deficiency payment system which would subsidise small marginal farmers without having to pay premia. It would cut over-production and the Community's agricultural budget substantially. The funds so released should be transferred to industrial intervention and support for progressive Third World countries.

Fifthly, much greater urgency must be given to introducing best practice in welfare provisions, trade union rights, the contractual conditions for labour, and redundancy and social benefit rights. Equally important are measures to take forward equal rights for women and 'guest workers'.

These policies are by and large incompatible with the current institutions of the EEC. The Treaty of Rome has at its very core a built-in force to extend the market and limit public intervention. The above policies could therefore only come about as the result of a major political shift within the Community, and a revision of the Treaty of Rome. The first Treaty resulted from the Messina conference in 1957. There is now a need for a new Messina conference, prepared to exclude those states who refuse to restructure the Community.

In the meantime the GLC should work towards these more general goals in whatever way it can:

We should continue to press London's case for receiving finance (of at least £400,000,000 annually) from the major EEC funds; Regional, Social, Esprit, Energy, Transport and the European Investment Bank. These funds should be used to finance the interventionist strategy developed by the Council to restructure London's infrastructure and industry. They should not be subject to Government agreement, or serve to allow the Government to make further cuts in London's public services. As one of the EEC capital cities without a Community institution, we should continue to campaign for the proposed European Trade Mark office, promising 200 jobs, to be sited in East London.

We should work together with other local authorities and sympathetic national governments, as well as the European Commission and Parliament, to support trade union intiatives to prevent multinationals playing off groups of workers and governments against each other, and cutting investment in the industrial heartlands of Europe. The Council is already engaged in action of this kind: it needs to be extended.

The Council should investigate co-operative trade with other public bodies in Europe, particularly as a means of strengthening industrial interventions undertaken by the Greater London Enterprise Board (GLEB) and parallel institutions on the Continent.

The Council should support the campaign for co-ordinated reflation of the EEC national economies against those governments following monetarist restrictiveness. It would be mistaken to see this as the principal answer to European recovery. The deep structural problems in European production reflected in the long term decline of profitability mean that reflation aimed only at the level of demand can soon run into problems of inflation. Nevertheless, a major programme of public investment in industry and infrastructure would expand demand in parallel with transforming supply.

The GLC should continue to support campaigns to alter the CAP with a view to maintaining Third World production rather than subsidising over-production by European agribusiness. From London's viewpoint the two most serious cases are the threat to the Tate and Lyle Silvertown refinery as the result of the EEC Sugar Agreement, and the threat to London's door-to-door milk delivery as the result of the Commission's ruling on long-life continental milk.

The GLC should support the campaigns for the adoption of the Commission's draft directives on part-time work, temporary work, occupational social security and parental leave, as well as the proposals widely supported in the European Parliament, for the 35-hour week, improved training for women, and equal taxation rights. The concerns of the EEC for equality of opportunity for women closely parallel those of the Council. The effects of the Commission's directives on equal pay and sex discrimination in extending the rights of women in Britain shows that there is some scope even within the current institutions for progressive labour policies.

In the gathering crisis of the EEC, progressive local authorities have a particularly important part to play in showing the directions which a new Treaty of Rome should follow in the field of public economic intervention. Local authorities have also been important supporters of the principle of a European nuclear-free zone, and have put this principle into practice as far as they can within their own localities. They have, too, been strong defenders of the principle of local democracy. The Council is a member of the Standing Conference of Local and Regional Authorities within the Council of Europe which has just produced a draft European charter of local self-government, which assumes immediate importance in the face of the British Government's authoritarian attack on local self-government and the GLC in particular.

Jobs, peace and local democracy — these three things unite many local authorities within the EEC. They face a common crisis, common problems, and in too many places a common monetarism. It is not surprising then to find close parallels in the policies we have been developing in the Labour cities and metropolitan counties in this country and those pursued in progressive continental localities: North Rhine Westphalia, Dortmund, Essen, Emiglia-Romana and so on. Contact between such authorities has been sporadic, and part of wider meetings of local authorities with conflicting directions and policies. National governments have reached a stalemate in carrying forward serious proposals to intervene economically and socially to counter the effects of the increasingly unrestrained European market. Progressive members of European parties have been trying to break this stalemate. So have trade unions, both through their national and European organisations, and through growing European action by trade unionists in multinational companies. Many local authorities, like London, have an urgent interest in contributing to this gathering pressure to radically revise the Treaty of Rome.

Chapter 11

The Dole Economy: Can we Plan our Way Out?

John Hughes

The main European economies have — notably in the 1980s — lurched massively away from any resemblance to earlier patterns of post-war 'full employment' and 'welfarism', defective as these may have been in practice. Latter-day capitalism is exhibiting new forms of instability, inequality, and industrial and financial crisis as the norms of its socially uncontrolled development path. This paper in particular probes the UK's situation, not to turn away from the problems of other European 'mixed economies', but rather with the sense that the UK stands as an extreme example of the socially devastating trends that are apparent. In doing so, the dangerously exposed position of workers' organisations and interests in the UK and across Europe, if uncontrolled capitalist development is not challenged, needs to be highlighted.

This paper does not assume that the structural crisis of the UK is primarily to be identified with the Thatcher Government, though Thatcherism as a phenomenon emerged exploiting politically the tensions in industrial development, public finance, employment, pay and taxation that were intensifying through the 1970s. After all, the 'peak' of manufacturing output in 1979 when Thatcher took office was already 5 per cent *below* the earlier peak in 1973 — the secular growth trend which had buoyed up the national economy since the 1930s had been replaced by decline. Nor is the development crisis of manufacturing in the UK — and Europe — simply to be traced back to the oil price shocks from 1973 onwards; though profound imbalances and surplus industrial capacity have for more than a decade arisen directly from that. In Britain, certainly, stagnation or decline of major industries (steel, shipbuilding, coal) was evident much earlier, the devaluation/inflation treadmill continued under successive Labour and Conservative governments, the curbing of public expenditure and deliberate demand deflation with the creation of higher unemployment was notably pursued by a Labour Chancellor in the late 1960s, there was greatly increased tension over pay determination, and growing regional imbalance. Thatcherism has more recently presided over the unresolved structural crisis, worsened it by grotesque mismanagement (e.g. the disastrous interest rate and exchange rate policies of its first two years), and consciously intensified the rapidly growing *inequalities* that in any case disfigure 'freer' capitalism. But we have to do more than criticise such policies as the Thatcher Government has; we need to analyse (if we can) the changed landscape of the 'mixed economy' that a future Labour Government might inherit.

Firstly, we need not just to *contrast* the massive growth in structural unemployment with the (particularly in Britain) equally massive rise in the profitability of industrial and commercial companies; we need to *connect* the two. On the most useful measure of profitability, the gross trading profits of industrial and commercial companies net of stock appreciation, the profits generated in the UK *doubled* between 1980 and 1984 (rising from £26 to £52bn. In 'real' terms this meant a profits increase of around 50 per cent. Over the same period the total wage and salary bill in the UK rose by only one-third, and in real terms it *fell* slightly. Actually over the 1980 to 1984 period the *number* of UK employees in employment *fell* by 8 per cent (by 1.8 million), while the real wages of those *in work* rose by roughly the same amount. Employers removed workers *en masse*, especially from manufacturing jobs, from their wages bills and pushed the cost of their maintenance on to public finance — while demanding through the CBI cuts in public expenditure.* A very considerable part of the profits recovery came from closing higher cost, labour intensive, units, and forcing through re-manning more widely. Little of it has been based on renewing the capital stock; in manufacturing, the official National Income accounts show net investment (i.e. fixed capital formation after allowing for the using up of existing capital equipment) as heavily *negative* from 1981 onwards (a deficit in net investment of over £5bn between 1981 and 1983). The capital was being run down and, overall, not replaced. The much vaunted profits recovery has therefore been heavily based on cuts in today's

*The 1983 *Family Expenditure Survey*, recently published, shows for the first time the *comparative* income position of the employed and the unemployed household. The average household with an 'unoccupied' head had less than 40 per cent of the income of the average 'employed' household. Wage and salary income in the 'unoccupied' household was (in 1983) *£189 a week lower* than in the 'employed'; benefit income was only £50 a week higher. It should be mentioned that the average 'unoccupied' household was larger, and had more children in it, than the 'employed'.

employment, but it has not led to investment *in the UK* to provide for tomorrow's employment; on the contrary.

Secondly, we should recognise the obvious characteristics of the capitalist firms that are surviving and growing. With the openness of capitalist markets and the substantially unrestrained movements of capital internationally, the modern cosmopolitan capitalist enterprise is a conglomerate managing a diversified portfolio of assets. The distinction between 'industrial' and 'financial' companies is increasingly blurred; many large companies (which means large multinationals) have piled up large cash surpluses and are pulled towards the aggressive use of such resources in financial transactions rather than in conventional 'accumulation' of productive assets. Increasingly, under mature capitalism the emphasis turns on the management of existing assets and portfolios of financial assets in pursuit of high real rates of return. All this links to the ever more frenzied use of capital markets to pursue mergers and take-overs, with the large-scale predator firms seeking companies temporarily undervalued by the market or which add in a strategic way to their existing product base (quicker access to new products, additional expertise and technology, etc).

The dominant enterprises — whether financial, industrial/commercial, or hybrids — are therefore caught up in strategic concerns that are cosmopolitan not national in their scope, and are heavily concerned with a power struggle to acquire existing assets rather than concentrated on new capital formation. (Indeed, new investment may be deterred since scarce management resources may be directed to re-grouping in the wake of extensive take-overs; cash and borrowing resources may be built up to engage in the merger power struggles, and consequently there may be less readiness to extend risky new physical investment). Neither the UK, nor physical investment in the UK, may appear in any long-term sense as central to such business strategies. Regional dislocation and imbalance, whole armies of structurally unemployed workers, are not elements of concern; the link with the health and balance of particular national economies is receding. In such companies' accounts (e.g. Unilever) the UK has all but disappeared, and become merely a constituent within an aggregated total recording turnover and profit continent by continent.

It is these conglomerate enterprises much more than the trade unions that are the power bargainers. This applies not only to the extraordinary pursuit of take-overs (or resistance to predatory attack) but to the countervailing pressures of powerful buyers and larger scale producers/sellers. It applies to bargaining with a whole succession of nation states over development finance, large contracts, environmental controls, industrial relations systems, and so on. It applies to the negotiations between financial institutions and other commercial enterprises. Power bargaining with the trade unions appears as merely one aspect of this 'managed' response by the enterprise to both competitive markets and relevant sources of power that they have come to terms with.

Thirdly, we should appraise carefully the weakened role of the state sector within the UK, and the loss of national autonomy in handling economic relations with other states. The European national economies in particular have become much more interdependent. This may be viewed as a constraint, if we are to worship the undiluted sovereignty of the nation state; it may be seen as an opportunity, if a wider alliance of socialist forces is to be pursued. Certainly, it seems unlikely that a narrowly chauvinist version of state socialism can be expected to match the dynamism of multi-national capitalist organisations.

What is more to the point is to recognise that current government policies in the UK are through successive waves of privatisation removing some of the 'commanding heights' from the public sector and from direct public control. Not only is there a constraint arising from the removal of most of the powerful revenue-generating public industries and services (some of them, such as telecoms and gas, retaining a high degree of monopoly power); there is a constraint on the planning of UK-based development strategies involving new technologies and products. Before we despair, we should perhaps reflect what inadequate use was made by earlier Labour governments of the vast, ramified, range of state industries they did command. But for the future, an alternative government may have to learn to give more emphasis to the role of the basic public services and local government in its development policies, and an emphasis much wider than the manufacturing sector in its deployment of inducements and controls to renew the growth of the economy.

The constraints on public finance are also significant, though not an overwhelming barrier to progressive initiatives in the future. During the period of the Thatcher regime the tax base has been eroded particularly by the fall of two million in the number of full-time employees in work. The dependent population requiring benefits to provide their income has grown massively, particularly through unemployment; a harsh regime of means testing and inadequate benefits has nevertheless seen total benefit expenditure rise by a quarter in real terms. An increase in the rate of many state benefits (e.g. for the long-term unemployed) would be an unavoidable priority for an alternative government. Besides, oil revenues — which so far under the period of Thatcher government have increased by over £10bn p.a. — are already falling in real terms and will fall steadily through the rest of the decade (estimate, from £12bn in 1985 to only £5bn in 1990, at constant 1985 prices). This removes over 4 per cent of current levels of total government revenue by 1990. Moreover, it can hardly have escaped anyone's attention that virtually *en masse* the millions of workers in the labour intensive public services have been and still are subject to a discriminatory policy of pay restraint, and that an alternative government would be confronted by the pressures of their demands.

This simply underlines the importance of setting out to win substantial public support for the priorities of an alternative policy challenging unemployment and inequality, and recognising the social discipline and responsibility (including tax and income policies) that go with this. For example, the Thatcher government that has so steadily preached the notion of the burden of public expenditure has, on its own published estimates of 'real' expenditure,* held down education spending to its 1978-79 level while *raising* defence programme spending by 29 per cent in six years, and 'law and order' spending by 38 per cent. There has to be the political will to *change* such priorities. Again, the welfare state of the *rich,* the elaborate and financially vast structure of allowances against tax (offered unconditionally without means testing!), has grown in scale under Thatcherism until the inequity involved is obscene. Take for instance the contrast between the £3.5bn withheld from tax revenues by mortgage interest relief, compared with the harsh means testing and high 'taper' of benefit reduction, as incomes rise, of housing benefit. Take the massive tax privileges of superannuation funds compared with Thatcher government proposals to renege on the modest state earnings related pension (SERPS) which does not benefit from such tax reliefs. (But note too the well rehearsed chorus of establishment *and* trade union opposition when the government recently floated the possibility of taxing occupational pension funds in some way). There *are* opportunities for major initiatives in public expenditure and taxation in a post-Thatcher world — but they have to be fought for politically.

The constraints on public finance extend also to borrowing. This is not to say that we know what the effective limits are exactly, nor to deny that there may be merit in redefining existing concepts

*Technically, current spending deflated by the general rise in costs (the GDP deflator).

(such as the PSBR, Public Sector Borrowing Requirement), in a principled way. But one grave problem we face, both in managing public finance and in seeking to stimulate new risk taking investment or construction activity, is that the *real* interest rate is uncomfortably high. (As one measure of it, the real rate of return on risk free government indexed stocks of shorter date is well over 4 per cent). In the main this was not true in earlier periods with Labour in office. Given the limits of this paper there is no opportunity to discuss at length why interest rates are so high (the phenomenon is international, though UK rates have been somewhat arbitrarily increased by recent government policies in the damaging pursuit — damaging to industrial growth and employment — of a 'strong' exchange rate). Nor is there scope to explain how considerably a general international regime of high real interest rates curbs a great range of physical investment spending. It should be noted, however, that the 'freeing' of finance capital's international movement (by total removal of exchange controls) makes it difficult to establish in the UK a *lower* real interest rate than elsewhere. Whether or not a general return to controls on capital movement by major savings institutions is possible, it does make sense to suggest that tax privilege (e.g. to the pension and insurance funds mentioned earlier) should not extend to any diversion of internal savings flows (encouraged by tax privilege!) to overseas investment on a scale, or in ways, not desired by a government in the UK that is to give priority to UK productive development. Some scope for increased public borrowing *without* an upward pressure on interest rates emerges from considerations such as these. Some might also emerge from a successful pursuit of a modest inflation rate in the UK, and a more stable and somewhat lower exchange rate; but that combination has eluded successive governments.

Recognising such contraints on the role of the state is no cause for despair. The opportunities for initiative, for bargaining about resource priorities, are tangible. Carrying more of the people, and particularly organised labour, with such initiatives will be a matter not only of the scale of resources deployed but also on the way the work is done, and how close it is to the direct participation (and learning) of ordinary people and working communities. Thatcherism's legacy is such that we *have* to turn the emphasis away from 'top down' state socialism towards building from below.

Fourthly, we need to look again at the realities of the labour market and of earned incomes. The analysis required has to go beyond — and behind — the aggregated and distorted unemployment figures. This is not just a matter of statistical manipulation; though it is worth noting that recent unemployment figures would have been some *450,000 higher* on the methods of measurement used up till October 1982, and that *in addition a further 450,000* were kept off the register by so-called training schemes.

The realities are more ominous still. Since June 1979 (measuring to Spring 1985) the number of *full time* jobs in Britain has fallen by some 2.2 million (1.7 million male jobs less, and over half a million full-time female jobs less). This should be contrasted with a growth in the population of working age of around three-quarters of a million. The loss of full-time jobs is of critical importance to the trade unions, since this must constitute their main organisational base. They should note that full-time male employment has continued to fall right through the Tory cyclical 'boom' from 1983 on.

What is *growing* is a secondary labour market made up of disadvantaged part-time workers (half the women part-time workers earn below the National Insurance threshhold and do not build up benefit entitlements related to work), and of the self-employed! The modern enterprise, large and small, is increasingly learning to shrink its established labour force and to manipulate contract and casual labour, and part-timers denied a whole range of rights and security. *Within* the fully employed labour force inequality has also been growing apace; within each main category (male manual, male non-manual, female manual, female non-manual) differentials have been widening in earnings terms, since 1977 for manual workers, since 1979 for non-manuals. More recently non-manual workers' earnings have been growing proportionally faster than those of manual workers. At one end of our pay spectrum we have the depressed and exploited workers in the secondary labour market in areas of heavy unemployment; at the other we have the powerful upward pull on 'top' professisonal salaries created by the cosmopolitan world of international finance based in London. Inequality and the disintegration of conventional pay norms (including old-style 'fair comparisons') could scarcely contain more extreme conditions.

To return to the official unemployment data, distorted as it is. Since the unemployed are assumed to be looking for and ready to take up *full*-time work, the real measure of the *rate* of unemployment should be the comparison with full-time work. In 1978 there were still in Britain as a whole 14 people in full-time work for each unemployed person. Today the proportion is only five in full-time work for each unemployed. Regionally the rate varies from three employees in full-time work for every one unemployed in the North Region to just over seven in full-time work for each one unemployed in the South East.

Moreover, the Tory boom has been experienced only by the southern regions of England, and even then only making modest inroads into the earlier loss of jobs. The devastation of the labour market in other regions is so extreme it is difficult to express. Northern region has seen a decline of one-quarter in male employment since Thatcher came to power; Wales a fall of one-fifth. Yorkshire and Humberside has seen a fall of one-sixth not only in male employment but also in full-time female employment. In six regions the decline in manufacturing jobs has been around 30 per cent. Overall, the increase in *long term* unemployment (continuously unemployed for a year or more) has been nearly *four-fold* in only four years. There are now over 750,000 long-term unemployed in the age group 25-54, that is in the middle years of working life. In Northern Ireland one male employee in seven is in long-term unemployment; in the northern region one in ten. Benefit discrimination against the long-term unemployed impoverishes the children in these households. Even so, by 1983, social security benefit income, inadequate as it is, accounted for 28 per cent of *all* household spending in Northern Ireland, 26 per cent of *all* household spending in the Northern region, 23 per cent in Wales and in Yorkshire and Humberside.*

For some time to come the raising of social security benefits — not least those to the long-term unemployed — will play a major macro-economic role in such regions in generating recovery and setting in train expansionary employment multipliers. (In general terms a given increase in total social security benefits would have up to twice the impact on regional household spending in the most disadvantaged regions that it would have in the South-East).

So much for the legacy of Thatcherite Britain. What might we do about it?

Shaping an Alternative

Perhaps the constraints we have to fear are those in our own thinking e.g. about development strategy rather than the constraints of our distorted and enfeebled economy. As an example, the last Labour government after 1975 had what it called an 'industrial strategy'. This, helpfully, made considerable use of *conditional, selective* aid bargained project by project or framed

**Source:* New Earnings Survey 1983. I have assumed that all social security benefits received are spent, which seems likely!

specifically for a particular industry. We will have to do the same again. What the last strategy did *not* do was to move very far at all beyond the manufacturing sector (which now accounts for less than a quarter of all jobs). Nor did it link the state financial aid to other major sources of development capital (financial agencies were notably kept out of the EDC structures). Nor did it establish any coherent *functional* links to tripartite planning and manpower agencies, while its attitude to local authorities potential role was predominantly negative. We should learn from what we didn't do last time, as well as from what we did do.

(a) Public Sector as Development Base

A number of general points might be made very simply here:

— Given the constraints of public finance, most additional expenditure directed to aid employment and development will have to be selective and conditional, both within the public sector and in dealings with private sector commerce. We express the language of priorities that way.

— To safeguard the balance of future public finance there should be considerable emphasis in the public sector development initiatives on revenue generating projects. This is not the same as using fully commercial objectives; e.g. an enlarged housing programme to meet urgent social needs, and not least the needs of those with lower incomes; improved environmental services such as leisure centres. In many cases such initiatives may be handled by developing combined public/private sector consortia (e.g. working with pension funds, including public sector pension funds, to finance part of the development with expectation of a fair long-term rate of return).

— Public purchasing should be concentrated more on UK suppliers who are prepared to place a strong emphasis in their own corporate strategy on UK development and employment creation (this could be expanded on a reciprocal basis with e.g. European associates).

— Priority in any public take-over of productive assets (e.g. elements of re-nationalisation) should concentrate on those that would play a key strategic role in accelerating advanced technological development (e.g. telecoms; aerospace) or to remove blockages to the strategic development of sectoral policy (energy policy for example).

— The existing gross regional inequalities must force a substantial re-ordering of priorities in co-operating with local government and development agencies in the most disadvantaged regions. A new and enlarged needs-based system for central government financial support to local authorities must weight resource allocation heavily towards the areas of severe unemployment; but a significant part of this would be conditional on Local Authority initiatives and co-operation in development priorities. Public service standards should also be levelled up in the areas of disadvantage.

(Given the demolition of the 'higher' structures of local government in England, there would need to be strong early encouragement to *federated* or consortium local authority development activity on a regional or sub-regional scale. This could be backed by authority for e.g. regional sales tax (on petrol for instance) shared among *co-operating* local authorities on agreed development/expenditure programmes).

— In areas of high unemployment encouragement should be given to the development of an 'intermediate' economy of co-operative and 'voluntary' (=non-profit orientated) community industry and services. This should offer opportunities for 'sheltered' contracts with local authorities and other public services, as part of additional provision, not at the expense of the level of existing direct labour or commercial contracts.

— Fair wage clauses, etc need to be restored immediately on coming into office.

— There will inevitably be tension between public service employees' pressure for improved pay, and the desire to concentrate increased public expenditure on employment creation. A crude 'restraint' policy is not suitable. The state (and its public services) should offer in return for limited pay advance the provision of enlarged additional resources to the service in question *and* direct sharing by the workers through their trade union organisations in shaping the priorities of improved resources (e.g. equipment and resources in schools; additional recruitment alongside increased in-service training; etc.) We may term this new element of industrial democracy *resource bargaining,* and assume it will be an element in development and employment strategy in *both* sectors.

(b) Influencing Corporate Behaviour

In the real world of corporate power it still *is* possible to establish a series of *effective* dialogues and bargaining around development and employment creation. There will *have* to be systems of inducement and subsidy (or waiving of elements of taxation), but they can be principled, and conditional on development matching the criteria of our development priorities, and subject to accountability and monitoring. At least the large-scale use of selective aid under the Industry Act in the second half of the 1970s showed how much could be done. But there must, legitimately, be an increased emphasis on public accountability; for instance a price increase by a powerful enterprise (private or public) is claiming for that enterprise additional resources, and in a constrained economy it is right to ensure that the claim on resources is necessary and that the resources will be used constructively. The second stage of the Price Commission from 1977 to 1979 showed that a powerful investigatory agency could be a major force in such accountability. To put it simply the development dialogue with business operates by both carrot and stick, by inducements and by rational elements of social control.

As the author of this paper has discussed such issues at length elsewhere,* it may serve the present purpose to concentrate on *four* areas of accountability that will most emphatically be needed. How far these would be handled by separate agencies, or in a more co-ordinated way, may be left for further discussion.

First, the Thatcherite policies of de-nationalising industries/firms with a strong element of natural monopoly (telecoms; gas; water; airways) means that an equivalently strong *Public Utilities agency* is needed to enforce the public interest. This is not only a matter of price control, but also service adequacy, and the guarantee of a sufficiently adequate and technically advanced UK development programme. (This is not necessarily an alternative to re-nationalisation, but an urgent and immediate requirement in any case).

Second, a strong agency is needed to develop standards of accountabillity to the public (and to members) on the part of all financial institutions that enjoy a privileged tax position in the accumulation and use of their funds. We may think of this as a kind of 'planning agreements' system in the finance sector. In particular, funds that act as trustees for the interest of millions of workers should be expected to act as socially responsible owners of assets, and can be stimulated to co-operate together more to bring more constructive influence to bear e.g. on companies in which they are dominant shareholders. The flow of funds for UK-based development and activities directly in the deployment of development and venture capital would be of major concern.

*In two Spokesman books. See the last chapter of John Hughes' *Britain in Crisis* (The Re-Industrialisation of Britain) and *Planning the Planners*, ed. T. Topham, chapter on 'Democratic Planning for an Enfeebled Economy'.

Third, in the main area of large-scale diversified corporate power — especially where international competitive pressures are limited — a return must be made to a strong investigatory Price Commission. This is the more necessary if trade unionists are to have any confidence in an overall economic strategy that puts more emphasis on priorities such as employment creation, renewing the public services, etc., and less on real pay advance. Such an agency is not to be seen merely negatively as a restraining force; it can (and did) probe industrial efficiency, and explore the link between prices and UK development needs.

Fourth, there will need to be a major shift in mergers policy. Much more emphasis will have to be given to scrutinising mergers to ensure that where they do proceed they will be followed by stronger UK performance and a more vigorous UK-based development strategy. There may well be scope for an active encouragement to 'de-merging' where this would offer a significant commitment to industrial democracy, and where this might liberate enterprises previously constrained by the conglomerate headquarters from pursuing major UK development and growth. Possibly the public agency given this more challenging and interventionist role should *also* have power to investigate independently major plant closures by companies, to carry through a social audit of the impact, and to explore alternative use of the assets. There should be some power to take over such discarded assets (in the name of the public) as a going concern, where this offers scope for renewal and viable maintenance of jobs.

Earlier Labour Government experience in the 1970s — notably with the 1977-79 Price Commission — demonstrated that a major advance in public accountability over powerful business enterprises, both private and public, could be achieved. So there is nothing Utopian in proposing the four major initiatives outlined above. And all of them could play an important role in strengthening the effectiveness of planning and development strategies. But given the multinational organisation and development of so much of large-scale business, the whole emphasis on establishing a more socially responsible and accountable system would be more effective if it were part of a wider European process. This is a process that would be assisted by stronger European Community initiatives, such as an effective 'code of conduct' for multinational companies operating in any of the countries involved, and a more vigorous challenge to aspects of monopoly power (including mergers involving more than one country). But this should not inhibit or delay the development of national systems of public control and accountability both inside and outside the European Community. Here, in particular, sharing of experience and comparison of systems of accountability and control could help all the countries that co-operated to establish a more effective development dialogue with large-scale enterprise.

Beyond these measures, and the development of selectively bargained systems of aid to commercial and social investment, planning for employment will mean 'signalling' priorities through changes to (and choices within) the structure of taxes and allowances that affect business cost structures and prices. In general it is better to redirect 'market forces' than to seek to override them. In terms of principle this means that the political community is identifying and quantifying elements of social benefit and social cost (that may not be properly reflected in existing costs or revenues in business accounts) and translating these into monetary costs/allowances that *alter* business decisions, e.g. on employment or the scale of capital development, as business pursues its goals of commercial viability and profitability. (A simple example is provided by the earlier system, now superseded, of influencing industrial training by a levy/rebate system, so that at low or nil cost to the Exchequer an expanded process of training would occur on controlled lines.)

It is certainly time, therefore, to look highly critically at the extent to which business finds itself — in the UK and in other European countries — facing a set of taxes and allowances which effectively *subsidise* fixed capital expenditures and *tax* employment. In a relatively fully employed economy there may be a degree of logic in such a biassed 'signalling' of costs and benefits. But in the context of mass and persistent unemployment it should be evident that we have to think again.

Moreover, as has already been argued, what is happening *within* employment is the *erosion of full-time* employment and in substitution for it the expansion of part-time, casualised employment, and the 'self-employed'. Much of this latter area of employment growth is not only subject to exploitation and discrimination by the employer but represents manipulation to *avoid* taxation (and other legal obligations involving costs) that is levied on full-time employees and on their employers.

So, the categories and norms of taxation in use act to create damaging 'substitution' effects. They direct the employer to even more capital intensive forms of investment and production than would emerge from the underlying levels of wages and capital equipment costs. They also encourage the substitution of 'secondary' labour market forms of employment organisation (part-time, labour only sub-contracts with nominally 'self-employed', etc.) in place of the employment of full-time employees.

Yet full-time employment is both the main organisational base for trade unionism and for the wider labour movement. Full-time employment is also one of the main tax bases for state revenues, and within that for the revenues that sustain the 'welfare' state of benefit payments in need (including pensions) and social services based on individual and collective need.

What is needed is a wide ranging discussion as to the scale and direction of changes that will be needed to alter the present signalling of taxes and allowances as they affect employment and capital formation and use, so that we develop a system less destructive of full-time jobs while still encouraging expansion of commercially oriented development. This is hardly the moment to be dogmatic as to what should be done. But the following possible directions of change might be considered:

(i) Employers should not be able to avoid the general structure of employment taxes by switching to using part-time labour for hours of work under tax/national insurance payment thresholds, or by manipulated use of self-employment. This points to new inclusive forms of payroll tax on employers, and to treating labour sub-contracts as equivalent to normal employment for payroll tax purposes. It means incorporating part-time workers into the general structure of worker rights, access to occupational pensions, statutory rights of protection, etc. It means therefore using changed legislation to extend *pro rata* pay, conditions, and other rights to virtually all workers (the European Community's intended Directive on treatment of part-timers, currently blocked by UK Government opposition, is one step on the way). The employer is still left with a rational choice as to forms of labour utilisation, but no longer on the basis of pursuit of tax avoidance etc.

(ii) There should be major experimentation with tax incentives to increase employment. For instance, a reduction overall of 1 per cent on employers' national insurance levy can be expected to have only vestigial effects on employment. But if the same scale of tax reduction were concentrated at the employment margin (e.g. offering a rebate of 10 per cent of the paybill on all additional employment — in relation to some earlier base period — for some period of years) the outcome could be more positive. As with the system of Regional Employment Premiums developed for a while in the 1960s, such signalling of the benefits of increased employment could be regionally differentiated (though not so that a conglomerate employer could switch employment between regions as the old REP system allowed to happen). Exchequer costs of such initiatives would be in fact very small, since to the extent they stimulate employment they also reduce state payments to the unemployed and increase tax revenues from the new employed.

(iii) As a long-term thrust of policy, the state should be encouraging employers and trade unions to negotiate and operate reductions of *actual* annual working time for full-time employees. This is not necessarily achieved by negotiated reductions in 'normal' hours unless there is an accompanying restriction on overtime working. Here too, payroll taxes and rebates could be used positively to reinforce pressures to reduce annual working hours.

This could include a system of surcharges on payroll tax imposed on all hours worked in excess of a given annual level (say 1,750 hours immediately, and 1,600 hours within three years). It could involve both levies on overtime hours and statutory constraints on total weekly hours worked.

(iv) There would be very obvious merit, too, in using a payroll levy/rebate system to stimulate the direction of greatly increased attention within each major enterprise — private and public — on the development of *human investment* in education and vocational skills, and in associated redesign of jobs and working environments. One way of doing this would be to rebate substantial funds to *joint* control by employees and employers at *enterprise* level for designated manpower development and work organisation plans. It would offer a new but important strand in earlier thinking about 'planning agreements', and help extend trade union functions and an industrial democracy that actually commands and allocates *resources*. Properly planned, such processes of in-service training, and wider personnel development, and redesign of jobs could not only increase efficiency (and encourage wider social responsibility) but also enable additional recruitment and employment (the educational system would itself provide an obvious example).

(v) In a similar way there would need to be a major re-examination of the existing system of corporate taxation and associated systems of 'allowances' against profits tax liabilities. One attractive possibility is to substitute a tax on net assets for some of the existing rate of tax on profits (so as to increase the incentive to function efficiently and profitably); this could be structured so as to tax more heavily low risk companies who could not switch their assets abroad (e.g. companies in the distributive industries, property companies) and to offer more stimulus to higher risk firms (e.g. manufacturing). But whether such a shift of the corporate tax base from income to capital assets is worthwhile, what *has* to be done is to make a substantial part of the system of allowances *conditional* and gear them to *future development.* There is considerable experience of such systems in countries such as Sweden. Such company level 'investment/development funds' can be built up either (or both) from diverting into them some of the tax revenues arising from standard arrangements for corporation tax, or by diverting into them some of the existing allowances for investment and depreciation. Release of such investment fund balances into finance for part (or all) of new development and employment creating projects would be conditional on meeting planning and development criteria and priorities. In other words there would be a much stronger and more rational basis for the future 'planning agreements' that we will need than that so feebly attempted by Labour in 1975. Moreover, some or all of these financial resources (waiting to be turned into material resources, investment in plants, reorganisation of activities, improved capital utilisation, and increased employment) could be made subject to 'resource' bargaining between the enterprise and the trade unions representing the employees; this could and should be more than the inadequate concept of 'consultation' that Labour added to its attempt at planning agreements in the mid-1970s.

In Summer 1985 the Labour Party and the TUC in their document *A New Partnership* endorsed the following general order of priorities:

"The first call on the nation's resources must be the creation of jobs for the unemployed. This will itself boost production and create wealth as part of a longer term industrial policy.

"The second call must be the improvement of living standards for those in most need, including pensioners, recipients of benefits and the low paid.

"The third call must be the improvement of living standards for those in work, both from earnings and from improved public services."

If we endorse such priorities we are under obligation to argue out how they could actually be implemented in the real world of commercial power *and* of power bargaining by trade unions as well as corporate business and government itself. What has been set out in this paper is a first attempt to argue both the principles and the methods that could be brought to bear. The kind of initiative called for would be better sustained, better defended against the opposition (and strikes) of organised capital if it were not an isolated UK struggle. If half of Europe were on the same path, we could win through. If most of Europe were on that path we would win through.

Chapter 12

What about Finances?

Richard Minns

I
Other Countries' Financial Institutions

It is ironic that some of the countries from which many foreign banks in London have emanated have domestic financial systems which offer interesting examples of alternative structures. The structures reflect historical needs which can be traced back to the industrial revolution (as in the case of Germany), post-war economic priorities (Japan), or localised economic pressures (Mondragon in Spain). There are also examples of extensive public ownership in banking (France) and examples of serious attempts at the introduction of the socially responsible use of pension funds (USA).

All these examples demonstrate that there are financial structures which are substantially different to those prevailing in the UK. Of course, each country has its own specific economic and political history and circumstances. The examples do illustrate, however, that the role of the financial system, or attempts to control the use of part of it, depend on decisions about its purpose. There are pressures and tensions within all the systems, especially with the current internationalisation of the lending and securities markets. Banks in Germany are not free from crises, and banks in Japan are rapidly increasing their overseas presence, especially in London's Euromarkets. Our argument is that, relatively speaking, these systems have developed radically different structures within capitalist markets. Some have been more successful than others, and there are progressive aspects to them which can be examined and developed in discussions about the control of finance in the economy.

The examples from other countries show different structures which separately or together:

1. Facilitate industrial and financial planning,

2. Increase public accountability,
3. Highlight the role of more localised institutions, and
4. Suggest mechanisms for the alternative use of pension funds in accordance with the wishes of contributors.

In the UK the various financial markets have developed separate institutions:

— the domestic or *retail market* for short-term deposits and liquid savings has been serviced by the clearing banks, and building societies too,
— the longer-term *savings market* has been channelled into investment institutions such as pension funds and insurance companies,
— the larger surplus funds of companies and other bodies passes through the *wholesale markets* dominated by merchant banks,
— the enormous sums of foreign funds flowing through the City — *the Euromarkets* — are largely managed by foreign banks.

The boundaries between the institutions in these markets are becoming less distinct. Merchant banks also manage pension funds as well as managing the wholesale markets for large sums of money. The clearing banks are merging with stockbrokers in order to capture more of the dealing business in the savings markets. Foreign banks too are taking over institutions in a similar way. The 'securities revolution' is the current stage in the historical role of the UK as a centre for international investment and lending.

Germany

In Germany many of the functions which have been the prerogative of separate institutions in the UK have been contained in one type of institution, namely, the universal bank.

The pre-eminence of the banking sector within the German financial system dates from the middle of the nineteenth century, when Germany was in the throes of industrialisation, and had to contend with strong competition from Great Britain which was at a more advanced stage of industrial development. It was recognised that to compete successfully, German industry could not afford to wait for firms to evolve from small to large concerns, financed by internally generated funds, as had frequently been the case in Britain. Moreover, technological advances indicated that to compete successfully investment in large plant was necessary. As a result companies had to be formed on a larger scale, which not only meant a greater financial outlay, but which also required mechanisms to facilitate the efficient collection and transfer of savings to the industrial sector.

Germany did not have large pockets of individual wealth,

amassed from colonial ventures which could be tapped as a source of capital. Furthermore, the banking system was unwilling to expand its operation to cater for the needs of companies with capital-intensive production techniques. The result was that German industrialists, with assistance from government, created their own 'industrial' banks.

Industrial banks, or as they are more commonly known, 'universal' banks, dominate the West German financial system. There are three groups of universal banks:

— the joint stock banks and private bankers;
— the regionally based Landesbanks and the savings banks below them;
— the credit co-operatives and their central institutions.

The universal banks have the capacity to offer a complete range of financial services such as: short-term facilities, medium and long-term loans, instalment credit, discount and acceptance credit, investment finance, mortgages for private and commercial purposes and the management of new securities issues. They can also invest in the securities markets on their own account, and issue bank bonds. The ability to offer such a broad range of services in-house meant that the banks were able to meet the needs of industrial clients and assist them in the expansion of their companies. The largest universal banks are now the 'Big Three' — Deutsche Bank, Dresdner Bank and Commerzbank.

German equity markets have been slow to develop. In part this has been due to the lack of strong institutional investors, but it is also because of the pervasive influence of the banks, who undertake the organisation of new issues, final placement with investors, and may possibly even provide a listing at a local stock exchange. In comparison, in the UK, security transactions, placement and new issues only minimally involve the commercial banks.

In Germany, Frankfurt and Dusseldorf are the main financial centres, but they do not dominate the financial scene to the same extent as the City of London. This is partly due to the fact that many of the German states (Ländes) have their own regional banks (Ländesbanks), and their own Bourses, or stock exchange, reflecting the greater degree of local banking and securities markets. Indeed the strong links between the financial and industrial sectors are maintained and strengthened by the many banks at the state and commune level.

Ländesbanks are organised at the level of the state and offer a range of financial services to the population, the institutions and the industries in the state. The range of services varies from bank to bank: some are highly specialised while others are regionalised universal banks. The majority do much the same kind of business as the large commercial banks. State banks are also able to carry out such operations as holding company shares and dealing in the money markets. The twelve Ländesbanks have between them accounted for 16-17 per cent of all lending to the private sector over the last ten years.

The Ländesbanks all maintain some kind of relationship with the local state. To take an example, the Hessische Ländesbank Girozentrale (HLG) is owned 50 per cent by the state of Hessen and 50 per cent by Hessen's Savings Banks. The State of Hessen also appoints 50 per cent of the members of a body guaranteeing the bank's equity. The solvency of the bank is underwritten by the State and the Ländesbank secures the State's debt. The shareholders' board meets annually and the supervisory board meets quarterly. The supervisory board appoints the managing director of the bank and approves loans over a certain limit. A third of this board is appointed by the State, a third by the savings banks and a third by the bank's employees. In HLG's statutes the prime objective is to provide the State of Hessen and its industry with the finance for development.

However, Ländesbanks have become increasingly involved in overseas lending. This may increase their relative independence from state economies. Some Ländesbanks have caused considerable concern to their States who have been called on to help solve serious shortfalls in capital, arising from bad sovereign debt. Involvement in property finance has been another important part of Ländesbanks' activities which has created problems. HLG, for example, required an injection of state aid after running into difficulties with property investment in the mid seventies.

As well as the main universal banks — the big 'three' — and the Ländesbanks there are 592 local savings banks and their 17,500 branches. Special savings bank laws still exist specifying that the traditional tasks of these institutions are to encourage savings and giro transactions, to provide credit for low-earners and the middle classes, and to fulfil the financial requirements of their local communities.

The Ländesbanks go for bigger customers accounts (this has meant them having to develop their services by providing Eurocurrency and other international facilities for the big customers in their State) leaving small company business to local savings banks. Two-thirds of all bank lending to small and medium enterprises is undertaken by the savings banks. Even though savings banks are individual, autonomous entities they do work together and co-financing takes place between Savings Banks and Ländesbanks.

Existing alongside the savings banks at the local level are the co-operative banks, which were originally self-help credit institutions set up for farmers and local artisans. The co-operative banks have increased their share of total domestic bank business volume from 5.6 per cent in 1960 to 11.5 per cent in 1983, mainly at the expense of the commercial banks.

A more detailed examination of the involvement between the financial and industrial sectors can be gained by looking at the financing of medium and small sized business sector, the 'Mittelstand'.

Table 1 shows bank lending by the three main types of banks to domestic businesses in total, and to the Mittelstand in 1979. The Commercial Banks, a heterogeneous group which includes the Big Three, the regional and other commercial banks as well as branches of foreign banks and the private banks, has the largest share of total advances, but the smallest share of advances to the Mittelstand. The share of the commercial banks in lending to the Mittelstand fell between 1970 and 1978; that of the savings bank fell slightly and that of the co-operative banks increased (see Table 2).

Table 3 shows that the role of the commercial banks in advances to the Handwerk sector (firms mainly employing nine or fewer persons) is smaller still in relative terms. The savings banks have by far the largest share and they seem to have been increasing at the expense of the co-operative banks.

Table 1
Bank lending by the three main types of banks to domestic businesses in total, and to the Mittelstand, 1979, Germany

	Total Bank Advances to Businesses 1979[1]		*Bank Advances to Mittelstand 1979*[2]	
	DM Billion		*DM Billion*	
Commercial Banks[3]	197.0	40.9	45.0	30.7
Savings and Giro Banks	191.0	39.6	52.3	35.7
Co-operative Banks	94.1	19.5	49.1	33.5
Total[4]	482.1	100.1	146.4	100.0

Notes
1. Includes mortgage lending.
2. Excludes mortgage lending.
3. Includes Banks with Special Functions.
4. Excludes lending by Mortgage and Hire Purchase Banks and the Postal Giro Systems.

Table 2
Percentage of total lending to the Mittelstand by each of the three main types of bank, Germany 1970 and 1978

	1970	*1978*
Commercial Banks	35.1	30.7
Savings and Giro Banks	36.3	35.7
Co-operative Banks	28.6	33.5
Total	100.0	100.0

Table 3
Bank lending to Handwerk by type of bank and total lending to Mittelstand, Germany 1970 and 1978

	DM Billions and Per Cent			
	1970		*1978*	
	DM m	*Per cent*	*DM m*	*Per cent*
Commercial Banks	1.2	12.5	3.0	12.1
Savings and Giro Banks	4.4	45.8	14.2	57.3
Co-operative Banks	4.0	41.7	7.6	30.6
Total Advances to Handwerk	9.6	100.0	4.8	100.0
Total Advances to Mittelstand	69.5	—	129.3	—
Per cent Handwerk of total	—	13.8	—	19.2

It is to be expected that smaller banks with more limited resources would be more likely to concentrate upon lending to smaller firms and that this tendency would be strongly reinforced by geographical factors. Small banks tend to be more deeply rooted in the community in which their directors are located, and the savings banks are obliged, by law, to restrict their activities to the local authority area in which they are located. The co-operative banks were limited to lending to their own members until 1974.

The extent of the voting rights held by German banks in companies is extensive. The banks directly own around five per cent of the voting rights of the top 100 companies. This ranges from three per cent in the top ten to over seven per cent in the 'bottom' 75. The banks also control the proxy votes for investment clients. This represents an average of 30 per cent in the top 100 companies, giving an average total of over 35 per cent of the equity of the top 100 companies either directly owned or controlled by the banks.

The German universal banks have been attacked for having too much influence over industry because of their equity holdings, the proxy voting rights they obtain from savings funds under their management, and their presence on the supervisory boards of companies. The banks have been accused of having sufficient power to make companies dependent on them, thus restricting competition. They have also been accused of using shareholder proxies under their control to advance their own interest, and of supporting this through the supervisory board.

Whatever the substance behind these debates, the banks have had various reasons to buy stakes and become involved in companies. A universal bank's shareholdings in companies may prepare the way for share listings, or may reorganise the shareholder structure, or may be used to avoid unwanted participation. On balance, the mechanism of universal banking has been a powerful tool in the development of German industry, albeit with enormous potential conflicts of interest.

There are also 'involuntary' share holdings and supervisory board membership which the banks have been forced to undertake. The most important recent crisis to hit West Germany's industrial sector has been that of AEG Telefunken (AEG). Its importance can be gauged by the fact that it was widely perceived as the first real occasion that West Germany's model of capitalist management had failed. Previously the Bonn Government's characteristic role in crisis management had been to rely on general measures of support for a sector rather than on intervention at the level of the firm (either for sectors under international pressure e.g. shipbuilding and mining, or for growth sectors e.g. the computer industries). This role left it up to the banks to engage in detailed intervention and monitoring of sector strategy. Central government had never allowed itself to become involved with a business in a booming sector but with serious problems arising out of bad management. This was all to change with AEG.

The last time in the 1970s that AEG paid a dividend was in 1973. The background to the losses AEG incurred from 1974 onwards was a series of costly and mistaken acquisitions of other companies, mistakes in the fields of nuclear power and computer development, and falling sales affecting a series of electronic consumer goods. In the autumn of 1979, led by AEG's 'house bank' — the Dresdner Bank — a huge rescue programme was mounted by a consortium that involved more than 20 banks, including the Deutsche Bank, and West Deutch Ländesbank, along with insurance companies and Daimler Benz, the motor car company. AEG received substantial financial aid in return for a restructuring programme. The monitoring of the rescue was to be facilitated by the election of Hans Frerichs of the Dresdner Bank as the chairman of the company's supervisory board in 1980.

AEG would have been insolvent in 1979 without a rescheduling of its debts and the subscription of new equity by the banks. Unfortunately, the problems of restructuring AEG proved obstinate, if not intractable. By 1982 the problems had turned into West Germany's biggest ever industrial disaster. The new management was unable to free itself from the burdens that had been imposed by the past phase of rapid empire-building, which had been based on borrowed funds and on the priority of increased sales over increased profits. This inheritance of enormous financial liabilities was aggravated by high interest rates after 1979. In 1979 the banks had pumped DM930 million into AEG at DM150 a share. By August 1982 the value of AEG's shares had fallen drastically to DM22.

The strategy of the banks and of management was to concentrate on preserving the viable areas of AEG by finding strong industrial partners for them. After the involvement of Bosch, Grundig and Mannesmann in the profitable telecommunications business, AEG management's restructuring programme sought to split the group into separate companies for capital goods and for household appliances. This programme collapsed in the summer of 1982 when the works council of AEG rejected the proposal that Britain's GEC should acquire an equity stake in the profitable capital goods business, in part because of concern about future personnel policy from GEC.

As a result of continuing losses and of the collapse of the rescue programme, the parent company AEG-Telefunken was forced to fight off bankruptcy in the autumn of 1982 by invoking the West German legal procedure known as 'composition' (Vergleich). The Vergleich is a court-supervised settlement with a company's creditors. Its objective is to relieve the external debt burden so that the company can gain financial room to restructure its loss-making operations. An administrator is appointed by the court to supervise the proceedings, which involve the attempt to persuade creditors to write off up to 60 per cent of the company's unsecured debts. Eventually the creditors are assembled to vote on a settlement. The Vergleich released AEG of 60 per cent of its debt burden, but committed it to pay back the other 40 per cent.

The experience of AEG during a period of economic crisis highlights some of the differences in mechanisms and approach between Britain and Germany to company restructuring. The banks took a leading role, aided by legal procedures which could be used to prevent precipitate action and to promote a restructuring. Naturally, as in the UK, the banks have been forced into rescues because they stand to lose more if they keep out. There have been a number of rescues in the UK where the banks have been forced to take action. In the rescue of Dunlop the banks converted some of their loans into equity stakes. But they also converted most of the long-term debt into short-term borrowings, so enabling the banks to call in all their loans within a year if they chose to do so.

The AEG case also shows that the banks could have perhaps identified the impending problems earlier. But the role of the banks in the rescue involved a substantial 'hands-on' approach, the lead bank taking over the chairing of the company's supervisory board, making it responsible for the future direction and rescue of the company. When problems remained and got worse after a year or so of the rescue programme the banks as shareholders acted as lead investors in the company, using legal procedures to prevent bankruptcy. This should be seen in the context of a banking and financial system in which the banks have played a much more important investment function, providing long-term funds and industrial support.

Japan

If Germany has had the experience of powerful 'universal' banks, Japan in contrast has had very segmented markets and institutions, with legislation providing for the separation of commercial banking and investment banking (like the US), and strict control over foreign banks and the management of pension funds.

The essential characteristic of Japanese finance after the Second World War was that it was designed to serve industry. This included government control of interest rates and credit allocation, but most important for our purposes, funds were channelled to industry from the private savings market through a range of financial institutions including commercial banks, long-term credit banks, regional banks and trust banks, each with a clear role to play in a system of segmented financial markets. In addition, exchange controls kept savings inside Japan; foreign investment had a minimal role to play and foreign institutions played only a peripheral role. This system was subject to pressures to change after the 1979 oil price rise. Japanese institutions have also been affected by deregulation and an opening up of the Japanese financial system to foreign institutions. We should note the importance of Japanese banks in the Euromarkets in London. With surplus funds in the domestic economy, as large parts of the corporate sector now have created sufficient internal cash flow, Japanese financial institutions have turned increasingly to the overseas recycling of Japan's excess of savings over investment and balance of payments surplus.

Much of Japan's success in economic growth has been attributed to a special relationship between government agencies and financial institutions. The government guided economic development by various mechanisms including the Ministry of International Trade and Industry (MITI); the Ministry of Finance; Japan Development Bank ; Export-Import Bank; the Trust Fund Bureau; by its control over the Bank of Japan (BOJ); and its control over commercial banks and regional banks.

The structures which have emerged combine a horizontal integration of financial and industrial planning at the national level, with a vertical integration of some national and local financial institutions.

MITI is the central government's mechanism for involvement in industrial and economic planning. Its formal objectives are the promotion of trade and the restructuring and modernisation of industry. Since being formed in 1949, MITI has gained the reputation of being the most important institution in Japan's industrial policy-making process.

MITI's various industrial branches (chemicals, textiles, heavy industry, mineral, oil and coal mining) deal with the planning and implementation of sectoral policies aimed at promoting the development of the relevant industries. The industrial policy bureau is concerned with the planning and implementation of policies which are common to all sectors, including industrial re-organisation and distribution and consumer protection.

The relationship between MITI and the various sectors of industry is not just imposed from the centre. The crucial element of reciprocity has always been a prerequisite to stable relationships with the state and finance. There are a wide variety of discussion groups, and, in particular, a formal consultative structure, under which business regularly participates in policy-making. This structure comprises a series of councils set up as advisory bodies to MITI and composed of representatives of private business, trade unions and academics. The 'industrial structure' council is among the most important since it discusses all basic MITI policy issues.

In Japan industrial policy must be approved by the Ministry of Finance which sets the limits on the scope of industrial policy at many levels, focusing on the stability of national currency; specific loans to business, sufficient government revenue as well as tax subsidies to particular sectors. The Financial Bureau of the

Ministry also manages the Fiscal Investment and Loan Plan which channels government trust funds into industrial sectors via public corporations such as the Japan Development Bank.

The Japan Development Bank (JDB) is an investment bank that was set up to play an important part in the government's strategy of reconstruction after the Second World War. JDB made low-interest, long term investment funds available to key manufacturing industries.

Obviously the role of the central bank in financial and industrial policy is crucial. The most important instrument of the Bank of Japan is the use of 'window controls' — informal persuasion employed to discriminate in favour or against certain borrowers, and to exert quantitative controls over credit. The Bank of Japan sets a limit on the amount it will lend to each bank. By raising or lowering these ceilings it attempts to control the supply of credit to priority sectors outlined by the National Economic Policy.

After the Second World War industrial and commercial enterprises were without liquid resources and turned to the commercial banks to finance their expansion. This high demand for liquid resources provided an 'over-loan' position, and commercial banks turned to the Bank of Japan for loans which strengthened the capacity of the Bank to control both the pace and the direction of development as advocated by the National Economic Policy.

After the Second World War the Allied powers had tried to eliminate the link between financial institutions and industry contained in the old Japanese Zaibatsu (bank-led industrial groups) but this only had a short-term effect. The prominent Zaibatsu, namely Mitsui, Mitsubishi and Sumitomo resumed their titles and links with industrial and commercial activities, although the number of these banks fell because of the effects of consolidation.

As a result of these developments the composition of the banking system consists of thirteen city banks and Zaibatsu banks; sixty-three local/regional banks; and fifty-four foreign banks. The commercial banking system has in fact been governed by economic policy aimed at the rapid growth of the economy by industrial expansion. The development of high technology, capital intensive industries meant the priority had to be given to capital investment. This led to investment as a share of the GNP being higher than any other industrial country (35 per cent in 1960, 38 per cent in 1971-3); and it was financed predominantly by the banks. In the 1930s 25 per cent of investment was financed by banks, while in the early 1950s 60 per cent came from bank advances. In fact most loans for industrial expansion have been advanced by the commercial banks (the city banks, Zaibatsu, and local/regional banks) from private sources, except in periods of 'over-loan' when commercial banks had to resort to borrowing from the Bank of Japan.

As in Germany, there is a tendency for the regional banks to finance small and medium-sized firms. They can only operate within a single prefecture (county) but they may operate several branches. In the 1970s 'window control' facilities and administrative guidance were extended to some local banks and in 1970 the Ministry of Finance refused to let city banks merge with regional banks. However, this very important segmentation of the financial system is currently under even more intense international pressure.

In conclusion, Japan has developed a complex set of financial institutions and mechanisms across both the public and private sectors of the economy for implementing industrial policy. The government's influence over industrial growth has been far reaching. Through the various financial institutions and mechanisms, continuous contact between government, industry and finance are of crucial importance in the formulation and implementation of Japanese industrial policy. Japan is an example of how a government can control, direct, persuade, guide and channel finance to industry through investment policies, banks and other financial institutions.

France

Germany is an example of a financial and industrial system in which the universal or industrial banks play the key role. In Japan the central state has a larger part in overall policy. In France we have an example of state intervention in the banking system, highlighted in particular by an extensive programme of public ownership, including the nationalisation of eighteen listed banks, twenty-one unlisted banks and two financial companies in 1981.

France had developed some of the original ideas behind industrial banking. In the mid-nineteenth century, the establishment of the Credit Mobilier as an investment bank for the promotion of enterprises and the provision of long-term finance, set a pattern for investment banking in Germany, Japan and elsewhere. Unfortunately, in France the financial system constrained the operations of the Credit Mobilier. The traditions of industrial banking, in which the provision of long-term finance is supported by active involvement and commitment to industry, did not become a central part of the financial system.

There were four key arguments surrounding the 1981

nationalisations. First, there was seen to be a need for a strategic strengthening of the position of the five or six large, state-owned industries such as Renault, Rhone Poulenc and PUK. In this way the government hoped to complement its industrial strategy towards these firms with a financial strategy based on a controlled banking sector. Second, the government wanted to influence long range planning through the creation of long-term credit facilities to industry. Third, the newly nationalised sector would begin a process of more flexible lending strategies where traditional criteria would be a barrier; for example to co-ops, to new businesses or to firms where less traditional factors in production were being considered such as non-polluting production processes. Fourth, and perhaps from our point of view most important, was the attempt to reorientate the banks towards acting not as lenders but investors. This would involve them in providing risk capital. This was seen as a key part of the government's industrial strategy.

The French banking system was renowned for being part privately and mutually owned and part nationalised. This dual-ownership structure stems from the period of the first nationalisations in 1945. The three largest nationalised banks, the Banque Nationale de Paris, the Societé Generale and Credit Lyonnais, had 36 per cent of the deposits and 30 per cent of the credits of the total banking sector in 1980. The size of the nationalised sector has always been significant and the nationalisations of 1981 can be seen as the completion of nationalisation of all private banks with deposits of more than FFr1 billion.

The experience of the nationalised sector since 1945 has been contradictory. Critics from the left have often accused the nationalised banks of being little different from their private sector rivals. Critics from the right have argued that traditional banking business practice has been undermined through nationalisation. The new nationalised sector now accounts for some 75 per cent of credits and 74 per cent of deposits, while the remaining private sector consists of 71 small banks (of which only 16 are genuinely independent) responsible for 1.2 per cent of deposits and 0.8 per cent of credits. The Mutualité, or co-operative banking sector, accounts for the difference, comprising 18 per cent of deposits and 22 per cent of credits, together with 5 per cent and 3 per cent respectively being held by foreign banks.

Thus the French Government has theoretically far more control over their banking system than any other OECD government. Indeed taken together with the controls and influences the French State exerts over the other institutions and processes of the French financial system, it is possible to argue that French monetary authorities had more freedom of manoeuvre relative to international monetary developments than, say, those of the UK during the 1970s. Exchange controls, for example, were much more stringent than anything that existed in Britain before their abolition by the Conservative Government in 1979, but proposals for easing these controls have recently been put forward.

From the start of the period of the new nationalisations various problems were immediately apparent. Despite changes in the very senior bank personnel, the broad majority of senior middle and lower management remained untouched and a whole range of practices within the system remained the same. In addition, despite the extent of control that nationalisation now gave the government, a detailed national plan for industrial restructuring, which would show how the control of finance could be used productively, was not forthcoming.

As a result of these factors the newly nationalised banks all had difficulties in coming to terms with their relationship to the state. Most are now engaged in a 'constructive bargaining' process with the government, particularly over its attempt to set up aid packages for state owned industry. Very soon after the nationalisations, for example, a new aid package was announced, and although unable to challenge the decision, the banks were able to negotiate better terms for the subordinated loan part of the deal; and the equity participations, making up half the total package, were agreed to be indirect stakes, via a holding company, in all the newly nationalised companies not just the loss makers. This gave the banks a reasonable assurance of receiving dividends in future years.

The most recent developments within the publicly owned French banking sector have been to provide nationalised banks with access to private capital. In 1984 Societé Generale, the third largest of the three banks nationalised after 1945, issued non-voting quasi-shares. This was the first bank since the 1982 nationalisations to offer its capital to private shareholders. In addition, France has introduced measures to encourage more long-term savings into the French market, aimed at promoting more long term investment in industry. There have also been initiatives by banks and other institutions to set up venture capital funds for funding private sector risk capital similar to the UK and US venture capital funds. The government also extended a tax relief scheme for personal investment in shares — a scheme very similar to the Business Start-Up and Expansion Schemes introduced by the Conservative Government in the UK. There have also been loan guarantee schemes to encourage nationalised banks to lend to state industry.

France therefore provides an example of some of the major problems to be faced in constructing a financial system which plays a central role in industrial planning and investment. It is easy to get trapped into making marginal changes in the existing savings and banking system, such as tax relief schemes and loan guarantee schemes, without being able to tackle the crucial constraints imposed by a financial system. To break the circle, public ownership was deemed to be a necessary condition, but we have learned that it is obviously not enough to cope with all the other changes which are necessary, especially a detailed industrial strategy which links the controls over the financial system with plans for restructuring.

Concluding Japan, Germany and France

In conclusion, there are problems with all the alternative structures we have outlined. We are not trying to argue that we should copy a German or a Japanese system, only to suggest that there may be positive and negative lessons in an examination of systems where, for various historical reasons, finance has, by and large, been used in a different way for the domestic economy. These other financial systems are still very much a part of some of the growing tendencies towards the internationalisation of bond and equity markets. German, Japanese and to a lesser, but growing, extent French banks play an important role in the Euromarkets with a significant presence in London. This has had major implications for the Japanese financial system which is now extremely active in financing international credits and bond issues at corporate and governmental levels. Japan has become one of the world's largest exporters of capital.

Nevertheless, in Germany and Japan at least, there is a history of a stronger relationship between finance and industry. In other words, different financing mechanisms have emerged. These can be the banks themselves, as in Germany, or the banks and state agencies, as in Japan. Germany shows that 'universal' banking, where an institution performs a range of financial functions, has benefited industry. On the other hand, Japanese industry has also thrived but on the basis of a very segmented banking and financial system, with strong central planning and control by the state.

In Germany and Japan therefore, in contrast to France and the UK, there has been a long tradition of investment, or industrial banking. As summarised by Yao-Su-Hu, industrial banking can be expressed as follows:

"1. the provision of long-term finance (long and medium-term debt, or such debt plus equity) to enterprises and entrepreneurs in the industrial and commercial sectors, in the form and combination that is most suited to their needs, as distinct from or in addition to the provision of short-term loans of a self-liquidating nature which has always been the province of commercial and merchant banking; and
2. a sense of purpose, a perceived role or mission, an institutional culture or a set of attitudes, which is reflected in:
— a readiness to promote, encourage and support industry;
— a willingness to accept a measure of responsibility for the performance of industry (for example, in recent years the German banks have devoted a lot of money and managerial time to the rescue of AEG-Telefunken; in Britain, the rescue of Rolls-Royce and British Leyland in the 1970s fell on the government, not the banks or shareholders); and
— an ability to understand the problems of industry, due to close relations with industry and the in-house employment of people with industrial experience and technical expertise, and therefore to accept what would be considered 'very risky' business by financiers who are ignorant of industrial realities".

Let us now take the examples a step further and look at a regionally based institution with close local links and a combination of financial and business functions aimed at company development, financing and restructuring. This regionally based institution is the clearest example of industrial planning and intervention by a financial institution.

Mondragon

A particularly interesting and innovative venture in financial planning, again with its own unique culture, has been created by the group of Basque co-ops centred on Mondragon in Northern Spain. This provides an important example of a regional institution. Central to their highly successful record of growth is the unique 'People's Bank', the Caja Laboral Popular (CLP). It co-ordinates financial flows to the co-operatives in its role as a credit co-operative or local savings bank, and it also acts as a strategic planning and consultancy body for the co-ops through its in-house Management Services Division.

In the CLP the Mondragon Group have developed a mechanism which combines a high degree of responsiveness to local economic needs with the discipline of financial expertise and planning. The Bank meets local investment needs through its management of local savings, maintaining close links between financial and industrial planning, allowing social policies to be pursued within a tight financial framework. This unique structure has protected individual co-ops from a number of the common problems affecting small and medium sized firms in the private sector.

The CLP was created by the infant co-operative group in 1959 to tackle the problem of raising investment finance. The co-operative venture in Mondragon was founded as a response to social and economic needs in the Basque region, which in the post-Second World War period suffered high unemployment and industrial decline. The first co-op was formed by five Basque graduates of a training school set up by a Catholic priest whose philosophy became the basis for the Group's policies on job creation, 'worker solidarity' in establishing wage rates, and the relatively low wage differential between the highest and lowest paid.

However, the Group recognised the need for a financial strategy. They wanted to increase the flow of investment into their local economy since their own cashflow yielded insufficient surplus to promote real expansion. The established banks refused help because the co-ops lacked sufficient assets to present as collateral and the co-ops themselves refused to accept outside shareholders. Hence the establishment of the People's Bank. Its role was to channel the profits of the co-ops and the savings of individual members back to the co-ops in the form of loans. The co-op's earnings were used to their maximum benefit and the traditional banks were by-passed. The CLP also played a wider role as a credit co-operative providing bulk purchasing facilities, marketing advice and running educational programmes. The central dynamic of the CLP is its desire to see a strengthening and extension of co-ops, who in turn are its major clients. As the CLP is also the strategic planner for the whole co-op group, their financial and industrial operations are brought together in one agency.

One result of this has been the impressive growth rates achieved by the Co-op Group. At the end of 1983 there were 162 co-ops in Mondragon, of which 88 were industrial, 8 agriculture and food, 14 housing, 44 educational, 1 consumer and 7 service and support co-ops. Between them they employed 19,000 people. The CLP itself is a fast-growing financial institution employing over 12,000 people in 141 local offices serving all four of the Basque region's provinces, handling 500,000 accounts. In 1982/83 it was taking £425 million worth of deposits from member co-ops and lent out £228 million backed by some £40 million of its own capital assets and reserves.

The fact that the CLP is a credit co-op has important legal implications for both its structure and its operations. In Spanish co-operative law, the controlling body in a co-op is the General

Assembly, which meets annually and elects a Control Board. The CLP Assembly decides all major financial matters such as the annual wage rates, the distribution of the surplus, and job expansion plans, while the Board deals with production and management issues on a day-to-day basis.

The growth of the CLP and the associated Co-operative Group over the last 25 years is a direct result of the tight financial policies that have been pursued. In many respects the CLP's Banking division acts as an ordinary bank, with standard charges and requirements. It acts as a clearing bank, an acceptance house, an agent for state funds, and as a lender. As well as the half million depositors, some 80 per cent of whose funds are on two year term deposits, a major source of funds comes from the Group's retail co-op, all of whose funds are held by the bank since their cash requirements are low. The principal sources of revenue for the CLP comes from interest on its loans and revenue from discounting bills, which are more profitable than the yields on state-authorised bonds, the only other outlet for CLP funds.

A distinctive feature of the CLP's banking operations is that the CLP and individual co-ops are linked by a legally-binding Contract of Association. Each individual co-op signs this in order to become part of the Mondragon Group. The contract outlines the financial aspects of the relationship, and also commits the co-op to various wider group policies on co-operative organisation.

The Contract of Association places clear responsibilities and constraints on the co-op, which surrenders some of its independence under Spanish co-operative law in return for the advantages of the CLP's financial and management services expertise. From the CLP's point of view the conditions reflect sound banking policies, which all individual co-ops must accept in order to avoid endangering the financial security of other members of the group. The CLP requires standard cover and guarantees from the co-op including a deposit of 25 per cent of the co-op's assets with the CLP. The co-op also has to submit regular returns and budget plans, in a format devised by the CLP, and accept an audit every four years. This enables the CLP to monitor both individual co-ops and the Group's overall performance. Any threat to loan repayment schedules on the part of an individual co-op could entitle the CLP to intervene.

The banking division of the CLP works closely with the management services division. Obviously complex planning is required to achieve successful banking operations that fulfil legal requirements that satisfy the Group's socio-economic aims, that meet the needs of individual co-ops and which also bring sufficient financial returns to meet long-term liabilities. All these depend on the health of the Group as a whole, and here the management services division plays a key role by providing expertise in all aspects of planning and development both for individual co-ops and the Group.

The success of the two divisions can be seen from the fact that the CLP has been able to show great flexibility in meeting the needs of co-ops in different phases of the Group's development. In the 1960s, the Group had relatively few funds. As a result investment priorities has to be determined carefully to minimise credit bottlenecks. The position was reversed in the 1970s due to the growth in co-op sales and the rapid expansion of accounts held by the public. The CLP then actively sought and helped create new investment outlets within the Group through supporting existing and newly-formed co-ops. The eighties have brought quite different problems, which will be examined below.

The management services division is organised around three main areas: promotion, assistance and engineering. Over 100 experts are employed, including economists, urban planners and engineers. The division charges commercial rates for services to the co-ops, but is not totally self-financing.

Promotion activities include the preparation of background product, market and sectoral studies, using an in-house product data bank, and help in launching new co-ops. This section was very active in the 1970s when 30 major new co-ops were launched. The assistance section offers services in exports, administration and accountancy, management staffing and commerce, whilst the engineering side focuses on town and country planning and the production and design of industrial buildings.

The activities of all three sections take place within a framework that prioritises both the needs of good banking practice and the wider socio-economic aims of the co-operative group. In the case of promotion activities, for example, the Group recognises that the investment of capital always has a socio-economic impact. It believes that the long-term needs of the local economy should affect investment decisions. Thus in the 1970s non-industrial ventures were included as co-ops to be supported. This had the advantage of allowing diversification in the Group structure, but also reflected wider aims including a recognition of the high level of ecological strain in an already highly-industrialised region; of the demand for low-cost housing and loans to purchase houses; and the need for promoting Basque culture and education.

The long-term strategy, on which investment planning in the 70s was based, continued to place most emphasis on co-operatives in the secondary sector. The main branches of activity are household consumer durables, machine tools and capital goods and house construction, with electronics a complementary branch. Foreseeing the problems that would arise in the eighties, priority was given to establishing an R & D Centre. The Group did not enter into extractive and capital intensive chemical industries, which were incompatible with the principle that new co-operators pay entry capital at 20 per cent of the total investment in the workplace. The Group only entered primary sector activities in areas of cattle farming and agriculture where there was a chance of developing independent chains, since much of the food sector is already organised by foreign multinationals. There was some commitment to tertiary sector co-ops in health and education.

A further factor affecting co-operative planning is that co-operative experience favours a maximum workforce of 500 in any single co-operative. Planning to achieve economies of scale therefore takes the form of forming links between groups of co-ops. Existing co-ops that are growing are encouraged to split off sections of their enterprise into separate co-ops.

Training has always had a high importance for the Group, and it runs its own polytechnic for industrial trainees and a management centre. Emphasis is placed on understanding the policy aims of the Co-operative Group and their implications for a particular job, as well as on the technical aspects of the work.

The Mondragon Group faces severe challenges in the harsher economic conditions of the eighties. Not only has there been a major recession, with saturation of existing domestic markets for several of its mass production lines, but there is also direct multinational penetration and competition in other product lines. The prospect of Spain's entry into the EEC threatens greater competition with other European producers.

Since the banking division of the CLP aims to maintain credit lines to co-ops in difficulty, the expertise of its management services division is vital. In 1983 an Intervention Agreement was established which states the terms on which the CLP can intervene in individual co-ops. Levels of intervention vary from weekly consultation through to the introduction of a CLP management team.

In 1983 there were 34 such interventions. This can involve 'reconversion', by which the management services division restructures the balance sheets of the co-ops. Where restructuring takes place the CLP will raise additional contributions from the co-op members. The CLP itself is prepared to make these up to £30,000 a job, when the long-term prospects are good. Intervention can also result in the CLP re-scheduling loan repayments. An alternative is recapitalisation whereby the co-op hands over an additional portion of its share capital to the bank.

The management services division has also been active in helping co-ops restructure their production lines. Whilst new entrants still pay entry capital, the labour/capital ratio has been relaxed to allow for major new investments in machinery. Ulgor, the oldest co-op, is preparing for a major role in the government plans for reorganising the white goods sector. The Group's R & D unit is already a pioneer of robotics in Spain. A major target for Ulgor is to bring production up to EEC standards, prior to Spain's entry into the Common Market. Ulgor reckons that 20-30 per cent increases in productivity are needed. To date increased productivity has been accompanied by transferring staff to other co-operatives rather than outright redundancy. In comparison other employers in the region have been cutting jobs.

Promotion groups are being set up to consider new ventures. These consist of management services division experts and individuals from the existing or would-be co-ops, under a CLP supervisor. The group undertakes a two year feasibility study, paid for by the proposers. The study has to be passed by a CLP joint-division technical committee before going to the Board of the banking division, on which management services division and co-op delegates are represented, for final approval. The Board must agree unanimously to the proposal before the new venture is funded.

In conclusion, it can be seen that with the financial and professional support, the CLP as a local agency has recycled savings into profitable business with a restructuring programme and employee involvement. A structure such as that of the CLP however does rely on the willingness of the workforce to continually reinvest rather than distribute its surplus. Critics have argued that this involves the workers accepting low financial returns which is another form of self-exploitation. Whilst interest yields are often below commercial alternatives, it should be recognised that this has been a deliberate and agreed policy based on the principle that long term wider socio-economic gains, including local economic growth, job security and job creation are more important than short-term maximisation of returns.

The United States and pension funds

So far we have looked at national and regional banking institutions which have various arrangements for linking finance and industrial planning, successfully or unsuccessfully. We now want to examine the alternative use of investment funds, namely pension funds. The growth of these initiatives in the United States is not state or bank directed but is the result of pressure from people themselves; the contributors to the pension funds who are concerned about the direction and use of their money.

American pension funds constitute one of the largest pools of private capital anywhere in the world. In 1984 the combined public and private funds' assets added up to approximately $900 billion and estimates predict they will increase to over $4,000 billion by 1990. Currently public pension funds make up about a quarter of this, and union-negotiated funds around a half, with the other quarter controlled by private employers. At the same time there has been growing concern from another direction about current investment policies. Out of the original upheaval of the civil rights movement in the 60s sprang several movements pressing for social change on issues such as links with South Africa, Chile, equal employment opportunities for women and concern for environmental damage. One common form of pressure was shareholder action, whereby groups bought shares or tried to influence major shareholders in the targetted corporation to put forward shareholder motions to change investment, sales, or production policies. Whilst these in themselves generated little direct change, an important spin-off has been the birth and growing importance of the concept of 'socially responsible investment', including the use of pension fund finance for local economic development. Activities and conflicts over the last decade have gone a long way towards clarifying both the legal framework within which pension funds should decide on local economic investment policies, and also on what constitutes 'socially responsible investment'.

The term 'socially responsible investment' (SRI) encompasses various economic, ethical and investment policy issues being presently discussed within unions, states, cities and the pension fund boards throughout the USA.

Socially responsible investments can be divided into two categories: first, where the investments are intended for the benefit of society as a whole, second where they are undertaken for strategic reasons, that is to benefit a particular section of the community.

The strongest advocates of SRI argue that economic returns may be secondary to the achievement of social results. The question of returns is crucial in the SRI debate with some critics arguing that the adoption of socially responsible criteria inevitably results in low financial returns. However a report by the Council on Economic Priorities on two large Californian public pension funds, whose assets totalled $17 billion in 1980, found that when two areas of investment in companies with corporate investments in South Africa and poor employee relations were excluded, this did not have any significant financial consequences for the fund's performance.

This conclusion has also been supported by a Franklin Research and Development Report, specifically prepared for the District of Columbia Hearing before its City Council Committee on Consumer and Regulatory Affairs. The study prepared an alternative portfolio of the DC Retirement Fund excluding companies in South Africa. It showed that over the previous nine years the Washington DC stocks related to South Africa had a growth in earnings and appreciation of 8 per cent p.a., while those not involved in South Africa averaged 11.2 per cent p.a.

But the South African issue is only a part of the general concern about using pension funds for productive purposes. The AFL-CIO, the US equivalent of the TUC, has established four principles of socially responsible investment:

1. To increase employment through reindustrialisation including manufacturing, construction, transportation, maritime and other sectors necessary to revitalise the economy.
2. To advance social purposes such as worker housing and health centres.
3. To improve the ability of workers to exercise their rights as shareholders in a co-ordinated fashion.
4. To exclude from union pension plan investment portfolios companies whose policies are hostile to workers' rights.

The AFL-CIO has recommended that a number of specific proposals be adopted:

1. That the unions take the initiative in working for the establishment of a new independent institution, partially supported by pension funds and aimed at the promotion of employment as part of a programme of reindustrialisation.
2. Encourage greater participation of union pension funds in programmes designed to increase employment.
3. Urge increased participation in the AFL-CIO Mortgage Investment Trust in order to increase the supply of housing for workers and other socially useful projects where there is a government guarantee of the investment.
4. Encourage pension fund trustees to exercise shareholder rights associated with the equity stocks held by individual pension funds and to explore the possibility of co-ordinating the

exercising of such rights.

5. Establish an information system to advise its affiliated organisations which companies should be considered unworthy of investment.
6. Establish a special training programme to assure that those responsible for determining pension fund investment policy have the knowledge they need.
7. Urge industrial unions, which traditionally have avoided involvement in the investment of their collectively bargained pension plans, to secure a significant role in such investment.

The American labour movement has managed to play an increasing role in the investment of pension funds for the benefit of workers and participants in a way which is consistent with legal obligations. It has maintained that within the area of equally acceptable investment risks, alternative choices are available so that workers' pension funds can be invested in ways that will achieve socially responsible policy objectives and still be prudent and attractive as investments.

But the alternative investment movement in the US has also developed positive strategies which will broaden the impact of pension funds. Work on formulating detailed proposals for local investment initiatives has been undertaken by task forces and special units in individual states by certain unions, and by independent research organisations. Whilst common principles are discernible, proposals have differed considerably in their details. This work proved that there are viable options for local investment which provide financially satisfactory rates of return. Particular interest has been shown in funding mortgages, small businesses and unionised companies.

Pennsylvania state has created a special investment fund to channel pension fund money to local businesses. The fund is sponsored by an independent agency created by the state in 1978 to foster local economic development, and which is made up of union, business and state representatives. The agency conducted a 12-month study to identify weaknesses in existing financial structures that were hampering potentially viable areas of the local economy. The study found that one-fifth of viable small to medium sized manufacturing companies could not obtain medium or long-term financing, and that some young high-technology firms could not obtain risk investment in the form of venture capital. The study recognised that pension funds might fill this gap because of their long investment time scale. It established various criteria for this including the requirement of a competitive rate of return; specialised investment management by a private sector firm; the pooling of investments with other investors; the opportunity to commit only a small percentage of assets; insulation from political pressures over investments and the ability to diversify in-state investments. The study commended that two funds be created, one to invest between $15 and $50 million in venture capital, and the second to invest $100 million in long-term fixed rate loans. The second fund was constituted in 1984 as the "Pennsylvania Private Placement Separate Account", managed by CIGNA Capital Advisors, part of a major insurance and financial services company with headquarters in Philadelphia, and a track record in this area of investments. Pennsylvania state employees' pension fund has agreed to invest up to $25 million in this scheme.

California State had its own in-house Governor's Pension Investment Unit from 1981 until early 1983. The Unit acted as a "public broker" between pension funds in the state and the capital needs of various sectors of the local economy. It also worked closely with unions to help them increase their influence and control over the private funds in which their members' pensions were invested. As part of the programme the State enacted legislation to encourage public funds to place at least 25 per cent of new money into housing schemes such as those which promoted low start mortgages for first time buyers. The Unit also developed plans for $280 million of investments in the federally guaranteed portions of small business administration loans, which could be originated by local banks and then sold off to the pension fund.

In Allegheny County, Pennsylvania, particular emphasis has been placed on job creation. The county encompasses Pittsburgh and surrounding suburbs where the effects of recession have been particularly severe. In response, the County Pension Board created a unit to supervise a programme whereby $1 million (equivalent to 1 per cent of total assets) of the fund is invested in federally insured certificates of deposit at a local bank, which then uses the deposits to make fixed-interest-rate loans to area businesses, whilst itself shouldering the risk of default. Eligible businesses include small manufacturing firms, retail shops, restaurants, food service businesses, office supply and equipment suppliers, and high technology firms.

Minneapolis Employees' Pension Fund teamed up with Minnesota based corporate controlled pension funds to finance new and innovative high technology businesses which offered long-term job creation in Minnesota. The pension fund invested $500,000 in "Minnesota Seed Capital Fund", entitling them to a seat on the Capital Fund's Board of Directors, with the right to review any major decision made by a company invested in, including labour practices.

Besides the public funds, many unions in America target projects for investment, both through the union structures and through their influence as trustee members on private pension fund boards. The New York State AFL-CIO at its mid-84 convention created a Pension Investment Policy Group whose brief is to assist and consult with public and private sector pension funds in establishing investment programmes which "could have a great and beneficial impact on economic and social well-being of union members and their families in New York". Pension investments formed the first item on the agenda at the confederation, in recognition of the fact that over $60 billion is invested in pension funds contributed to by union members in the state.

The UAW (United Auto Workers) have bargained with major employers, including Ford and General Motors, as part of their 1984 contract agreements, not only on company investment programmes but also on the investment of pension fund money. The agreements include the establishment of a joint UAW/GM committee to identify new businesses in which UAW members can be employed, for which up to $100 million of GM investments will be targeted. A similar agreement was made with Ford. The UAW/GM 'New Venture Fund' will receive proposals for new business ventures from local union-company bodies, so that existing skills and plants can develop new production lines. A second programme agreed was to invest up to $1 billion in a job bank designed to protect workers against job losses resulting from the introduction of new technology. The money will be used to retrain and reassign displaced workers. The joint committee will make specific recommendations to the GM's board of directors for final approval.

The 1984 agreements also contain clauses that alter the ways in which the pension funds for all the UAW employees in Ford are invested. GM and Ford have committed themselves to invest up to five per cent of new monies in housing and other socially desirable projects. In the GM case this is equivalent to $20 million in 1983 figures. Both agreements stipulate that funds will invest in residential mortgages in communities where there are substantial numbers of UAW members, as well as in loans to non-profit nursing homes, nursery schools, and hospitals in these communities.

Further, UAW will have the right to designate up to seven companies in which funds should *not* be invested. In the GM case this is left to the union's discretion, but the Ford agreement specifies that the designated companies will be those that have not endorsed the "Sullivan principles" which are codes of conduct for companies operating in South Africa. UAW has, since 1979, had the right to submit the names of five companies to be excluded from the Chrysler pension fund's new investments, based on their South African policies. Although the recommendations are not binding, the fund's trustees have so far complied with the request, and in the 1983 contract negotiations this was extended so that the union can now designate up to ten companies which have not signed the "Sullivan principles".

In conclusion, it can be seen that the attempts both to explore the boundaries of socially responsible investment, and to implement practical schemes, particularly those which channel money into local economic regeneration are still in their earliest stages. In particular, many of the local initiatives that have been created reflect the safest channels — such as mortgages and guaranteed business loans — in a narrow range of sectors, predictably including high technology. Our own experiences show that progress is necessarily slow in many of these areas, but the US demonstrates the broad spread of feeling by contributors that pension fund investment should be taken very seriously in any discussions about the use of finance.

II

New structures and policies: the GLC proposals

Analysis of the role of financial institutions and their functioning in the economy shows that the City fulfils certain tasks, many of which raise serious questions about their relevance to the needs of London and the British economy. In this section we want to argue that in order to meet economic and social needs and objectives a radically different structure of financial institutions is necessary.

Financial institutions have become larger and more centralised. There has been an increasing dominance of these institutions by overseas activities and a massive rise has taken place in the huge flows of global money which pass through Britain via the City. Despite the vast sums of money tied up in savings and deposits held by these institutions, there continues to be insufficient added to investment in productive industry in Britain's economy.

Indeed, with the growing trend towards deregulation, it is difficult to focus on the shifting boundaries between the institutions themselves. Mergers too contribute towards the growth and size of internationally based financial conglomerates, and the dangers of financial speculation and crises raise fundamental questions about control and regulation. The risk of financial crashes makes the GLC extremely concerned about the costs which will be imposed on people in London. Third World debt also imposes massive strains on the financial system. Already people in Third World countries are paying for this serious international problem.

The GLC is therefore concerned about the implications of existing financial structures and policies for:

a. the control of funds for long-term investment in the restructuring of British industry;
b. the control and regulation of the speculative tendencies in the financial system;
c. the control over the dangers and costs of financial crashes.

Social control

The role of the financial system is so crucial in the direction of economic activity that a thorough-going introduction of social control is necessary in order to meet our objectives. Social control would be necessary in order to achieve:

a. proper and meaningful accountability
b. democratic and popular involvement
c. investment in restructuring industry
d. better financial services for different groups in society
e. better employment conditions for those in the financial sector, and equal opportunities treated as a priority.

Traditional approaches to both public and private control of the financial system have serious limitations. Private attempts to link finance with industrial restructuring have floundered on lack of commitment and the lack of appropriate structures to plan and finance on the necessary scale. Proposals to regulate the financial system as it develops into a structure of conglomerates are based on private, self-regulatory structures with statutory backing. The history of self-regulation in the City does not provide convincing evidence that proposed structures can control the changes which have occurred in the financial system during the 70s and early 80s. The whole structure of accountability and democratic involvement needs a fresh approach.

The history of alternative proposals for the financial sector by the Labour Party and trade unions has swung from nationalisation to the establishment of minor public bodies offering cheap credits. In 1976 the Labour Party conference called for the nationalisation of the big four clearing banks and the top seven insurance companies. By 1982 the conference had amended its proposals to public ownership of one or more clearing banks if the banks failed to make appropriate changes in lending policies to support British industry, to improve services and bank supervision. What occurred between the 1976 and 1984 conferences was the establishment of the Wilson Committee to Review the Functioning of Financial Institutions. This was set up in 1976 by the Labour Government in response to the 1976 Conference proposals on public ownership. It recommended against nationalisation in the financial sector. A minority report of the Committee advocated the establishment of a National Investment Bank, following a TUC proposal to the Committee. The TUC advocated that 10 per cent of the cash flow of pension funds and insurance companies should be directed to the NIB. The funds would have a guaranteed rate of return. The objectives of the NIB would be to invest in companies and projects in Britain, but the mechanisms for investment and restructuring were left unspecified.

The proposal for a National Investment Bank, and other proposals such as sanctions on the clearing banks, if they failed to perform, go some way towards exploring the options for alternative investment strategies. However, the problems of accountability, control and supervision, of mechanisms for industrial restructuring, and of employment and services, require further substantial measures.

Some people argue that a National Investment Bank which provided cheap money and guarantees to industry, supported by strict exchange controls and credit policies, would provide an adequate framework for promoting investment in UK industry. They argue that radical measures such as public ownership in the financial sector would face massive opposition and would be prohibitively expensive. They also argue that the experience of Japan and Germany shows that an industrial policy, supported by the financial sector, does not require public ownership.

We do not agree with this. There is no doubt, as we have indeed argued, that the examples from other countries demonstrate alternative structures. They present powerful evidence that the relationships between finance and industry in the UK need to be transformed for a successful industrial policy. But one problem is whether they can be transposed from one country to another. The experience of Japan and Germany is based on such radically different historical circumstances, involving different long-term divisions within the industrial and financial classes which suggest that controls and cheap credits would not overcome the basic approach of finance in the UK. Subsidies or guarantees to banks and investment institutions are not sufficient to change approaches and policies (recall the loan guarantee scheme). It is also not clear that piling up pools of money to force-feed industry provides the means to direct or promote investment in the right areas and on a sound financial basis without a broader reorientation of the whole financial system. Another problem is that we want to develop financial policies and services, as well as employment policies in the financial and industrial sector which are more progressive than just replicating a German or Japanese system.

On the other hand we recognise that social control through public ownership poses the problems of strategy as much as it solves them. First there is the cost of the exercise. The cost of the 1976 Labour Party proposals would amount to around £14 billions (at 1985 prices), far greater than the public sector borrowing requirement. Should this amount of expenditure be switched to buy up the UK financial institutions all at once? Should there instead by a phased programme? If so, how should it be phased? Or is there an alternative which involves no cost? We have some proposals on this which will be discussed below.

Second, the experience of France suggests that public ownership is not a sufficient condition for industrial regeneration. It needs to be part of a detailed industrial strategy, with structural links between finance and industry. Public ownership, of itself, is simply not enough. We need detailed plans for investment in industry, and this means looking at the mechanisms proposed, regardless of whether we are discussing public ownership or some other proposals. Discussions and proposals on investment banks, public ownership, exchange controls, fiscal changes to encourage institutional investment in the UK, and many other proposals designed to promote industrial investment, leave a gap when it comes to the details of an industrial strategy. Many proposals offer cheap money to industry or they attempt to trap financial capital in the UK on the assumption that the demand for that finance will automatically appear. What is required is an industrial strategy, sector by sector, dealing with R & D and product diversification, marketing strategies on a company or sectoral level, and many other detailed matters on the basis of which finance can be applied productively.

Third, public ownership requires the personnel to carry out alternative financial strategies. Again, French experience suggests that there is a real problem in running the institutions once their ownership has changed. We may want to develop our financial initiatives in a way which gives people the confidence and training in the operations and management of alternative policies and institutions.

Fourth, there is serious opposition to public ownership. The trade unions in the financial sector have not been in favour of nationalisation, although they are not necessarily against it in principle. Trade unions are concerned about possible job losses as a result of nationalisation, although the implications of technological changes in the financial sector suggest that there have been and will be substantial job losses under private ownership. In the face of these losses, a changed system of ownership and control could enable employees to negotiate an appropriate structure of industrial democracy which would extend the power of employees over their working lives. In addition the recruitment and promotion of female and black employees could be radically advanced under new management policies consequent upon a change in ownership and control. The evidence we are aware of shows a marked absence of female and black employees at senior positions of responsibility within the financial sector. In our view, the prospects of these employees would be greatly enhanced within a socially owned and controlled institution. But these arguments have got to be won.

Fifth, public ownership, however defined, would also create the danger of reprisals on the foreign exchanges. The French raised interest rates in order to prevent speculation against the Franc but this can only survive as a short-term measure. A threat to impose stringent exchange controls will just force the money out of the country sooner rather than later.

These five points are fundamental to the debate about social control. Policies on public assessing pose issues of cost, of industrial strategy, of personnel, of trade union attitudes, and of financial reprisals. We need *a strategy* on social control.

We believe that there is a key role to be played by local, decentralised structures developing investment strategies, by the greater use of pension fund finance in a socially responsible and democratically accountable manner, and by expanding other local financial services. These decentralised structures should be part of a national policy of intervention in the financial sector aimed at increasing democratic accountability, but which raise new possibilities for addressing some of the issues raised earlier.

Local structures

As part of policies for increased social control, we see the need for more locally based, socially responsible and democratically accountable financial institutions. Through the development of new locally based institutions with an enhanced role for local authorities, we believe it is possible to extend the debate about the control and direction of the financial institutions.

What, then, are the principal arguments behind a locally based dimension to the financial sector?

First, the size of the tasks of formulating and implementing a strategy of industrial recovery will be immense. To expect this task to be solely organised at a national state level is both ineffective and impractical. The history of the 1974/79 Labour Government's industrial policy clearly emphasises the weaknesses inherent in a centralist approach. The perspective was inadequate and even contradictory in relation to the objectives it sought to achieve. The development of the 'popular planning' movement of workers plans, industrial democracy, user control and the other attempts to create a basis of grass roots influence over the organisation of economic relations, is testimony to the problems of statist conceptions of economic planning. There needs to be a powerful extension of this movement not least to consider the questions of financial institutions too.

Second, the very nature of the impact of Britain's economic recession raises the importance of a locally based approach to alternatives for recovery. The evidence available points to wide disparities and inequalities in the impact of deindustrialisation; despite the generality of unemployment, marked territorial differentiation exists. Indeed the different consequences of the recession for different localities necessitates a differentiated policy response by alternative economic and social strategies. It is by recognising the way in which regions and localities are particularly affected by the recession that enables the development of a more responsible set of policies to operate. Responses to employment change, trends in local labour markets, seasonal shifts of trade and production, the crisis of company restructuring, the generation of new products and new patterns of distribution; these factors require a strong input from regional and local level.

Third, we believe that a more socially controlled and thus publicly accountable financial system will be helped by measures which promote a more locally based dimension. This will facilitate greater popular involvement by savers and borrowers, by companies and their workforces, coupled with more public discussion and political debate. In short, the extension of a local dimension to the financial sector will open up opportunities for exercising greater social control, thus facilitating wider public accountability and involvement in the role and direction of financial institutions. But this dimension is easily ignored in debates about the control of finance.

As we have seen, the dominant tendency in the history of British banking and investment has been towards centralisation. The latest threat to regionalised institutions can be seen in the Conservative Government's policy on the future of the Trustee Savings Bank. The Government's proposals on the Bank also form another link in its strategy of privatisation.

The Trustee Savings Bank has long been an anomaly in the eyes of the banking establishment. This is due to the Bank's unique objective of putting its customers' interests first, and its ability to gear its services towards working class communities. From the 1950s the Bank grew in size, and wanted to offer new services, such as cheque books and lending facilities. On these and other issues it was vigorously opposed by the traditional banks and the Treasury. In response to the pressure from the TSB's management and customers on the one hand, and the pressure from the clearing banks on the other, the Treasury set up a special committee to consider the TSB's future. The view of the committee was that the TSB should become a people's Bank, and in the proposals it made a central point that the Bank should be made into a 'mutual' organisation as part of a structure of regional banks — run for the benefit of the staff and customers, as opposed to outside shareholders. The depositors would own the TSB and elect at least some of the board. As it was unclear who owned the Bank, the committee decided it should become a 'People's Mutual Bank' operating under Friendly Society law (like co-ops).

However in 1982 proposals for selling shares in the Bank were announced. This will help to destroy the individuality of the Bank, encourage it to pay less attention to the poorer social class groups, and undermine any possibility of a more regionalised network. The shares will end up with the big centralised investment institutions. Banking, Insurance and Finance Union (BIFU) members within the Bank fought against the sale but failed.

Our argument is that there may be a strong case in the interests of employees, consumers and local economic development, for a local dimension to policies aimed at the reorientation of the role of finance. Some of the limited practical examples already exist in the UK. We should build on the more positive aspects of these cases in considerations of central and local policy for private sector finance.

Yorkshire Bank The Yorkshire Bank is owned by three of the big high street banks (plus Williams and Glyns), but operates some different policies. In 1983 current accounts increased by 24 per cent. It concentrates on the Yorkshire region and offers free banking, in contrast to the big four who (with the exception since

November 1984, of the Midland Bank) insist on a minimum £100 to qualify. In 1983 it was the top performing bank in the industrialised world in terms of returns on assets. This is despite aiming for the 'unbanked' population in the North. Its expansion has in fact led it to open more branches and recruit more staff.

Motherwell Municipal Bank This Bank was founded in 1924 and is owned by Lanarkshire County Council. It was set up in order to bring banking to the working classes and to give the Council an alternative source of borrowing. A recent accountant's report found that interest saved by the Council as a result of borrowing from the municipal bank, rather than the Public Works Loan Board or the private money market, was £75,000 a year. Depositors also received a higher rate of interest than they would have obtained from commercial bank deposit accounts. However, the bank is constrained in its activities by the requirement from the Bank of England that it lend only to the council. But there is a proposal to promote the bank further amongst potential depositors by establishing a bank office which would be both a bank and a rent and rates collection point.

Royal Bank of Scotland The main reason for considering the Royal Bank of Scotland is the way in which it can be described as a regional bank, not controlled from London or overseas. Within the UK, Royal Bank holds about five per cent of the total assets of the clearing banks. In 1981 both the Hong Kong and Shanghai Bank and Standard Chartered Bank (a British registered bank with predominant overseas activities) made bids for the Royal Bank of Scotland. The Bank of England had previously agreed to a bid from Standard and Chartered. However, the Monopolies and Mergers Commission examined the proposed mergers, looking at, amongst other things, the desirability of 'maintaining the balanced distribution of industry and employment in the United Kingdom'.

The Commission recommended against the mergers, stating that there was value in preserving such independent local centres of business initiative as survive in the United Kingdom. "The links of the Edinburgh financial community would no longer be with a major Scottish bank with complete power of decision, and personal contacts would not be with a chief executive of a genuinely independent clearing bank". The report amplified this:

> "We foresee a detriment to the public interest in Scotland in the case of either merger arising from the removal of ultimate control from Edinburgh. Major decisions on marketing, investment, company strategy, risk-taking and expansion would naturally and rightly be the concern of the centre, whether it was in London or Hong Kong. No doubt a great deal of responsibility would be delegated to the local

> management in Edinburgh; we do not envisage large scale intervention day-to-day by the centre. But it would be unreasonable to expect either parent to give full autonomy to a part of the business which, however substantial and well-run, was at the policy level dependent on and linked with the overall operation of the group. The vast majority of individual business decisions would continue to be made on the spot in Scotland. But we would not expect the general policy stance of a London or Hong Kong based owner in relation to the expansion of Scottish business and the support of Scottish initiative to be as sensitive to local interests as a native management based in Edinburgh. Nor would we expect management to be as quick to respond".

In other words, there was a clear opinion that a regionally successful bank could operate outside the general trend of mergers and concentrations of decision-making power. It was deemed to be economically efficient for Scotland to retain a locally based institution. A *local and independent* financial system was a crucial ingredient for local economic development. As mergers and deregulation proceed, institutions lose their local identity. A growing concentration of power among few financial institutions means that people and communities have less influence over the direction of capital.

These examples provide further clues as to the scope for alternative financial structures and alternative policies.

They show us:

a. local banking opportunities for the 'unbanked';
b. socially responsible use of finance;
c. the importance of local links between finance and the community;
d. employment opportunities in expanding local services;
e. profitable opportunities in areas which avoid uncontrolled international lending.

We want now to explore three themes which will bring out the implications of a local dimension to our approach; we will concentrate on the following issues:

a. a more *socially responsible* use of finance for people;
b. *closer links* between finance and industry; and
c. how links between finance and industry can be forged by *establishing interventionist bodies* where industrial restructuring and investment can be matched by the funds required.

Local investment

If decentralised structures are to be an important part of our strategy for social control let us deal with an important aspect of this, namely local authority pension funds.

We have seen how powerful the role of pension funds and other forms of institutional savings can be. Our argument has been that these huge sums should be directed towards new objectives. A later section of this chapter considers the establishment of a Pensions and Investment Resource Centre one of whose inspirations has been the potential role to be played by local authorities. Here, then, let us examine briefly how local authorities can help the diversification process of the institutional funds' investment into real opportunities at local level.

In our view pension fund investment in the increasing number of local initiatives now under way would help to provide long-term capital for companies in different areas of the UK. These local initiatives aim to bring together the companies, sectors, and industries in need of restructuring, marketing, diversification, and so on, and match these plans with the appropriate finance.

The last point is particularly important. One of the arguments put forward by pension fund managers is that there is a shortage of investment opportunities in the UK. Local enterprise boards could provide some alternative vehicles for pension fund investment because they offer funds local information about investment opportunities and are involved in an active way in promoting investment.

It is clear that many companies are in need of financial restructuring because of the heavy debt commitments they have taken on in recent years. As we have seen, the approach of the banks is all too frequently to call in the receiver and close down the company regardless of the long-term prospects of the company. Local enterprise boards can perform a crucial role in acting as leading investors in companies, providing risk capital which enables a company to operate on a more secure long-term basis. Pension funds would obtain the benefit of real growth in these companies.

So far, the Greater London Council, Lancashire County Council, Merseyside, West Midlands and West Yorkshire County Councils have established enterprise boards. Other local authorities are moving in the same direction. A network of such local boards would offer pension funds a range of investment opportunities in British industry which would lead to the promotion of economic growth and employment opportunities.

Local authorities administer over £15 billion of the £100 billion of pension fund investments. Investment agencies which mobilise local authority pension funds for local investment could help to bring together local economic development policies and the investment requirements of local authority superannuation funds, as well as the other public and private funds.

The development of Enterprise Boards should be aimed at creating local investment banks with full merchant banking and investment functions, extending their role so as to provide a full range of financial services for companies. The mobilisation of pension funds makes a start in the creation of local institutions with a powerful role to play in the channelling of public and private funds.

Responsible investment and local authorities

But this still leaves untouched the large block of shareholdings and other investments held by the savings institutions — the pension funds, insurance companies and various trusts. What are the issues which arise from consideration of the broader economic and social relevance of these investments? What if we are concerned about the activities of companies (and banks too) that we invest in with our savings? Have we a right to consider whether these companies act in the interest of the local and national economy, whether they pollute the environment, promote equal opportunities, trade with unstable or unacceptable regimes, and so on? Local authorities have a very significant role to play as administrators of over £15 billion of pension fund investments. They may be particularly keen to ensure that investment practices are consistent with broader public objectives.

Of course, it is often argued that taking such factors into account will damage the financial rate of return on investments. Pension funds, we are told, as well as other investors, have a duty to invest where the return is highest, and broader economic or social concerns are not necessarily relevant to this. As the National Association of Pension Funds and the Confederation of British Industry have stated:

> "Pension funds should have one duty only — to their pensioners. They should not be obliged to concern themselves with any outside interests, even the public good".

Well, firstly, it is a mistake to pose as alternatives, 'financial investment' and what is defined in a derogatory way as 'social investment' or 'the public good'. This is because there may be a range of 'social' factors which affect the performance of an investment in financial terms, even assuming that there is one objective definition of narrow financial investment. These factors may mean that a company which is likely to have unsatisfactory industrial relations, that could create consumer enquiries into the quality of its products and services, that could generate government and legal concern over its health and safety, equal opportunities, and race relations provisions, that could suffer setbacks through trading with South Africa, that could be disinvesting from a local area or being taken over through poor management, that one or all these things make a company a more unsatisfactory long-term investment. This may be the case, it may not. But what these factors establish is that it is legitimate to take into account broad areas of corporate activity in making investment decisions. This means that a prudent pension fund trustee should consider all aspects of investment decisions.

Of course, implementing broader criteria of more social and economic concern is scratching the surface of the problem. The main issue is the mobilisation of funds at the national and local level to become more involved with domestic production, and to become less internationally based, less part of the flows of capital between multinational companies and banks. The 'responsible investment' debate has a deeper relevance to discussions about the accountability and use of money for local and national needs. In this sense a broader system of social control is vital if the local initiatives are to be made more relevant to social and economic needs.

GLC initiatives

The role of local authorities in the development of an alternative financial strategy has been considered crucial. The way in which local authorities have extended their role in tackling the problems of deindustrialisation, employment and company collapse is not new, but the recent period has shown how new and more interventionist approaches can be developed. The link between the work of the GLC on formulating a London economic and industrial strategy, and the approach outlined in this document is being made by the work of the Council in particular projects. In this section we outline projects which are a small beginning to some local financial initiatives which should be part of a new strategy. We deal in turn with local investment of pension funds; with local, socially responsible investment policies; with local banking possibilities; and with the specific issues raised by local finance for black business. We then move on to say more about the initiatives which we feel should be considered for national policy.

The London Development Capital Fund

The London Development Capital Fund has been formed as a Unit

Trust with a life of ten years to enable pension funds, in particular those for employees of local authorities and organisations with strong regional involvement in the Greater London area, to promote investment in a number of unquoted United Kingdom companies based mainly in the Greater London region. This initiative has been pursued under the joint auspices of the Finance and General Purposes Committee and the GLC Superannuation Fund Investment Staff Joint Panel.

The Fund will draw on investment proposals from a range of sources, including Enterprise Boards and Economic Development Units in the local authorities in London. Such investment will assist with the retention and stimulation of employment and the expansion of the economy of the Greater London region.

There are three components in the management of the Fund; the managers, an Investment Panel and a Supervisory Board. The managers, who are a small merchant bank, will be responsible for the day to day management of the Fund; to identify, research and negotiate investment propositions for consideration by the Investment Committee; to monitor and assist in the development of companies in which the Fund has invested by means of close liaison and board representation. They are also required to keep the Investment Committee fully informed of the progress of the Fund's investments and to prepare half-yearly reports to unitholders on the progress of the Fund.

The Investment Committee will meet on a regular basis to ensure that the investment policies of the Fund are properly implemented and to keep the progress of the Fund's portfolio under review. All the investment transactions of the Fund require the approval of the Investment Committee. The Investment Committee comprises five members; two appointed by the managers and three independent appointees who have experience of industrial investment.

The Supervisory Board enables unitholders (pension funds) to maintain liaison with the managers and the Investment Committee, and will consist of up to eight members of which five will be elected by and from unitholders at the Annual General Meeting of the Fund.

This Fund provides a unique opportunity to bring together local authority pension funds in the London region with employment retentive or generative projects. There will be a clear link through the local authorities and the Fund, for projects that arise from the work of the authorities.

The Pensions and Investment Resource Centre

The origin of the Pensions and Investment Resource Centre lies in two recent developments taking place amongst local authorities. First, a number of local authorities are expressing growing interest in the way pension funds affect local and regional economic development. Second, local authorities who themselves manage their own pension funds, are becoming more concerned with the way that the activities of companies they invest in affect the other functions and responsibilities they carry out on behalf of their constituents.

The proposal to set up the Pensions and Investment Resource Centre emerged as a result of Local Authority Pension Fund Conferences held by the West Midlands County Council in 1982, by Merseyside County Council in 1983, and by the GLC in 1984. This annual conference, which brings together representatives from local authorities who manage pension funds on behalf of their local authority employees, had established two working parties which studied the questions of socially responsible investment by such funds, and the potential resources of these funds for productive investment in UK industry.

In this way, a broad approach evolved which sought to explain the relationship between the investment strategies of local authority pension funds and other functions and responsibilities of these authorities. Over the last few years a new philosophy of investment strategy has been debated amongst local authorities. This is based not only on sound commercial investments able to provide a suitable financial rate of return, but also takes into account the responsibilities of local authorities to promote and maintain certain standards in social and economic life on behalf of their constituents.

Under the impact of economic recession and with the associated process of local and regional economic decline, many local authorities have been considering how they could shape their pension fund investment strategies towards those opportunities which may have direct or indirect effects on their local and regional economies. With the emergence of local and regional Enterprise Boards and other direct investment agencies, local authorities have begun to determine new parameters to their investments. Many local authorities are now developing new initiatives to invest pension funds in their localities, either through enterprise boards or through mechanisms organised around specific projects. These initiatives are based on the need to mobilise pension fund resources for viable companies that require selective intervention to provide appropriate financial resources for consolidation, expansion and restructuring.

Coupled with these developments with regard to economic

regeneration, many local authorities have also begun to be concerned with socially responsible investment (SRI). Socially responsible investment is a way of combining the traditional pension fund investment principle, or matching future liabilities with real assets, with the promotion of social and economic benefit, and the avoidance of social and economic injury. At the local authority pension fund conference, a speech given by Dr Robert Schwartz, from an American bank, outlined the American experience of SRI. The speech has been published in pamphlet form by the GLC.

Consequently, the services provided by the PIRC do not relate solely to a local authority's responsibilities in the field of economic and industrial regeneration. Local authorities come into daily contact with companies in their constituencies in a variety of ways. The establishment of commercial contracts; the management of planning permissions; inspections (environmental, consumer, legal) for example, all involve knowledge, analysis and monitoring of companies, their operations, their structure, financial viability and product/service suitability.

There are also new demands that many local authorities are now making: in relation to positive action policies on sex and race: occupational health and safety standards; and employment, industrial relations and training requirements. The interaction between local authorities and companies operating within their constituencies seems likely to increase.

The PIRC provides a unique service under one roof and a mechanism for democratically elected bodies to promote responsible investment policies.

Local banking and other financial services

We have dealt so far with pension funds, an important part of the British *savings institutions* which include the local authorities. People in London and other areas, including the employees of local councils, not only save through pension funds, they also use bank accounts for their more immediate needs. Companies not only need long-term investment capital from pension funds and Enterprise Boards, but they also need bank finance for long or short-term borrowings. Can local authorities mobilise bank-type funds from the private sector for local lending?

A municipal bank could be aimed at attracting deposits from those sympathetic to an alternative and local banking institution which is distinct from the main clearers. These deposits could come from public bodies, trade unions, individuals and pension funds; it could offer a banking service for the 'unbanked'. Although the proportion of the population which has a bank account has increased to over 70 per cent, this varies from 89 per cent in the highest socio-economic group to only 17 per cent in the lowest. Furthermore, by providing overdrafts and loans for community/co-operative/women/ethnic initiatives, the bank could offer a real alternative to the existing banking system.

However, in the establishment of the new trade union bank — Unity Trust — it was clear from the experience of the trade union banks in Israel and Germany, that a bank should nevertheless aim at a broad deposit and lending base in order to survive and grow. Within this broad base it is possible to specialise and direct funds to particular areas and groups. In this way a municipal bank could be complementary to the investment activities of GLEB and the proposed GLC/London Borough pension fund consortium in providing a range of short, medium and long-term financial instruments for London projects.

A municipal institution could use various outlets for its deposit taking and current account business: e.g., housing offices on council estates, a giro system for rents and rates bills offering the bank as administrator of half-yearly or monthly payments.

The German trade union bank (BFG) deals primarily with short and medium term deposits and credit operations and offers a full range of banking services. About 10 per cent of banking business involves trade unions and co-operatives. The argument is that if it were just a 'housebank' for the labour movement, it would be dealing with one customer group on each side of the balance sheet. Instead, a bank's function is to accept money from as many people as possible with as varied repayment dates as possible and to make loans with varied maturities to a broad customer base. The greater the explicit specialisation, the greater the reserves necessary to cater for the higher liquidity ratios required.

A bank also requires a large equity base to facilitate expansion in lending. But there is a need to retain control over the institution if it is to be locally accountable. The Israeli Bank Hapoalim has a two-tier structure of equity, only one of which is voting.

Credit unions are different from banks in that they are aimed at enabling a specifically identifiable community group to pool financial resources for that group's benefit. They cannot accept deposits from the general public, and they cannot lend outside that group. They are important and relevant for particular groups, but we also want to extend the scope of local banking.

The GLC and other local authorities would be crucial in marketing the concept of a regional bank in London, using town halls and other municipal buildings as local branches. Londoners would also be able to subscribe for equity in a London-wide appeal to contribute to 'your local bank'. The total equity of such a bank would be about £2-4 million. A small number of voting shares could be distributed to individuals. Further capital would rank as non-voting equity, with the majority of shares held by the local authorities.

Local enterprise boards, local authorities and other bodies and individuals, would have a London regional bank to use. The Bank could also establish a pension fund management service for investing in British projects. This will therefore give Enterprise Boards a further source of funds, perhaps in some cases for projects that cross local authority boundaries (e.g., larger companies).

A first step in moving into the area of tapping local funds might be for enterprise boards to issue local bonds. This would help overcome one of the biggest problems with the existing financial system, namely, a clear identification between local savers and the responsible investment of their money in their own locality. Such local bonds could have wide local appeal, enabling people to see their savings coming back into their own area.

Local banking is not economically inefficient. There may be opportunities for smaller banks, with a local base, to have a more flexible approach, to identify particular local markets, and to avoid the huge fixed costs of the large clearing banks. It might be assumed that small banks would fail to compete, and would not therefore be economically efficient. They have certainly been taken over in their droves over the last century and a half.

But this is to confuse, in part, market power with economic efficiency. A local bank may play an important part in the local economy, as described earlier by the report from the Monopolies and Mergers Commission. It may provide a particular type of personal service as with the Yorkshire Bank, which is difficult although not necessarily impossible for a larger and more centralised bank. The local bank would need a national clearing system for cheques and for surplus deposits. In this way, local banking is at least complementary to a national system.

Lending to ethnic minorities

In recent years the problems of bank lending to ethnic minority enterprises have received increasing attention. This has been partly an attempt to understand and resolve the factors which have contributed to the marked absence of a strong black business sector in the UK. It is also in part a response to the problems of mass unemployment, the incidence of which is much higher amongst the ethnic minority communities. A further and important contributory factor has been the importance attached to self-help measures, that stimulate confidence, economic independence and political strength, and release the massive untapped energy and creative potential that exists within these communities.

The problem of ethnic enterprise has been succinctly summarised by the Runnymede Trust who, in surveying a cross-section of Asian and West Indian businesses, found that small firms owned by Britain's ethnic minorities suffered serious disadvantages and were seriously under-represented amongst businesses in Britain. Such disadvantages include difficulties in obtaining finance, premises and business advice generally. The most intractable of these difficulties is that of finance, which is exacerbated by the lack of communication between the ethnic minority communities and the financial sector, the clearing banks in particular. As Clive Woodcock, the *Guardian*'s small business correspondent notes, this is as much a product of "the banks' insensitivity to the needs of black firms, particularly in the marketing of bank services, the essentially negative views of bank managers about their black business customers and the attitudes of black firms to bank borrowing".

However, once such 'difficulties' are overcome, black and ethnic minority enterprises often find collateral requirements for loan and overdraft facilities excessive. For example, a survey of ethnic enterprises by Hackney CRE found that for an overdraft facility of £25,000, the ethnic minority firm was required to provide collateral of five times that amount.

The banks vigorously deny that such discrimination exists. They argue that the only criteria used are financial. Morever, they argue that the intensity of competition, and the pressures on bank managers to increase branch profits necessarily precludes the rejection of any viable project. The problem they suggest rests with the ethnic enterprises themselves, who seldom produce basic accounts, cash-flow forecasts or coherent plans to justify their proposals.

Although it is not denied that such a problem may exist, this only partially explains the difficulties ethnic businesses have in obtaining finance. "The simple if unacceptable truth is that too many of those responsible for the running of our financial institutions have a prejudiced stereotype image of the ethnic minorities. As a result, Asian, West Indian and other ethnic business people find that they are required to fulfil exacting conditions in return for receiving less financial and investment support than small businesses set up by members of the majority community in Britain'' (*Black Business: Redressing the Balance,* GLEB).

There are a number of alternative policies being explored to deal with these problems:

i. A variety of business start-up schemes with funds earmarked for black enterprises and allocated in a conventional banking manner or in some instances through grants.

ii. The GLEB schemes — GLEB FIN and GLEB LAA, which emphasise the interventionist investment approach, rather than the more traditional banking approach, in their support for black enterprises. GLEB FIN provides finance for a range of feasibility studies. GLEB LAA has started with an initial £300,000 to be invested in targeted sectors, where GLEB's sectoral knowledge and the material expansion of black enterprises in those sectors can give much greater support and thus prospects of success than the normal small firm financing schemes.

iii. A black Enterprise Board. This could build on the experience and principles of GLEB LAA and implement it on a wider scale.

iv. A black bank. One such proposal is the Afro-Caribbean Bank. It has five objectives. First, to establish a financial institution to serve the needs and requirements of the Afro-Caribbean community in London through the provision of high street banking facilities, including taking deposits from and encouraging saving amongst that community. Second, through such an institution, to give sympathetic consideration and positive assistance to the business development needs of members of the Afro-Caribbean community who wish to establish or develop business in London. Third, to enhance the expectations of the Afro-Caribbean community by establishing a financial institution staffed progressively from amongst its members. Fourth, to ensure, as far as possible, through its financial structure, that such an institution is primarily owned and controlled by the Afro-Caribbean community. Fifth, to seek to influence the criteria and lending activities of existing banks by evidence of the success of such an institution.

The crucial factor that will determine the ACB's financial success or failure would be its ability to acquire a strong deposit base. This would be determined by the marketing skills utilised and the support it can raise from amongst the Afro-Caribbean community and the wider black and ethnic minority communities. If banking facilities are required, the experience of trade union banks in other countries suggests that a bank should aim at a broad deposit and lending base in order to survive and grow. Within this broad base it is possible to specialise and direct funds to particular areas and groups.

Questions have arisen, however, as to whether the objectives of the bank are compatible with the proposed structure. It is said that an ethnic minority bank would have to be very cautious in its lending decisions, especially if operating with a narrow deposit base. Banking operations are subject to requirements, by the Bank of England, in particular affecting debt to equity ratios. So, 'positive assistance' and 'sympathetic consideration' may well be restrained by financial conservatism. This will be reinforced by the need to provide dividends for bank shareholders, which may be the antithesis of positive assistance to the business development needs of the Afro-Caribbean community. The more restrictive the bank is in its operations, the less able will it be to meet the business development needs of the black community. In this light we would want to maintain the importance of financial policies for ethnic minorities as part of the investment and banking strategy of a broader based institution, both at local and national level.

These issues are in need of detailed examination. GLEB has funded a feasibility study which should provide additional information on options for a black bank at the local level.

These then are our proposals for introducing a local dimension to new policies on finance which start to deepen the debate about social control. But they need to be placed in a national context which also takes into account our earlier discussions on the parameters of policy.

National policy

We have outlined some practical proposals being undertaken by the GLC. These proposals are related to our concern about the decentralisation of investment decision-making. They also say something about our concern for a change in the relationship between finance and industry, and about accountability of investment. They suggest a new dimension to discussions of social control. The new dimension includes a role for local democratic bodies as part of a reorientation of the financial sector. Local structures are essential as part of a national strategy for social control. But these proposals only take us so far. Policies for finance and industry, and for accountability, need to be developed at the national level.

1. Regulation and accountability

We have argued that the changes taking place in the financial system in the 1980s make the issue of regulation a crucial one. The danger with bank crashes and financial collapse is that taxpayers and savers have to pay for rescuing the system. We have experienced the nationalisation of some secondary banks after the 1973-5 financial crisis and the nationalisation of Johnson Matthey Bank in 1984. This is nationalisation to rescue banks. At the same time the City and the government have proposed mechanisms for self-regulation, with varying degrees of statutory support, in order to promote fair competition and consumer protection.

The main points of the Conservative Government's policy can be summarised as follows:

— the promotion of competitiveness and efficiency; freedom for market forces to stimulate competition and innovation;

— self-regulation within a new statutory framework, to be provided by new legislation in 1985/6;

— two regulatory bodies are proposed, one to regulate the securities, investment and future industries, and one to regulate the marketing of life insurance policies and unit trusts;

— action by the financial institutions themselves is proposed in order to make the self-regulatory proposals a reality; in other words, the new regulatory structures should be devised and administered by the financial sector itself;

— the new structures will rely heavily on existing regulatory mechanisms such as the Stock Exchange.

The Government hoped that regulatory systems could emerge which command broad support and co-operation: this would make it "the more likely that the arguments of those who call for close, detailed Government control over the financial services industry will be confounded".

The problem is extremely important when we consider the changes occurring in the City. The securities business, the stockbrokers and jobbers, along with pension fund management, and often insurance too, will be increasingly controlled by one newly merged group, headed by a foreign, UK, clearing or investment bank. Regulation has become a more general problem, affecting banking, securities, fund management, insurance and unit trusts, all of which will be subsumed under conglomerate institutions. It is debatable whether regulation based on *functions* (securities management and so on) can cope with an increasingly complex system of mergers between what were once separate *structures* or institutions.

It is argued that it is 'outsiders' that cause all the problems for the regulatory systems. It was the 'fringe' banks in 1973-5, Johnson Matthey in 1984. It is argued that the clearing banks and the rest of the banking system have been operating relatively satisfactorily. But there are two problems with this argument. First, the clearing banks have some of the major over-exposures to Third World debt which could threaten the rest of the financial system if the debt 'crisis' became a major financial crash. And second, some of the new financial groupings are being formed by 'outsiders', namely, foreign institutions. It is not at all clear that the regulatory proposals and procedures can cope with the potentially explosive implications of Third World debt, as well as all the other potential problems of conflict of interest and fraud which can only increase as a result of the merger between different institutions.

For example, the 1979 Banking Act gives the Bank of England the right to information from banks. It can establish lending guidelines, but these are not legally binding. The Bank's main powers lie in the approval of new banks, and in cajoling others, where it has relevant information. If it is not given the appropriate information, it cannot act. This is a perfect example of the weakness of voluntary regulation. On the other hand, setting up a public supervisory body, a quango run by a selection of 'the great and the good' does not increase the ability to control and direct in a detailed and accountable manner. The experience of the Bank of England underlines this.

Regulation refers to the prevention of criminal fraud, and to unfair practices which may affect the consumer. Under a monopolistic regime with restrictive practices, as the City used to be — brokers having their monopoly, merchant banks their's and so on — there was abuse. Under a liberalised regime there will still be fraud and there will still be unfair practices. The crucial question is therefore, how publicly accountable are the regulatory bodies themselves? This accountability should include a greater degree of public involvement, perhaps through democratic accountability.

We therefore argue strongly for more public sector involvement in the financial sector. Regulatory mechanisms need strengthening to enable people to know that the institutions are accountable. There is a clear need for more democratic accountability. *We propose that there be a public sector stake* in a clearing bank-led financial group, a merchant bank-led financial group, and a foreign institution-led financial group. This would substantially strengthen regulatory mechanisms by involving the public sector in the constantly evolving nature of financial services. It would make the public sector a part of the financial system in a way which would increase public accountability. The public sector would not *run* these institutions on a day-to-day basis. But it would have the power to increase accountability in order to protect deposits and savings. We argue below how this can be done at minimal cost.

These proposals are a logical and technically coherent way of providing information and control over developments in the financial sector. Liberalisation or deregulation has enormous potential dangers for ordinary people as savers, taxpayers and depositors. The world-wide move towards internationalisation of bond and equity markets must be accompanied by effective public control. This public control can lead towards the financial sector becoming more a part of the national planning of the direction and use of finance which is more consistent with the needs of consumers, employees in the financial sector, and different social groups and minorities.

2. Finance and Industry

There must be a national planning apparatus which creates methods and vehicles for restructuring industry and providing investment funds. As well as a revamped National Enterprise Board for industrial reorganisation and reconstruction there should also be a National Investment Bank, but one with rather different powers and functions than proposed hitherto.

Just as initial stakes in financial groups are an important part of a satisfactory structure of accountability and broader direction of finance, so stakes in industrial companies should be part of a successful strategy of industrial restructuring. We have seen the close links between companies and banks in Germany as lenders and investors. German banks hold shares in companies as well as acting as lenders. Large Japanese groups have their own banks as part of a close system of co-operation between finance and industrial planning. How then can we create these close links which form a *qualitative* basis to a new relationship between finance and industrial restructuring? We need planning bodies with stakes in finance and industry in order to create the appropriate mechanisms. Below this national apparatus for finance and industry the local and regional investment organisations will operate, providing a fine-tuning and locally sensitive approach to investment and finance within the parameters established by the NEB and NIB, which in turn would have to be democratically accountable, with political representation on the Board.

Let us first of all try to link the need for interventionist bodies at the national level with the need to consider the investment functions of the pension fund system, since investment funds must be closely linked to the mechanisms for industrial reconstruction.

The structure of occupational pensions is usually divided into its three component parts: the private sector, the local authority sector, and the rest of the public sector. It is anomolous that within the public sector there is a pension scheme for civil servants which is non-contributory, which has no 'fund' for investment, and which pays benefits on a 'pay-as-you-go' basis whereby pensions are paid as and when they arise, out of taxation. In the nationalised industries, public corporations and local authorities, there are separate 'funds' which are invested. There is the National Coal Board Pension Fund, one for staff and one for mineworkers. There is a local authority pension fund in each county, with the constituent district council employees contributing to a fund administered by the relevant county council. In London, the boroughs have their own individual funds, and the GLC has its own separate fund. London Transport also has a separate fund while outside London, the Passenger Transport Executives and their staff contribute to the metropolitan county pension fund in their particular area. Teachers and the fire service also have different arrangements within the public sector.

In spite of all the differences in contributory or non-contributory schemes, and whether the funds are administered by county council, borough, transport authority, or nationalised industry, the pension *benefits* are very similar, particularly insofar as they are underwritten by ratepayers and taxpayers, and they all provide for inflation-related, or index-linked benefit. Basically, therefore, despite all the differences in the administration of these public sector funds, the benefits are the same, and they are all underwritten by the state, or rather by taxpayers and ratepayers.

However, whilst these schemes are part of the public sector, they, like private company schemes, are influenced or directly controlled by the City. They are a part of the financial system which could be part of a national plan to benefit industry and the economy *without any* effects whatsoever on benefits.

We propose that local authorities retain their pension funds because of the scope for democratic accountability which already exists. The rest of the public sector pension schemes should be merged into one pay-as-you-go system based on the civil service model. The assets, or investments, held by the public sector pension funds, their holdings of shares and other securities, should be vested in the state.

Public sector pension funds, the nationalised industry and public corporation funds, are amongst the largest in the UK. They represent about a quarter of all pension fund assets. Since pension funds as a whole own 30 per cent of all quoted equities, about 7.5 per cent of the stock market would be owned by the state; in other words 7.5 per cent of ICI, 7.5 per cent of National Westminster Bank, and so on. Obviously these are only average figures, and the precise percentage in any one company will vary around this norm; some are much higher, some lower. We suggest that this shareholding should have certain special rights, based on the concept of the 'golden share' introduced by the Conservative government in its privatisation of companies like British Telecom. This special shareholding entitles the owner to be consulted and to control certain activities of the company, which we would extend to investment and employment policies, and to appoint Government Appointed Directors. The role of the special shareholder would concentrate primarily on overall policy parameters and monitoring, rather than day-to-day management.

We further propose that the shares in the financial sector be placed under the control of a National Investment Bank, which would operate as a state holding company with stakes in the financial system in a way which follows on from our earlier proposals on regulation. The stakes in industrial companies would be placed under the control of the National Enterprise Board. The shareholdings under the control of the NEB would then be used as part of sector planning and industrial restructuring.

We would therefore develop two powerful institutions with stakes in the financial and industrial sectors to further the policy objectives outlined in GLC strategies.

Our proposals for national policy are therefore as follows:

1. Public ownership, or public stakes in key financial groups to increase accountability and regulation.
2. Public corporation pension schemes to be changed to pay-as-you go schemes, and their funds' investments vested in the state.
3. The public sector pension fund shareholdings in the financial sector would be placed under the control of the National Investment Bank. The shareholdings in industrial companies would be placed under the control of the National Enterprise Board.
4. The National Investment Bank would become an important arm of the state in the financial sector. The National Enterprise Board would use its shareholdings to further sector strategies and industrial restructuring.

Chapter 13

An Alternative European Strategy

Stuart Holland

In the 1970s several socialist economists active in their own European parties realised that the demise of Keynes and the rise of the New Right meant loss of commitment to full employment policies, and a crisis of ideas and institutions threatening the principles of a welfare state and society. They also grasped that the economic crisis triggered by the OPEC price increases from 1973 was not short term or cyclical, but structural and long term, reflecting fundamental changes in the previous balance of power between national governments and national capital. Sovereignty itself was in question with the rise of multinational industrial and financial capital, yet the European communities aggravated rather than remedied such sovereignty loss. New policies were needed to mobilise a project which could counter the crisis of monetarism and market forces with a new European agenda which could defend jobs and welfare and extend effective sovereignty through joint international action.

The result was *Out of Crisis: A Project for European Recovery* (Spokesman 1983), sponsored by key members of the incoming socialist government in France in 1981. This process of research, reasoning and dialogue involved several meetings of not only the initial group (many of whom now are in parliament or government) but also of political economists and trades unionists from over a dozen European countries (including Scandinavia). The arguments of *Out of Crisis*, on the imperative for recovery, restructuring of power and redistribution of resources, became part of the new thinking of the European Left and were endorsed in the opening statement of the joint manifesto of the Confederation of the Socialist Parties of the European Communities for the 1984 elections to the European Assembly. More recently, the main theme of *Out of Crisis* has been adopted and extended by the *Global Challenge* report of the economic committee of the Socialist International, chaired by Michael Manley (Pan Books, 1985).

A 'Euro' AES

In itself, the *Out of Crisis* argument was already familiar to activists in the British Labour movement since its arguments amounted to an extension of the Alternative Economic Strategy originally shaped and endorsed by the Labour Party in the early 1970s. If it advanced on these it did so by making the case for joint action international rather than simply national, and by extending the reasoning of the AES from the case for an alternative economic strategy to an Alternative Economy and Society. Nonetheless, *Out of Crisis* did not address specific institutional issues in the European Community framework. This was both because it first was necessary to make the case for joint recovery itself, and because its arguments ranged wider than Community Europe alone — including Scandinavian countries and parties and unions in countries which are not members of the EEC. In line with long standing analysis on the European Left, it claimed that the key issue was a realignment of social and economic forces for change, rather than whether — or not — one was a member of a particular institutional grouping within part of Western Europe.

Thus the *Out of Crisis* project paid special attention to the social and political base for economic recovery. This is made plain in particular in Part 4 of the project on 'Forces for Recovery'. It also stressed that short-term recovery of spending and jobs alone would not shift Europe out of crisis without a related shift of resources through redistribution and a restructuring of the prevailing imbalance between unaccountable private and accountable public power.

Restructuring is a highly contentious issue. Faced with the Japanese industrial challenge and dollar dominance in the international arena, it is clear that no recovery programme can gain political credibility if it follows European Community lines in insisting that the same policies be pursued in the same way in the same countries at the same time. However, in the *Out of Crisis* report itself and in the discussions which led to it, we stressed that unanimous multilateral agreement by all countries was not necessary for a recovery dynamic to be sustained. Joint recovery programmes pursued by some key countries would promote recovery in others. Also, while some countries may choose to seek to stimulate recovery by indirect means such as fiscal and monetary policy, other countries will undertake direct public expenditure programmes and adopt a range of complementary planning instruments.

Redistribution nonetheless is crucial to a major recovery

programme over the medium term. This must mean (1) redistribution within countries between different social groups and classes of wealth and power, of working time, (2) between the private and public sector in different democratic forms covering both spending and enterprise, (3) and between urban areas and regions. But it also must mean redistribution between different countries within Europe and in the global economy. This links directly with the current phase of the North-South dialogue and the degree to which like minded governments can and should take joint initiatives for the recovery of spending, income, welfare and trade.

Regional and Social Redistribution

Employment is a key argument for recovery of the European or global economy. Yet with the impact of new technologies such employment cannot simply be seen in a return to 40 hours a week plus overtime for all. It must mean planning as a process of social negotiation of change in employment structures, with public action to ensure that the productivity increases from new technologies are redistributed to defend and extend prevailing levels of both personal and social income. But if this case is to be supported by joint action between parties, unions and governments of the Left through Europe, it also means jointly addressing both common *and* uncommon problems in our respective countries.

For instance, faced with the axe in government spending on urban programmes in the UK, Labour controlled metropolitan and local authorities have applied for EEC funding for inner city projects under the Community's social programmes. None of the Labour councils see this as a substitute for adequate national government funding to finance employment. But it has a role to play now, just as joint action by Left governments to sustain mutual recovery could offset foreign trade constraints and help generate resources for real renewal of our inner city areas. But for some of the main parties of the European Left such de-industrialisation of inner city areas and urban decline is secondary to rural poverty. Much of the political base, whether in France, Greece or elsewhere, comes from poor or unprosperous self-employed farming families — often organised in producer cooperatives — rather than multinational agribusiness.

At present it is the Common Agricultural Policy which supports such marginal income groups through an inflated price and protection level which allows them to survive, while agribusiness makes an institutional monopoly profit, and consumers everywhere pay inflated food prices. The British Left with reason has criticised the CAP on these grounds for years. What is needed is a joint policy which reduces support prices for agriculture yet ensures that the marginal farming families are not shifted off the land nor consigned to rural poverty.

Regional and Social Funds

This implies either national intervention by member governments, or Community intervention or both — on regional and social funds. There are two main problems with the regional and social funds of the EEC. The first is the manner in which the Commission — rather than Community member states — dominates the administration of the funds. The second is the altogether derisory resources involved — partly through understandable member state reluctance to transfer major resources to the Commission on regional and social funding where each member government has its own major programmes.

For instance, the total EEC budget on own resources is one per cent of Community VAT which is itself a fraction of one per cent of Community gross domestic product. Since agriculture now dominates some three-quarters of total resource spending, the regional and social funds have been reduced to less than five per cent (and more recently around 3.5 per cent) of the Community budget. In other words they amount respectively to one twentieth of the budget as a whole. In addition, only around one tenth of the regional budget takes the form of net transfers between countries. Thus the net transfer of resources between European countries and regions resulting from the regional fund of the Community represents between one two-hundredth and one two-thousandth of one per cent of Community GDP.

As can be seen from such ratios, a nominally major political initiative such as a 'doubling' of the regional fund would amount to slightly more than two × zero. It would in no sense represent the kinds of resource shift needed for the recovery of Europe's most problematic regions, far less for the recovery of the European economy.

By the same token a 'Marshall Fund' for the Mediterranean countries, if equivalent only to the resource transfer of the regional fund would be entirely cosmetic. While no doubt representing worthwhile individual projects, around a half of the regional fund spending of the Community at present takes the form of infrastructure investment in roads, irrigation, water control systems etc, several of which have in any event substituted for domestic programmes undertaken by individual member states. In the British case, the refunded rebates from the Commission are not distributed to the regions but are taken off the public sector borrowing requirement by the government.

Another key criticism of the Social Fund at present reflects the retraining and redeployment context in which it was first shaped in the 1960s. In other words, the social fund can pay resources to employers who are undertaking retraining programmes for workers. In the current slump syndrome, it is not surprising that such claims on the fund are limited. Certainly it in no way confronts the problem of social funding the fiscal deficit faced by all member governments as the slip from recession to slump means declining real wages, declining social security and pension contributions, and an inability (compounded by the lowering of effective taxation on private sector companies) to finance social security and unemployment benefits for the growing mass army of Europe's unemployed.

There is no way — even by doubling or trebling the resources allocated to the Community's *own* funds — in which they can contribute through redistribution to the economic recovery imperative for the survival of international cooperation at the European level.

Redistribution and Recovery

But real redistribution is an essential component of recovery. It is central to the needs of Left governments which face a fiscal crisis due to rising unemployment, lowered direct and indirect tax revenue, and an increased social security and unemployment budget.

In these respects there is a central link between a joint recovery programme and effective financing of either social or regional budgets spent by member states (supplemented by the Community) over the medium-term.

There are national and regional differences in the fiscal argument. For example, it has been estimated for the United Kingdom that for an unemployed couple with two children gaining unemployment benefit, supplementary benefits and family income supplements, it costs no more to create employment for at least one member of the family (thereby reducing the state's unemployment expenditure and gaining both income tax and indirect VAT) than to maintain the persons concerned on the dole.

This is a powerful argument directly relevant to the situation in not only Britain but also in the more developed Northern European member countries such as Denmark and the Netherlands which are facing a major fiscal crisis and anticipating the reduction of real social benefits. Compounded through at the macroeconomic level, this aggravates the under-consumption dimensions of the present crisis and further deepens the slump syndrome.

In Southern Europe by contrast, where a welfare state and society framework is much less developed, similar arguments could not be applied. Nonetheless, the priorities for establishment of a social welfare framework in the Mediterranean countries implies long-term expenditure programmes which can only be afforded within a major European recovery framework.

It is in this context that the arguments of the *Out of Crisis* report are directly relevant to the question of social funding by the member states of the Community (supplemented by Community action). In other words, if European recovery both is to occur and to be sustained, the central areas of the Community should be able to support development deficits in those countries which need major long-term expenditure in order to sustain their recovery from slump.

While it is difficult to change the prevailing perceptions of subsidy in some of the Northern European countries, the basic Keynesian argument on circularity of income and expenditure is relevant to the centre-periphery dimensions of social and regional spending in the Community. If Left governments in Europe proceed with social welfare programmes implying raised real consumption over the medium term, this implies higher import demand and thus mutual export trade between European countries. It is the social and wider European regional dimension of the import-export dualism and the fact that one country's imports are other's exports.

Such wider social and regional redistribution of resources by member governments cannot meaningfully be accommodated within the framework of the present European Commission. The sums are too large and the challenge to own resource spending — with reason — too strong. The 'own resources' issue, with its federalist implications, gets in the way of feasible joint international action for recovery. Apart from which a major increase in the Community's own resources arguably should be opposed in the medium term until it has been demonstrated that improved mechanisms for its accountability can be established and adequately monitored by both the European Assembly and national parliaments.

International versus Supranational

The argument for a 'Euro' AES focused on recovery *through*

redistribution therefore implies an alternative strategy for Europe. It means recognition that the present Communities are stalemated both by their ideas and their institutions. There has been as much a 'false start' for European cooperation after the war as there has been a 'false start' elsewhere in many Third World countries. Much of the problem lay in the supranational and federalist pretensions of its founders.

Undeniably the founders — including Jean Monnet — both thought big and for the long term. But they also found it hard to escape the framework of past failures in political co-operation. On the formation of the European Coal and Steel Community in 1952, Robert Schumann famously declared that through such integration "a future war between France and Germany would be not only morally unthinkable but materially impossible". Even this declaration was without real foundation: when hostilities had begun between France and Germany with Guderian's tank push through the Ardennes, the electricity grids of Western France and Eastern Germany already shared a power switching arrangement. When German bombs damaged a French power station, French engineers telephoned their German counterparts, asked for the switching of so many megawatts through to the French grid, and got it.

The illustration is not facile. It demonstrates that economic integration *per se* does not lead to political co-operation. Again, as is well known, in 1961 the first President of the EEC Commission Walter Hallstein stated bluntly "we are not in economics at all — we are in politics". The politics of such founding fathers were supranational and federalist. Aiming to avoid the weakness of the League of Nations in the face of prewar fascism, the founders of postwar European cooperation aimed for a federal framework which would bind even major member states. Federalism was embodied in detailed constitutions (including the Paris and Rome Treaties). Its actions would be initiated by independent supranational bodies, and infringements tried before a supranational Court of Justice.

The political vision was for a United States of Europe. This had a pleasingly familiar ring to those in the United States of America who sought closer political cooperation between predominantly 'moderate' or Centre-Right governments in an unsettled Western European countries which only recently had seen Communists in coalition in government in major countries such as France and Italy.

If West European integration in the early 1950s had been seriously concerned with avoiding war, it would have looked at the two main protagonists in Europe at the time and determined that a Third World War in Europe between the new superpowers of East and West should be not only morally unthinkable but materially impossible.

Had they so wished they could then have built on the foundations of a wider East-West European economic co-operation through the United Nations Economic Commission for Europe, established in 1948 in Geneva and for some eight years under the inspired chairmanship of Gunnar Myrdal. Potentially the most influential regional economic commission of the United Nations, the ECE was marginalised by the dynamic of the 'first' cold war. Its outstanding characteristic of including all the West and Eastern European countries, was lost for a generation, and its potential never realised. Both sides of Europe must share some of the responsibility for this.

Meanwhile, rejecting the most promising framework for economic cooperation between East and West Europe, the West European federalists pushed hard for not only economic integration, but also the integration of European defence and politics. This political drive linked the formation of the Coal and Steel Community in 1952 with the proposals for a European Defence Community in 1954. Blocked by the French parliament, this was followed by equally abortive proposals for a European Political Community made in 1955 by the Dutch. In 1957 when Euratom and the EEC were agreed it was widely considered at the time that the integration of joint research and development in the field of atomic energy would be far more important than the customs union and economic union proposals made in the Rome Treaty. In a real sense, the EEC was the sixth compromised start for European economic cooperation.

Further, the efforts at postwar European integration were unrelated to wider social and political forces in Europe at the time. The reasons for this lay not only in the heightening of the 'first' cold war but also in the difference between the main parties of the European Left. Although it is worth recalling that virtually every major Left party either opposed the Rome Treaty or expressed profound qualifications on its introduction, there was less convergence and alignment between the wider European Left at the time than is evident on a broad basis for recovery and employment now.

An accent on free movement of trade and factors of production was more acceptable in the full-employment 1950s when investment, employment, incomes and trade were expanding at unprecedented rates than today in conditions of international economic disintegration and slump.

Also, the federalist pretensions of the founding fathers were only *implicit* in the Rome Treaty itself. The Treaty did not refer to a United States of Europe as such, even though its proposals for procedure to majority voting in the Council of Ministers was supposed to take place from January 1966, i.e. precisely the date at which De Gaulle having left an 'empty chair' in the Council of Ministers the previous summer, forced through agreement on the Luxembourg compromise on unanimous voting.

Cooperation versus Integration

The issue for Europe now, deep in crisis, is not whether to cooperate but what to do in common. Similarly, the aspirations of Europeans — East and West, North and South — are not whether to fiddle with farm prices but to determine joint alternatives to poverty, low pay, the decimation of welfare benefits, and mass unemployment. The European agenda should be less concerned with butter mountains and wine lakes than with shifting the money mountains of Europe's collective resources into projects for the joint creation of jobs, security and welfare.

The real criticism of the EEC is that it is not European. Its failure to include most of Scandinavia, Austria and Switzerland consigns it to only part of Western Europe. Eastern Europe is subject to technology dependence on US multinational capital and to debt trap from the IMF rather than opened to real economic and financial relations with the rest of the European continent.

The EEC also has failed its own main objectives. The CAP was supposed to be the prelude to a CIP or Common Industrial Policy, leading through economic to monetary union. No meaningful progress has been made by the Community on the industrial front in a quarter century. It has not even properly defined a European Company Statute, and has recently gelded even the anodyne Vredeling proposals for economic democracy in multinational companies. In twenty five years it has failed to restrain the growth of multinational capital or make it genuinely accountable. While the Commission has sought to liberalise trade between countries in the community the main beneficiaries of economic integration have been big companies — less than 150 of which now account for a third of its gross domestic product.

As attempted through the EMS monetary union has been a fiasco. Ten years into the current crisis, it has failed the key function of aiding expansion of individual European economies.

Meanwhile, multinational capital has integrated Europe's money markets on its own terms. The Eurodollar and Eurobond market is a money mountain. Now in excess of $1,000 billions — a sum equivalent to the national income of some half dozen community countries — it is a monument to the power of unaccountable private capital and the failure of the community to harness private finance to public need, dwarfing butter mountains and swamping wine lakes. An equivalent sum put to work over ten years (a net addition to West European expenditure of $100 billions a year — on the lines of the *Out of Crisis* project) could create the 20 million jobs which Europe needs to avoid mass unemployment over the next decade.

Put simply, as already stated, the Community has been integrating the wrong things in the wrong way. Joint policies against monetarism and to harness multinational finance capital are imperative for European job creation. Left European governments — in and out of the Community — need a framework in which they can jointly plan for the recovery of spending, employment and welfare. Agricultural integration is virtually impossible when the productivity differences between Portugal and Denmark for comparable farm products are as much as 1 to 15. France cannot easily allow Spain in the Community because this would undermine the economic base of the small peasant (rather than rich capitalist) farmers on whom the Socialist Party has depended for a century for support.

The EEC's institutions also prevent rather than promote joint international action. The Monnet vision of Europe depended on a supranational body — the Commission — making proposals. Neither the Council of Ministers nor the European Assembly can propose action to the Commission. What should be a springboard for action has become a bottomless letter box.

One reason undoubtedly was the over-ambitious federalism of the original Coal and Steel Community and Rome Treaty proposals. The Community Treaties entail not only formal acceptance of majority versus unanimous voting, but also specific powers given to the Commission in the form of directives which are supposed to be binding on member states. Such directives range through the main Community policies enshrined in the Treaties, and specifically in coal and steel, transport and agriculture. In purely legal terms they give precedence to the Treaties and the Commission's powers over any national legislation.

Re-shaping Europe

However, a new Messina conference should address itself not only to the process of decision-making inside Community Europe but the wider issues of how to relate the at present relatively disintegrated parts of Europe, East and West, North and South.

1. A *real* Community of Europe would mean institutions which include representatives from the East, the North and South of the continent: i.e. those countries within Comecon, Scandinavia and Iberia which at present constitute the periphery of Europe, yet should be central to its agenda for action.
2. Such a Europe would find a way of bringing together the issues jointly confronting this wider Europe and the wider world. It would seek to relate the roles of the UN Economic Commission for Europe in Geneva (which already includes all the West and East European countries) as well as EFTA and the OECD, and make a reality of the North-South Dialogue.
3. The European Assembly is a talkshop rather than a workshop. But an Assembly of the whole of Europe — however hard to achieve — would be a project worth promoting. It could promote issues for joint international action, put before the institutions of the EEC, EFTA, The Economic Commission for Europe, and OECD — real issues of countering monetarism and harnessing finance capital rather than harmonisation of rear view mirrors and vehicle registrations.
4. Such a Community would be explicitly international rather than supranational. Proposals from a new more representative Assembly would carry support by merit of their argument and the social forces they can mobilise at a European level. Endorsement would be by national parliaments which would remain sovereign for the peoples they represent.
5. Implemention of such proposals should be by those governments which support them, rather than the lowest common denominator approach of either unanimous agreement in today's Council of Ministers or the would-be majority voting favoured by the supranationalists.

Re-Shaping Instituions

Europe's major institutions present a picture of relative disintegration. EFTA and the EEC are not directly or systematically related for joint policy initiatives. Similarly, while the COMECON countries are part of the United Nations Economic Commission for Europe, and while this nominally includes all the West and Eastern European countries, both COMECON and the ECE have been marginalised relative to the main political dynamic of the European Assembly and the Council of Ministers.

We need to focus the argument on a possible potential role for a new European Assembly and a new Council of Ministers, relating to the four main economic institutions of which the European countries either separately or collectively are members.

The representation again indicates the marginal role of the Economic Commission for Europe, but it nonetheless is striking that the two institutional bodies of which all the Western European countries are part are the ECE and OECD.

A new Assembly and Council in this wider sense could represent *all* Western European countries. Inversely it would not imply that all COMECON or Eastern European countries should be members of the Assembly and Council. Clearly this is nowhere near the agenda of practical politics. By contrast, however, the possibility of those countries which would elect delegates to the wider European Assembly and send representatives to the wider Council of Ministers (a Pan-European Assembly and Council in substance if not in name) would mean that as Western European members of the Economic Commission for Europe they could both propose initiatives through the ECE secretariat in Geneva and also in principle dispose of resources in terms of mutual finance and credit arrangements as well as joint Technology Agreements within a wider European programming framework made possible by both the existence and technical skills of the ECE itself.

Re-Shaping Decision-Making

Clearly any new European institutional framework of this kind needs to confront decision-making and issues for feasible joint action. Such issues include countervailance of multinational capital, on joint reflation, social and regional policy, where European countries should be able to shape common policies. This implies three principles for common European policies.

1. Joint policies should be sovereignty extension rather than the sovereignty loss implicit in federalism. Joint policies based on common interests should be actively pursued at the European level, just as they are pursued — in principle, through other international organisations. But if such policies are to prove effective, they must be based on an identification of specific common problems as the basis for joint international action, rather than the assumption that all problems are common, demanding comprehensive integration.

2. The concept of sovereignty extension means international rather than supranational institutions. This implies a major change on the principles of majority voting which should be forwarded by like minded governments within the key institutions affecting Europe — and especially the EEC. This is the principle that

unanimous voting should still apply for any policy which is supposed to bind member states, but that majority voting should be possible for those states which intend jointly to pursue common objectives such as economic recovery and job promotion. Thus as opposed to the necessary negative veto on measures which individual member states cannot accept, affirmative positive voting for joint action should be possible for those like minded governments which wish to pursue alternative policies.

Such policies could include not only recovery programmes which could be self-sustaining if implemented by enough countries — as elaborated with quantitative support in the *Out of Crisis* project. They also could encompass joint policies accounting for and gaining greater accountability over the multinational companies which now command so large a share of Europe's output and employment, on the lines of the Planning by Agreement approach already endorsed in Labour Party policy in Britain, and by the socialist governments of France, Italy, Greece and other countries. They could include multinational joint ventures between public enterprise (whether national, regional or local) in different European economies, backed by the share of Community resources represented by those governments which voted to support them, rather than no common industrial strategy worth naming at the Community or wider European level.

Those who do not wish to take part — such as the Thatcher government in Britain or the Kohl administration in West Germany — could duly vote against without being bound by the policies, even if, in the case of recovery — and if they last long enough — they would indirectly be beneficiaries through increased exports to other European economies pursuing expansion.

3. The principles of sovereignty extension and international decision-making also further imply the principle of provisional versus irreversible power. As with the right to differ, this is a basic condition of democracy: it implies the right not only to changed views, in changed circumstances, but also the right to reverse administrations and policies.

Clearly, one reason for the failure of majority EEC Council voting lay in the view of France and its role held by De Gaulle. But De Gaulle's opposition to majority-voting reflected a real difference on the role of State power between France and other governments in the Community. Such differences are important not only in the sense of avoiding a banal and uniform Europe where social life and institutions become homogenised to the lowest common denominator, but also are essential to the working of the democratic process itself. Democracy depends both on the right to differ and to be different. Granted not only the unequal economic power, but also the differences between Left, Right and Centre in the Community, the defence of difference and the right to differ at a European level is crucial.

As with the right to differ, provisional power is not simply a Right-Left issue. Even US federalism does not imply irreversability. With the support of Congress, an incoming US President can reverse policies of a previous administration. European Community integration is exceptional in the irreversability implied by both the Treaties themselves and the powers of directives granted to the Commission.

To some extent, such admission of the principles of (1) sovereignty extension, (2) international decision-making, and (3) provisional power reflect the *de facto* situation in the European Communities.

The role of national parliaments and governments could remain sovereign inasmuch as governments decide and parliaments endorse or reject through a widened Council of Ministers on policies in the European arena.

By the same token national parliaments jointly with the European Assembly debate issues but also proposed initiatives to the Commissions and secretariats of the EEC, EFTA, OECD and ECE, with recommendations also made by them to the joint Council of Ministers.

There is a parallel between this approach and the variable geometry concept, or different shapes and configurations for different speeds, levels and roles — whether for aircraft or institutions. It has the advantage of allowing differences to be respected within a common political framework (like in a common airframe). It transforms the two speed Europe proposals to rationalise an inner fast and outer slow area into a more plural Europe within the concept of a real Community.

This would be a Europe of common geography and culture, a convergent Europe working for consensus where it can be achieved, but allowing and even encouraging differences where these best suit the economic, cultural and social diversity of the countries or areas concerned. It would introduce political choice for changed options into the structures of hitherto unaccountable Euro-institutions.

Re-Alignment

Such changes would amount to an institutional re-alignment, a change of form and substance in Europe. They would complement and reinforce the case for other major initiatives such as European nuclear disarmament. Just as a nuclear free zone does not depend on a single decision taken by NATO or the Warsaw Pact, but can be built through free zones reinforcing those already in place in Scandinavia and *(de facto)* in Iberia, so progress to full employment and welfare through Europe could be pioneered by those countries willing to counter the crisis through joint action.

Re-alignment complements non-alignment. But re-alignment stresses the process of working towards a more autonomous Europe with an authentically independent role in world affairs. It does not mean that we are anti-Soviet or anti-American. It means that we are able to harness our own talents, skills and experience in shaping our own destinies. It means not relying on US recovery before we shape our own strategies against the slump, nor waiting for an outcome to US-Soviet negotiations — such as those at Geneva — before opting for non-nuclear defence.

Such re-alignment cannot come from the top alone. European nuclear disarmament is a live issue because it is supported by millions of people through Europe across sectarian and national divides: women, the churches, academics, peace activists, trades unionists and politicians. The European recovery project stemmed from socialist economists many of whom now are members of parliament or of governments. But it also reflects strong trades union interest through the regional and local level in individual countries, and now has broad support in the ETUC and the Socialist International.

Nonetheless, re-alignment will not succeed unless it shifts the European debate beyond the EEC and its limited terms of reference. It must relate more directly to people's real needs and offset their real fears. Through Europe these are essentially jobs, welfare and survival. The real security for Europe does not lie in reductions of some warheads or weapon systems but in restoring the right to security of employment, housing, health, education and social services, as well as non-nuclear defence.

Such issues should put the current squabbles over the EEC budget into perspective. Everyone is divided on the budget as it is — fiddling with farm prices while Europe slowly burns with mass unemployment. The real European budget, on which broad agreement exists — outside Thatcher's Britain and Kohl's Germany — is for joint spending on a scale which can recover welfare and trade, restructure the social sector of the economy and redistribute resources to eliminate poverty and low pay. This is the $100 billion a year budget of the European recovery project. Such re-alignment means shifting our thinking from the Rome Treaty and the eye of the needle in Brussels to real joint action to spend our way out of the slump.

Ends and Means

Faced with such issues, whether individual countries are members of the EEC as it now is should be a secondary rather than primary question. Any continued membership should be conditional on joint action to promote major changes within both the Community and the wider Europe spelled out above.

The aim of European nuclear disarmament is obstructed by the socialist government in France. But much of the socialist party is opposed to tactical nuclear weapons and some Giscardians (certainly with some dissent) have criticised the government's independent nuclear deterrent policy as 'suicidal', calling for a non-nuclear defence policy.

The aim of European economic recovery by contrast is unanimously shared by all the main parties of the European Left. More urgently, their governments face political oblivion if they cannot deliver real change within the next few years by joint action to counter the slump.

In such a context an Alternative European Strategy itself should be a means rather than an end in itself. As already stressed, the end objective for the new European Left — in France, Greece, Spain and Scandinavia — is nothing less than an Alternative Economy and Society. As the Right replaces the welfare state by the warfare state of cruise missiles, Pershing II and first strike, the European Left has to offer an alternative to blood, sweat, dole and tears. In principle a Labour government in Britain could go-it-alone farther and faster than other European economies, for a time, due to energy self-sufficiency. But if we go-it-together we gain mutual 'better my neighbour' increases in trade and spending rather than the 'beggar my neighbour' defeatism of deflation and devaluation.

What we now need is both debate and increasing support for such a political project, reinforcing rather than reducing the power of governments and movements to act in the international economy. Such an Alternative European Strategy widens rather than narrows the options for the peoples and parliaments of Europe, and complements the major new initiatives taken in the Socialist International's *Global Challenge* report. Its methods and agencies — including proposals for a more genuinely European assembly — are important but secondary. The primary task is to shake Europe loose from its inertia and the threads which bind from Brussels, by placing joint action to transcend the economic and social crisis, by new means, onto a new agenda.

Afterword

Ken Coates

The reason that some Labour movements have been cautious about the growth of economic co-operation in Europe is not difficult to pinpoint. With all their faults, European national governments have, since the second world war, operated under a series of effective democratic restraints. For decades of near full employment, the growth of social consensus and welfare persuaded a majority of working people that real democratic achievements were possible within the given constitutional framework. In some countries the Common Market offered real scope for economic growth. In others it presupposed important economic changes, which were by no means welcome among large sections of the population. But whatever the reaction of workpeople to the threat or promise of EEC membership, until recently it has been generally assumed that nation states acting independently or even alone, have offered an adequate framework both for macro-economic management and such reforms as were thought to be necessary.

Slump has undermined these expectations without charting alternatives. Some socialists believed, two decades ago, that a severe economic recession would provoke capitalist corporations to look for international institutions in order to recover initiatives which were no longer possible on the reduced national scale. In the event, multinational capital has been more than tardy in fulfilling such prophesies. Beyond doubt, nation states bear the responsibility for maintaining vital infra-structures in education and communications, and equally beyond doubt, slump has rendered this task more and more impossible. But multinational capital has obtained such marked advantages from the collapse of national regulatory mechanisms that it betrays no anxiety to render feasible their recreation at an international level.

Transnational business derives power and wealth from the freedom to operate where it will. Joint action to create a countervailing power is difficult in the extreme. While companies have annulled frontiers, trade unions and labour movements have not. It is easy to internationalize a balance sheet, because figures are an international thing. It is difficult to internationalize trade union organization, because democracy respects different traditions and cultural heritages, and speaks different tongues. If those who work for the great international corporations are difficult to organize, how much more difficult is it to organize the unemployed, or the poor?

To accept this challenge is to accept a long commitment. Joint democratic action requires that we link up as we are, respecting one another's differences. It invites us to build co-operation and trust in a process of common effort and discussion. None of this comes easily. But delay will only render it more difficult.